# The Colonial Fortune
## in Contemporary Fiction in French

Contemporary French and Francophone Cultures, 46

# Contemporary French and Francophone Cultures

## Series Editors

EDMUND SMYTH
*Manchester Metropolitan University*

CHARLES FORSDICK
*University of Liverpool*

### Editorial Board

JACQUELINE DUTTON
*University of Melbourne*

LYNN A. HIGGINS
*Dartmouth College*

MIREILLE ROSELLO
*University of Amsterdam*

MICHAEL SHERINGHAM
*University of Oxford*

DAVID WALKER
*University of Sheffield*

This series aims to provide a forum for new research on modern and contemporary French and francophone cultures and writing. The books published in *Contemporary French and Francophone Cultures* reflect a wide variety of critical practices and theoretical approaches, in harmony with the intellectual, cultural and social developments which have taken place over the past few decades. All manifestations of contemporary French and francophone culture and expression are considered, including literature, cinema, popular culture, theory. The volumes in the series will participate in the wider debate on key aspects of contemporary culture.

### Recent titles in the series:

OANA PANAÏTÉ

# The Colonial Fortune
# in Contemporary Fiction in French

LIVERPOOL UNIVERSITY PRESS

First published 2017 by
Liverpool University Press
4 Cambridge Street
Liverpool
L69 7ZU

British Library Cataloguing-in-Publication data
A British Library CIP record is available

ISBN 978-1-78694-029-2 cased

Typeset by Carnegie Book Production, Lancaster
Printed and bound in Poland by BooksFactory.co.uk

# Contents

# Acknowledgments

This work has been supported through a faculty fellowship at the Center for the Study of History and Memory, a summer faculty fellowship awarded by the Office of the Vice-Provost for Research and an Individual Research Award from the Institute for Advanced Studies, all at Indiana University-Bloomington. At the same institution, my research has been generously recognized, productively challenged and always stimulated by faculty members and graduate and undergraduate students, especially in the Department of French and Italian and the Center for Theoretical Inquiry in the Humanities.

My visiting position at the Chaire des Amériques following an invitation from the Institut des Amériques and the Centre d'études des langues et littératures anciennes et modernes (CELLAM) during the Fall of 2013 allowed me to initiate and, in some important cases, to resume a fruitful dialogue with students and colleagues at the Université Rennes 2-Haute Bretagne. A thought-provoking exchange with the faculty and graduate students who organized and invited me to participate in the Interdisciplinary Approaches to Modern France and the Francophone World Workshop at the University of Chicago afforded me the unique opportunity to clarify some important points and put the finishing touches to the final draft of the manuscript.

My gratitude also goes to a select group of MA and PhD students in the French/Francophone Studies program at IUB, with special thanks to Georgy Khabarovskiy and Amanda Vredenburgh, who assisted me in researching and editing the manuscript, as well as Flavien Falantin and Loïc Lerme, who read and commented on certain sections. The index has been prepared with Jessica Tindira's careful assistance. The anonymous readers of my work, especially those of Liverpool University Press, deserve to be recognized for their constructive criticism and valuable suggestions.

Among the colleagues and friends who on many occasions and in countless ways have lent me their generous encouragement and whose research and ideas have inspired mine, I would like to thank in particular Akin Adesokan, Hall Bjørnstad, Emmanuel Bouju, Margaret Gray, Alison James, Eileen Julien, Vera Klekovkina, Valérie Loichot, Lydie Moudileno, Grace Musila, James Ogude, Yolaine Parisot, Ioana Popa, Alison Rice, Tiphaine Samoyault, Agathe Sultan and Sonia Velázquez.

This book is the continuation of a project that began many years ago under the thoughtful guidance of Jean-Yves Tadié and Jacques Neefs. The seeds of my passion for French language and Francophone literatures were planted years before by two very different but equally exemplary mentors: Lacramioara Petrescu and Elena Popoiu.

For my parents, Zâna and Virgil, who always listen, care and hope
For Craig

# A Primal Scene:
# The Colonial Fortune

Ai-je quelque ascendant qui fut beau capitaine, jeune enseigne insolent ou négrier farouchement taciturne ? À l'est de Suez quelque oncle retourné en barbarie sous le casque de liège, jodhpurs aux pieds et amertume aux lèvres, personnage poncif qu'endossent volontiers les branches cadettes, les poètes apostats, tous les déshonorés pleins d'honneur, d'ombrage et de mémoire qui sont la perle noire des arbres généalogiques ? Un quelconque antécédent colonial ou marin? (Michon 9)

Pierre Michon's *Vies minuscules* (1984) recounts a provincial young man's Proustian journey toward literature in the second half of the twentieth century, for whom becoming a writer is an undertaking ridden with guilt, desire and despair. The beginnings of *Vies minuscules* take the form of a rhetorical question pointing to the phantasmatic projection of a romantic genealogy and adventure-filled family saga in which the colonial past plays an ambivalent role. It is both central, as one of the key reasons for the writer's project of recasting the humble lives of his ancestors in a new light, and marginal, since it is never fully addressed in the literary work that it has engendered.

This study has originated in an observation: the subtle yet persistent presence of the colonial in narratives not directly concerned with colonial history or issues such as immigration, multiculturalism or neocolonialism. In works written by metropolitan or French continental writers such as Claude Simon, Pierre Michon, Laurent Gaudé, Stéphane Audeguy, Marie Darrieussecq or Régis Jauffret, the reader is surprised to discover references to colonial or postcolonial history, geography and civilization. "Ces images, fugaces et évanescentes" (Havard and Vidal 9) are disseminated throughout the narrative and dialogues and discreetly woven into the fabric of the authorial discourse, indicating that the process of colonization and its aftereffects are not the main focus of these books. Nonetheless, they engage with colonization in oblique and ambiguous ways. This is epitomized in this excerpt from Régis Jauffret's *Microfictions* in which a Frenchman's empathy with the gendered, racial and historical subaltern paradoxically and sarcastically paves the way to solipsism, moral relativism and indifference:

> Peu importe que je sois né Blanc en 1976. J'aurais pu naître Peau-Rouge en 1804, jaune prostitué sous la dynastie des Ming dans un bordel de Pékin, ou Noir dans un zoo humain au début du XXᵉ siècle. La roulette des races, des sexes, et du temps nous a distribués au hasard. On ne peut pas demander à des numéros tirés au sort d'être solidaires les uns des autres, ou d'éprouver de la compassion pour les chiffres les plus faibles. Je suis ma seule patrie. (Jauffret 300)

In this respect, these writers' approach seems to mirror the rhetorical and ideological attitude exhibited by non-metropolitan writers or those who claim a non-Hexagonal heritage and who envision the colonial story arc (first encounters, slavery and the plantation culture, the struggle for decolonization and the postcolonial present) as a "transpersonal" experience that describes, according to Marianne Hirsch and Nancy Miller, "a zone of relation that is social, affective, material, and inevitably public" (Hirsch and Miller 5) recounted from a "transindividual" (Bessière 9) perspective that cuts across national, political and moral categories. In the novels of the Martinican Édouard Glissant and the French-Mauritian Jean-Marie-Georges Le Clézio the colony is configured by the interrelated phenomena of escape, encounter, imprisonment and empowerment, in which the experience of the colonizer is inseparable from that of the colonized and the master's story is predicated on the slave's. The Guinean writer Tierno Monénembo recounts the story of a nineteenth-century French explorer of Africa in what I call an "alternal" *roman d'archives* that espouses the point of view of the Frenchman, relying on a poetics of empathy for the colonizer's experience. Born of a French mother and an absent Senegalese father, Marie NDiaye resists the label of Francophone, yet her fictional world is haunted by the ghost of a radical – not only social or racial, but also ontological – otherness. In the autobiographical writings of the French–Algerian author Leïla Sebbar and the Algerian-born Jewish–French author Hélène Cixous colonization appears as a phantom that is "always already there," closely woven into the fabric of the subject's identity and guiding her literary path. The Cameroonian Léonora Miano engages with the shadows of secrecy, shame, guilt and suffering that taint the memory of slavery in Africa, while the Haitian writer Lyonel Trouillot uncovers the striking continuity of secrecy, shame, guilt and suffering characteristic of the neocolonial experience. While the body of works examined here is by no means comprehensive, it is representative of a trend in French-language literature that started in the 1960s in the aftermath of the French colonial empire's collapse and whose visibility and public recognition has increased notably since the 1980s thanks to the increased participation and recognition of non-metropolitan writers in the national and transnational literary field.

My choice of writers and texts has been guided by my belief that today's fiction writing is a transfrontier process, understood as a creative undertaking by authors who travel and share their lives between two or more countries, languages and collective memories (Panaïté 2012). Furthermore, these artists partake of a common artistic memory, an immanent result of the political and economic process of globalization, which they nonetheless transform in specific and individual ways, remodeling into what Édouard Glissant called "Tout-Monde." Literature's fictional engagement with the legacy of the empire stands in contrast with the silence of history that, even in its most ambitious iterations, epitomized by Pierre Nora's monumental *Lieux de mémoire*, evinces a "fantastic" (Gregory Mann in Forsdick and Murphy 2009, 277) exclusion of the colonial past; thus, artistic imagination both reveals and fills in the *lacunae* of the historical imaginary. At the same time, the fundamental ambivalence of the concept of "colonial fortune" also allows me to call attention to the pitfalls of subaltern cosmopolitanism, self-exoticization and memorial mortification present, in explicit or implicit forms, in these works. The expression "colonial fortune" refers to a rhetorical, narrative and aesthetic configuration implying an interconnectedness between the notions of chance, luck, destiny and wealth simultaneously present in the works examined here that can either reinforce or disrupt the narrative flow. This approach sets the emphasis not on a set of colonial themes, conceived as static phenomena, but on colonial tropes that draw on the lexicon and semantics of fate (destiny, adventure, vocation, happiness or vicissitude), economics (wealth accumulated or lost, inherited or self-made), legacy (built, squandered, ignored or ill-honored) and debt (claimed or owed, payable or inestimable).

This reading engages with what I call paracolonial aesthetics, which describes a double phenomenon. On the one hand, it refers to the revival, resurgence and remanence, remanence of the colonial in today's political and cultural imaginary; in other words, a variety of forms indicating a residue or discrete permanence.[1] On the other, it addresses the reimagining, revisiting and reassessment of the colonial in works of literature. All of these gestures are fraught simultaneously with danger and opportunity, as they entail the custodial task of maintaining and even instilling new life into colonial culture in the material, emotional and ideological sense without discounting the moral responsibility toward the human and experiential sustenance of the past. Such an approach remains mindful of Nicholas Harrison's caution to the critic or theorist who

> even in a field such as postcolonial studies, needs to go beyond the search for depictions of representative minority experience, if she or he wishes to deal with the literary at all, to treat texts in their specificity (and so to avoid falling into incoherence), and to respond adequately to the work of new and old writers alike. (Harrison 2005, 15)

The "colonial fortune" offers an ideological and affective configuration that seeks to transcend the historical and conceptual limitations of the binary between "colonialism" and "postcolonialism" while attending to "the mundane, complex, and ambiguous psychic space between subjugation and submission" (Aching 65) and between domination and oppression. For this purpose, I engage in a critical investigation of the evolving process of the "paracolonial." In using this term I am aware of adding to the taxonomical inflation that affects our field while drawing little intellectual benefit. However, as John Michael Archer argues in his study of early modern travel writing, the "para-colonial" enables us to gain a more comprehensive and nuanced perspective of the colonial phenomenon or, to paraphrase Mignolo's formulation, of the colonial *gnosis*:

> A proper consideration of Europe amidst the Old World during the early modern period requires a concept like *para-colonial* studies, where the Greek prefix means 'alongside of' without precluding either 'before' or 'beyond', and can suggest both 'closely related to' and 'aside from', as well. An understanding of the para-colonial, conversely, might help us to develop nontotalizing or nonessentialist understandings of colonial power in the New World and in the world of today. (Archer 16–17)

Moreover, Amar Acheraïou uses the term "para-colonial" to contend that, while Conrad, Foster and most other British modernist writers adopted openly anti-colonialist attitudes, they also consent to its principal tenets:

> They challenge imperialism, but prove at the same time tacitly collusive with colonial ideology and culture. This ambivalence in relation to empire may account for the modernist authors' espousal of a para-colonialist discourse, which I define as a fractured enunciative split between a covert endorsement of the imperial major narrative of progress and an open support for the minor rhetoric of (anti-colonial) resistance. (Acheraïou 116–117)

The word's own etymology denotes the refusal of a "nontotalizing" and "nonessentialist" stance on account of the prefix, which suggests a supplemental, marginal, accompanying, but closely connected and potentially subversive meaning. Among the definitions the Merriam-Webster dictionary offers for the prefix "para" one finds: "beside," "alongside of," "beyond," "aside from," "closely related to," "faulty," "abnormal," "associated in a subsidiary or accessory capacity," "closely resembling" and "almost."[2] In order to retain the full force of this semantic constellation, I propose to use the non-hyphenated version of the term in order to capture both the heterogeneous temporal continuity of colonialism, its *before* and *after*, its *pre-* and *post-* reverberations, and the ideological ambivalence of the discourses surrounding it.

In my analysis, I proceed from the same critical premise formulated by Gerad Aching in his book *Freedom from Liberation*: "that subjects achieve self-consciousness while already embedded in societies and institutions that coerce them to act in or react against certain regulated ways" (Aching 91–92). While Aching derives his theorization from the study of slavery narratives in colonial Cuba, his contention that "the subject emerges as a subject already embedded in coercive circum-stances" (Aching 92) can be ascribed to all narratives stemming from the colonial encounter. Such an approach invites us "to shift our understanding of the struggle for freedom away from an overemphasis on or sole understanding of freedom as the elimination of external coercion and toward an analysis of the internal grappling with forms of coercion that constitutes the struggle for self-mastery" (Aching 15). To envision these works from a paracolonial perspective makes possible a transversal reading that cuts across distinct poetics, national boundaries and colonial and postcolonial interpretive models.

## "Littérature-monde" as World Creation

In pursuing the transfrontier investigation of literature introduced in my previous research, I contend that there is a non-theorized consensus among specialists of contemporary – that is, late twentieth and early twenty-first-century – fiction regarding the distinction between "committed" and "artistic" writing. Even as the 1980s witnessed the end of this modern divide, thanks to the "narrative turn" marked by the demise of experimental and collective literary movements, on the one hand, and a growing interest in "obsolete" literary techniques such as storytelling and characterization, on the other, a new line of demarcation emerged, separating Metropolitan, or French proper, from "Francophone" writers. While the former are associated in mainstream scholarship (in both "French" and "Francophone" literary fields) with a variety of genres, including autobiographical, social and historical fiction (inspired in particular by European and more generally Western history, such as the two world wars), the latter are often confined to a limited set of topics and genres pertaining to non-European history and ethnographic, testimonial and documentary writing.

As Charles Forsdick points out, recent decades have witnessed an intense questioning of the disciplinary structures and values of French studies, which has presented scholars with a host of potential configurations:

> The traditional division of the French studies field into chronological or generic fields has been challenged by a new historicospatial model, and the uneasy co-existence of these often divergent understandings poses a major challenge at a time of increased uncertainty generated by perceived crises in undergraduate recruitment. What has been the impact of the increasingly popular study of postcolonial literatures and cultures in French on traditional notions of French studies? The answers one might propose are diverse: a loss of coherence tending toward fragmentation and dispersal; an assimilationist and centripetal approach whereby the non-metropolitan is progressively normalized; the perpetuation of a centre–periphery binary whereby the non-metropolitan is marginalized, or objectified and transformed into what Graham Huggan, triggering very necessary alarm bells, has perceptively dubbed the "postcolonial exotic"; or, finally (and perhaps most constructively), a more fundamental response, epitomized by Lawrence D. Kriztman's contribution to Yale French Studies, that involves a more general restructuring and an integrative understanding of the interaction between "French" and "Francophone" dependent on "hermeneutic strategies that

are both comparative and dialogic in nature". In short, the development of a Francophone postcolonial studies may permit the elaboration of a genuinely postcolonial French studies. (Forsdick 2005, 528)

That Francophone or postcolonial studies should emerge as winners of these institutional struggles and conceptual reassessments has been further called into question by the 2007 collective manifesto "Pour une littérature-monde en français," published in the newspaper *Le Monde* and the volume *Pour une littérature-monde*, edited by Michel Le Bris and Jean Rouaud for Gallimard. The polemical tone adopted by the forty-four French-language writers in the first document and the more scholarly stance of the book have spawned a sub-field itself fraught with ideological disagreements and critical ambitions. For all the debates and quarrels surrounding it, the idea of world literature has brought to the foreground a number of important issues, such as the development of new aesthetic and critical models (transcultural, transcontinental and transfrontier), the recognition of "minor" literatures and the importance of rethinking the conceptual framework and value system of French writing today. In an article that examines the cultural and political context in which the manifesto and its "produits dérivés" came to be, Lydie Moudileno underscores the political potential, "la puissance politique" (Moudileno 2013, 24), of world literature in French for today's writers, who find themselves in a precarious situation between "le potentiel centrifuge de la littérature-monde, forcément transnationale, et [...] les forces centripètes du nationalisme hexagonal" (Moudileno 2013, 22).

The most important contribution and measure of "littérature-monde" consists of its ability to reveal hidden or overlooked aspects of the world it seeks to reimagine and represent. Pheng Cheah redefines several key terms that are commonly used to talk about the notion of "world literature" and underscores literature's potential to act as a counter-force to the process of globalization and the existence of the global market, which subjugates human beings to its demands. In a philosophical sense, world literature opens up the possibility for other worlds to come into being and constitutes an alternative to the threat of globalization by "craft[ing] new stories of world-belonging for postcolonial peoples" (Cheah 214). Kant's original understanding of the term cosmopolitanism and his definition of the world affect the way we understand these terms today. Kant's work suggests imagining the world as a global community of (all) human beings in which individual self-importance diminishes as a result of awareness of others' perspectives, a world with a sense of mutual responsibility. While Kant himself is suspicious of literature, his understanding of cosmopolitanism underscores the importance of the role of literature in a global community, as literature "brings humanity into being by integrating individuals into a universal whole by means of the sociability it occasions" (Cheah 44). For Goethe, "[w] orld literature is an active space of transaction and interrelation" (Cheah 38), whereby transaction is understood not in economic terms but rather as a process that allows different nations to coexist with, interact with and understand each other. Goethe ascribes a key role to translation and translators in making possible and promoting world literature. Before discussing Marx in the context of world literature, Cheah clarifies a common misunderstanding surrounding the term "world": he insists that it is impossible to talk about world literature if by "the world" we mean "the globe." The critic argues against the widespread conflation of the two terms, insisting that the world is not a geographical space but a means to conceive of a way in which human beings exist together. The globe is "the thing produced by processes of globalization" (Cheah 42), whereas the world is "an ongoing dynamic process of becoming, something that possesses a historical-temporal dimension and hence is continually made and remade" (Cheah 42). Literature constantly negotiates with the materiality of the world, reconfigures its symbolic shape and reveals other ways of seeing reality: it is "an inexhaustible resource for reworlding and remaking the degraded world given to us by commercial intercourse, monetary transactions, and the space-time compression of the global culture industry" (Cheah 186–187).

A powerful echoing of this point comes from Susan Buck-Morss's examination of the changing definition of art and the role of the artist in contemporary society. If modernist art reached far beyond museums and exhibitions and exerted a tremendous influence on social and political life, in today's post-modern world art, or, rather, what she calls post-art, despite being available to anyone, does not have much concrete political effectiveness. As Buck-Morss aptly puts it, the impact of art is "neutralized and domesticated" (Buck-Morss 548). In an attempt to counteract the logic of the global market and to pull artists, critics and the public out of their self-absorbed state, the philosopher suggests a turn to "radical cosmopolitanism" (Buck-Morss 549). The members of the artistic community should thus recognize that they can no longer monopolize the space of culture and that, as creators of cultural content, they have a responsibility not to their community – an erroneous idea that perpetuates isolation – but, in a broader sense, to humanity at large.

I situate my study in a critical horizon where the move to expand the sphere of French literature is tempered by the attention to the ethical dimension of such a move. As the editors of the 2010 volume *French Global* point out, scholarly efforts to account for the transnational, mainly non-Hexagonal, literary production of the last decades of the twentieth century and the early twenty-first century have succeeded in challenging "French literature's national borders as well as France's traditional self-image – that of a republic where 'all citizens are equal' with no attention paid to ethnic or other differences" (McDonald and Suleiman xi). Against the monumental and monolithic idea of French literature, *French Global* redefines it as a multifaceted process fraught with differences and contradictions and bearing the stamp of transnational movements. The editors' introduction cautions against a unified and totalizing image of the new literary space: "While we challenge the notion of a seamless unity between French as language, French as literature, and French as nation (let alone French as 'universal spirit'), we do maintain the idea of literatures in French" (McDonald and Suleiman xix). Categories such as spaces, mobilities and multiplicities encourage a non-monolithical idea of writing in French and a concern for the relational or, as I have argued elsewhere, dialogical (Panaïté 2016) reading of texts separated by geopolitical or disciplinary borders.

## The Colonial Remains

The goal of this study is not to propose a typology or a classification of texts, nor is it to claim the emergence of a new literary paradigm. While it resonates with recent studies such as *The Colonial Comedy*, in which Jennifer Yee offers a persuasive reassessment of nineteenth-century French realism through readings that reveal "colonial projects" in the works of canonical writers such as Balzac, Flaubert or Zola (Yee 25), my approach does not, for instance, directly engage with the generational distinctions between the authors examined here and does not operate with categories such as literary movements or schools. Rather, it emphasizes the effects of discrete continuity between writers separated by literary chronology (such as Claude Simon and Laurent Gaudé or Marie Darrieussecq) or geopolitical sensibility (such as Pierre Michon and Tierno Monénembo). My study focuses on a network of texts that, though distinct in style, thematic concerns and ideological stances, share a number of discursive and narrative features crystallized around the proprioceptive and remanent dimensions of the colonial. I contend that, through dissemination, empathy, indirection, obliqueness and mediation, the colonial situates contemporary narratives in a larger historical framework while also reminding readers of the many layers and force fields that constitute their textual fabric.

The "colonial fortune" writing also emerges from the interplay of two dynamics introduced by Jane Bradley Winston in her discussion of Marguerite Duras's work:

> The first of these dynamics are the *representational efforts* designed and deployed to conserve (or to destroy) the French colonial order and its subject. The second dynamic is *displacement*, whose intentional forms assured 19th-century France's colonial implantation, but [...] whose more accidental and directionally inverses 20th-century manifestations increasingly subverted the French colonial subject and its cultural orders to produce their ongoing "Francophone shifts". (Winston 4)

On the surface, colonial resurgence and remanence are readily associated with the Hexagonal imagination, which channels the long-standing collective unwillingness to relinquish what Kate Marsh and Nicola Frith have dubbed "France's lost empires" and the reluctance to engage in an open, nationwide conversation about the "colonial fracture," according to Pascal Blanchard, Nicolas Bancel and Sandrine Lemaire. Instead, responses span from the escapist retreat into epiphenomena such as nostalgia, melancholy and denial, examined by Paul Gilroy, Dennis Walder and Kate Marsh, to ideological diversions such as the partially repealed 23 February 2005 law about the positive role of the French presence abroad (especially in North Africa) and the debate on national identity. Moreover, the critical postcolonial stance is commonly, and sometimes exclusively, attributed to Francophone works of literature, history or philosophy. While this reflects a long-standing political and aesthetic tradition epitomized by the emergence of the influential Négritude movement in the 1930s, scholars such as Abiola Irele, Paul Gilroy, Christopher L. Miller and Dona V. Jones have studied extensively its historical and ideological underpinnings in order to expose its ambiguous connections with Western ideas. As Jones points out in her study dedicated to the influence of the French philosopher Henri Bergson on the early twentieth-century anticolonial thinkers:

> The *Négritude* poets Leopold Senghor and Aimé Césaire defined colonial revolt by fusing the *Lebensphilosophs* with ethnography and surrealist experimentation. The core of their poetry, a mythical founding of

> a unified African people yet to be, was a deep feeling for a deep
> conviction of the consanguinity of all forms of life, obliterated in modern
> consciousness by the positivist classificatory method focused on the
> empirical differences of things. But with this form of life mysticism they
> also inherited the political dangers of life philosophy. (Jones 10)

Vitalism, racialism and irrationalism threaten to tear the fabric of the
anticolonial discourse in Senghor's essays on African humanity and
civilization and in Césaire's poem *Cahier d'un retour au pays natal*. As
convincing as Jones' analysis of this philosophical genealogy may prove
when applied to demonstrative or deliberative writings, its instrumentalization of poetic texts raises the question of how we can *read* and
what we can read *into* literary works.

Such discussions bring to the fore the issues of the continued presence
or, rather, the remanence of the colonial imaginary as well as the
importance of colonial culture today. The editors of *Colonial Culture
since the French Revolution*, which covers a vast and variegated body of
evidence (from colonial exhibitions, war policies, schools and museums
to literature, the press, postcards, posters and songs), remark that "[t]
he place of the colonial in our institutions, our political culture, and
our imaginary was not simply a product of state propaganda, but also
the result of an array of influences, intermediaries, and interactions of
which we are only beginningto understand the importance" (Blanchard
et al. 2014, 6). In this study, I tarry with colonial *survival* in the narrative
writings of the period dubbed "The Time of Inheritance" in the above
cited volume. This includes composite phenomena such as corrective
or nostalgic gestures and attempts at recreating the past motivated
by cognitive, moral or affective reasons and serving political agendas
that can be progressive, reactionary or even both. Colonial survival
carries over into the postcolonial present and dovetails with E. Said's
notion of "latent Orientalism." Upon recapitulating the characteristics
of Orientalist tenets, the critic makes an important distinction between
latent and manifest Orientalism. Latent Orientalism is described by Said
as "an almost unconscious (and certainly an untouchable) positivity,"
while manifest Orientalism is indicative of "the various stated views
about Oriental society, languages, literatures, history, sociology, and so
forth" (Said 1978, 206). While latent Orientalism foregrounds the advent
of colonial ideology, the survival of colonial thought today accounts
for its belated, posthumous, postcolonial reverberations. It indicates
an impossible yet irrepressible longing to recognize the colony as the
colonist's native land. Moreover, rather than feeling compelled to offer

a translation or to fill in the blankness of a signifier awaiting its scholar to populate it with images and meaning – that is, rather than following the colonial principle that "the Orient is all absence" (Said 1978, 208) – today's literature assumes a more skeptical, almost nominalist position, the essence of which was captured by Roland Barthes at a time when the memory of colonization, violent decolonization and their many discontents were fresh in the French public's consciousness:

> L'Orient et l'Occident ne peuvent donc être pris ici comme des 'réalités', que l'on essaierait d'approcher et d'opposer historiquement, philosophiquement, culturellement, politiquement. Je ne regarde pas amoureusement vers une essence orientale, l'Orient m'est indifférent, il me fournit simplement une réserve de traits dont la mise en batterie, le jeu inventé, me permettent de 'flatter' l'idée d'un système symbolique inouï, entièrement dépris du nôtre. Ce qui peut être visé, dans la considération de l'Orient, ce ne sont pas d'autres symboles, une autre métaphysique, une autre sagesse (encore que celle-ci apparaisse bien désirable): c'est la possibilité d'une différence, d'une mutation, d'une révolution dans la propriété des systèmes symboliques. Il faudrait faire un jour l'histoire de notre propre obscurité, manifester la compacité de notre narcissisme, recenser le long des siècles les quelques appels de différence que nous avons pu parfois entendre, les récupérations idéologiques qui ont immanquablement suivi et qui consistent à toujours acclimater notre inconnaissance de l'Asie grâce à des langages connus (l'Orient de Voltaire, de la *Revue Asiatique*, de Loti ou d'*Air France*). (Barthes 1970, 10)

For Barthes, far from being an essence or an object in itself, the "Orient" – and, for that matter, the "Occident" as well, which, wrapped up in the "compactness" of its "narcissism", awaits the history of its own "obscurity" – is a set a features, an *other* system of symbols which holds the possibility of a difference capable of transforming one's experience of knowledge. The example of the *satori*, the Zen event, makes the subject tremble, shakes up its rational foundation and evacuates the word, giving way to writing: "il [the *satori*] opère un *vide de parole* [...] qui constitue l'écriture" (Barthes 1970, 12).

In 1956, as the war in Algeria was underway, Jean Sénac wrote "Lettre à un jeune Français d'Algérie." This powerful document seems to espouse the legitimist perspective of the young Pieds-noirs while at the same time calling for a historical and political awareness necessary to transcend the ideology of colonial nativism:

> Tu aimes l'Algérie où tu es né, où tu as grandi, comblé; tu as sur cette terre tes parents et tes morts, tes souvenirs et ton espérance, le seul

endroit pour toi de l'acte et du repos. Pour tout dire, l'Algérie est ta patrie et ta raison de vivre. Tu sens que cette terre t'appartient, qu'elle chemine dans tes veines, que vous êtes liés indissolublement. Tout cela est vrai, cela est juste et bon. Mais puisque tu aimes cette terre t'es-tu vraiment demandé ce qu'elle est, cette terre, ce qu'elle est réellement? (Brun and Penot-Lacassagne 202)

In an article tellingly entitled "Postcolonial Remains," Robert J. C. Young contends: "Something remains, and the postcolonial is in many ways about such unfinished business, the continuing projection of past conflicts into the experience of the present, the insistent persistence of the afterimages of historical memory that drive the desire to transform the present" (Young 2012, 21). (It is worth noting that, in the spirited rejoinders elicited by Young's and Dipesh Chakrabarty's articles published in a 2012 special issue of *New Literary History*, the semantic network of remanence was further developed by the use of terms such as "debris" or phrases such as "Empire's present" and "What is left in postcolonial studies?"[3]). From Young's perspective as a historian, postcolonialism should be construed as "neither Western nor non-Western, but a dialectical product of interaction between the two." Such a stance allows reseachers to "articulate new counterpoints of insurgency from the long-running power struggles that predate and post-date colonialism" (Young 2001, 68). Refusing to give a teleological account of postcolonialism or to treat it as a continuum extending from colonialism through anti-colonialism to postcolonialism in a straight line, he highlights the importance of multiple components that make it up, as well as the unresolved tensions within the field of postcolonial studies. By treating postcolonialism as a material rather than a textual space, Young stresses the fact that postcolonialism is by no means a totalizing discourse. He offers instead a *disjunctive* account of postcolonialism by "articulating it in the context of other less determinate positions" (Bongie 2002, 262). Achille Mbembe also refers to the "compositeness"of the "postcolony," a concept he applies to the contemporary state of affairs, particularly as it concerns Africa. He further explains the discursive and symbolic dimensions of this hetero-geneity, insisting that the "African present is formed by an assemblage of signs and symbols and artefacts that mean different things in various languages and contexts. These signs, symbols and artefacts are then organised around multiple central tropes that come to function as both images and mirages, parables and allegories."[4] However, when it comes to literature, Young minimizes its importance in understanding the phenomenon of (post)colonialism, placing it in the margins of (post) colonial discourse, since, in his view, the production of literary texts does not follow the same rules as those that govern other discursive practices. As Chris Bongie points out, while historians and postcolonial theorists may regard literary studies as secondary, they are nonetheless "potentially disruptive of any understanding of colonialism and postcolonialism" (Bongie 2002, 267). In raising the question "What's colonialism/ postcolonialism got to do with [literature]?" Bongie contends that the boundaries between literary and non-literary should, after all, matter (Bongie 2002, 266) and that scholars of contemporary literature should not consider themselves to be working on the margins of postcolonial studies, "applying" postcolonial theory to literary texts at the expense of losing sight of their object ("literature"). The present study subscribes to Bongie's call for the more productive approach of bringing theory and literature into dialogue with each other. Beginning our enquiry with the text itself allows us to grasp the ways in which it problematizes the existing accounts of postcolonialism or disrupts the logic of colonialism, even if it explicitly supports it. In actuality, the issues Young singles out in order to illustrate the limits and contradictions of postcolonial analysis can be found at the center of contemporary texts that are also grappling with "the politics of invisibility and of unreadability: indigenous struggles and their relation to settler colonialism, illegal migrants, and political Islam" (Young 2012, 22).

In addition to the opposing versions of the past and clashing interpretations found in current debates over the beneficial effects of colonialism for the people and the lands that once formed the French empire, over the recognition owed to former colonial officials and their native auxiliaries, such as the Harkis in Algeria, or over the debt France owes its former colonies, such as Haiti, "literature has surprising perspectives to add to the questions that history raises" (Miller 2008, 93). As Christopher L. Miller observes in the case of the literary treatment of the slave trade, "acts of projection by French authors [...] by no means fill the historical void nor remedy the silence of the captive or the slave. But they try to" (Miller 2008, 93). Moreover, by unraveling the pact between language and nation (Rouaud 21) – that is, by transcending national borders to include writers from different parts of the French-speaking world – the present study seeks to establish a "dialogue" or "trialogue" (Miller 2008, 92) between "the various imaginations at work on all points of the triangle" (Miller 2008, 96). This approach meets with but also supersedes and complicates the historian's call for a tricontinental or "transculturated" Marxism as a renewed "foundation to postcolonial theory" (Young 2001, 169). It avails itself of the contrapuntal reading through an "awareness both of the metropolitan history that is narrated and of those other histories against which (and together with which) the dominating discourse acts" (Said 1994, 51) while remaining mindful of the pitfalls of a hermeneutical dialectics that would seek to resolve these tensions in the harmony of the text's ultimate meaning or message. In Charles Forsdick's view, a contrapuntal reading would

> present comparatism with an unrestricted field of enquiry and without any implicit hierarchies. Central to it is the desire to elaborate a critical practice that is "neither completely at one with the new [...] nor fully disencumbered of the old".[5] In exploring the "interval between what we mean by "France" and what we mean by "French" – an interval central to understandings of the relationship between the French and Francophone – such a nuanced approach would seem invaluable. (Forsdick 2005, 529)

## Writing for (which) Humanity?

In the current climate of increased economic and axiological precariousness within academic institutions, whose traditional core disciplines have been gathered under the designation of humanities, literature is faced with the question of its own survival, tantamount, for some, to the survival of humanity itself: "L'avenir n'a plus alors d'autre figure que celle de la survie elle-même: ce qu'on ne parviendra pas à sauver va mourir, non se transformer en une autre chose, non *devenir*" (Merlin-Kajman 2003, 18). For Jacques Rancière, the literary and the political are inextricably linked by the figurative and persuasive power of language: "L'homme est un animal politique parce qu'il est un animal littéraire, qui se laisse détourner de sa destination 'naturelle' par le pouvoir des mots" (Rancière 2000, 63). Grounding her approach in the idea of *homo ludens*,[6] Nancy Huston also ties the survival of humanity to the ability to imagine fictional alternatives, which not only provide an escape from everyday reality but allow the reshaping and rethinking of reality in order to better understand and inhabit it: "Pour nous autres humains, la fiction est aussi réelle que le sol sur lequel nous marchons. Elle est ce sol. Notre soutien dans le monde" (Huston 29).

In her recent essay *Ayaï! Le cri de la littérature*, Hélène Cixous reflects on literature's intrinsic ethical gesture as "une défensive d'urgence contre le pillage, le massacre, l'oubli. Contre notre propre auto-immunité. Notre terrible système d'adaptation, notre affreuse soumission à la réalité. Notre exécrable économie spirituelle" (Cixous 2013, 25). Proceeding in an anthropological and ontological vein, in a book tellingly entitled *L'Animal ensorcelé*, Hélène Merlin-Kajman indexes the difference between the survival or salvation (survie/salut) of humanity, of its future and its human values, which denotes a sense of danger and urgency that, in turn, betrays, on the one hand, a lack of preparedness and, on the other, survival as "survivance" in the sense of keeping alive or maintaining a legacy as a specific type of literary intervention in the world. Borrowing from Aby Warburg the term of *Pathosformel*, a form evoking pathos, which relates to the artistic expression of an affective experience through its exaggerated re-enactment or reactivation, Didi-Huberman uses the expression "ghostly time of survivals (survivances)" (Didi-Huberman 53 in Merlin-Kajman 2016, 72) to call attention to the double movement of the irruption of an emotion that is always beyond our reach and of the artistic language that seeks to capture it as in a still shot (*arrêt sur image*) to better preserve its intensity, always ready to be released.

I draw on these reflections about the political and anthropological function of literature in order to argue that colonial tropes that have shaped the imagination of metropolitan and non-metropolitan writers alike, through the shared experience of class readings, could be read as pathos-evoking forms. Many a writer born and bred in the colonies, from Césaire and Senghor to Djebar and Chamoiseau, recounts his or her own unique experience of the encounter with the French literary canon. Major literary works, from Rabelais, Ronsard, Pascal and Molière to Hugo, Baudelaire, Rimbaud and Proust, are credited with opening the gates of literature to little children for whom France was an absent presence, both very near through her symbols (her flag and national anthem) and agents of authority (teachers and administrators) and distant, insofar as the local surroundings did little to reflect and, in fact, clashed with the geo-cultural description of the political motherland. Literature and (Other)Worldliness are thus discovered together and remain inseparable in the imagination of the future "Francophone" writers. Furthermore, the process of acculturation and alienation can be attributed to an even greater extent to lesser-known authors and works, those "minor classics," such as Jules Verne, Pierre Loti or Louis Boussenard, who accompanied the childhood of entire generations of readers and future writers from all corners of the empire, populating its center as well as its many peripheries. The question then becomes: Having been used as an instrument of ideological and political domination, is literature itself, as an artistic form, a verbal practice and a cultural institution, colonial?

These questions touch the very core of the idea of literature. The crux of the matter is that ideas in literature or poetry are conveyed in ways distinct to those used in an ideological pamplet or a philosophical treatise. To state that literature thinks in a mysterious, enigmatic or inexplicable way is to beg the question by retreating into an essentialist aesthetic.[7] Derek Attridge offers a solution for overcoming this circular logic by envisioning the singularity of literature not as an intrinsic and static quality but as "constitutively impure, always open to contamination, grafting, acidents, reinterpretation, and recontextualization" (Attridge 63). This perspective enables us to grasp key notions such as creation, invention, responsibility and ethics without subordinating them to the constraints of a particular philosophy or ideology. Moreover, Attridge paves the way for professional and common readers to press beyond the question of a work's truth-value and adopt a "post-aesthetic" point of view. Drawing on Heidegger, Adorno and Derrida, he reworks the relation between truth and art in a non-univocal and dynamic manner, placing the emphasis on a signifying form, tone or style. It is through the event of the meeting between the work and the reader that truth manifests itself as actualization of meaning.

Nevertheless, to contend that literature presents the truth in a manner that is at the same time proper (inherent to a sensible form), singular (untranslatable in a non-literary way) and global (irreducible to the sum of its parts) does not assuage the concerns about its intelligible content comprised of factual and verifiable information, logical, axiological and moral arguments and judgments.

"La littérature, c'est la monarchie" wrote Barthes in 1971,[8] quoted by Merlin-Kajman in the context of the debate sparked by the remarks of presidential candidate Nicolas Sarkozy in 2006 about the seventeenth-century classic *La Princesse de Clèves*. In Merlin-Kajman's opinion, Sarkozy's attacks on a concours reading list that includes such an elitist, outdated and anti-democratic text unwillingly echo Barthes's remark about the totalitarian, "monarchic" nature of classical literature. Several decades of Postcolonial studies would also authorize us to add, following in both Barthes and Sarkozy's footsteps: "Literature is colonialism itself!" Quoting literary texts, such as Marguerite Duras' book for children *Ah Ernesto*,[9] alongside numerous anecdotal examples drawn from the current French education system, the critic discusses the widespread idea that the very act of learning represents a form of violence and alienation. The study of French language and literature, in particular, has been portrayed in children's literature and textbooks and has been theorized by pedagogues as a spiritual vampirization or colonization of the young. Thus students find themselves torn between the injunction to learn and the call to reject or resist learning, a double bind that leaves them powerless and confused. Merlin-Kajman thus states:

> Dans mon livre *La langue est-elle fasciste?*,[10] j'ai essayé de montrer comment des exercices, des choix de textes, des romans pour enfants ou des albums de jeunesse, révèlent la présence insistante d'une idéologie éducative, supposée émancipatrice, qui consiste à apprendre aux enfants à se méfier du langage, de l'éducation et de l'instruction, de l'autorité parentale et professorale, et plus largement des adultes, de leurs ordres et de leur ordre. Les enfants, sortes d'éternels colonisés de l'intérieur, sont poussés à regarder le monde dans lequel ils vont grandir, dans lequel des adultes voudraient les faire entrer, comme un monde ennemi où un pouvoir tyrannique diffus les guette pour les dominer et même les écraser, et dont ils doivent se libérer par le rire, l'insubordination, la *délinquance*, en principe symbolique. (Merlin-Kajman 2016, 65–66)

And yet, however convincing such an analysis may be, it sets aside rather than addresses the epistemic violence to which the subaltern (youth, women, colonized people) have been subjected. It also does little to invalidate the ongoing need for a hermeneutics of suspicion toward any discourse that purports to overcome past dichotomies by overlooking or negating their historical reality. As Sara E. Melzer contends in her study dedicated to France's conflicted legacy as an ancient colony and a modern colonizer:

> The French colonizing strategy in the New World borrowed the Roman colonizing strategy toward the Gauls. In sum, these two stories mirrored each other. In the first, the Gauls/French were the colonized *other*, who were then civilized by the Romans. In the second, France became the colonizer, assuming the same role as the Greco-Romans before them by colonizing the New World inhabitants. By creating a "New France" in the Americas, France would become a "New Rome." (Melzer 3)

Moreover, she insists on the necessity of examining the traditional separation between national cultural discourse and colonial critique. By working against the "dominant paradigm for early modern French culture" which "has severed colonization from its cultural discourse about itself, as if it belonged on a different planet," Melzer shows "that culture and colonization were always conjoined, so interdependent that each enabled and shaped the other" (Melzer 3).

If certain strands of contemporary criticism recognize the need for bridging the interpretive–affective gap, for practicing "surface reading"[11] and for setting down literature's distinctive and "double-edged weapon: the critique of literature versus literature as critique" (Felski 16), other voices warn against the risks brought on by non-agonistic approaches to notions such as "storytelling"[12] and the lures of interpretive polytheism. Forsaking critique and espousing an affective stance toward literary texts and practices carries within it the risk of exposing oneself to misunderstandings and seemingly abandoning the political dimension of our discipline. Yet, as Ulrich Beck points out: "the presentation and representation of the other calls not only for sound and image, but also for meaning. It presupposes an understanding of the alien Other, *cosmopolitan understanding* – or, in the humanities and social sciences, *cosmopolitan hermeneutics*" (Beck 2009, 4). To adopt a logic of risk thus opens literature to new, "unsafe" spaces while preventing it from resorting to an economy of return. Such a "risky" project can be found in Gerard Aching's choice to read a slave narrative from the point of view of what he calls, borrowing from Frederick Douglas, "the tender point" of a slave's condition, composed of all the moral duties and emotional ties overdetermining his condition. These connect him to his friends and family, thus maintaining him in a state of submission despite his will for freedom generated by the "turning point" of his defining act of rebellion against his master. In Aching's view, Douglas's seminal narrative "acknowledges how such personal deliberations transform the slave into a reflective subject of and in the struggle to be free. He demonstrates how the 'turning point' and the 'tender point' vied for dominance in his bid for freedom" (Aching 16–17).

The question then stands: If literature is both integral to humanity's survival and inseparable from its conflicted historical legacy or its inhumanity, how can we attend to the "turning points" of emancipation, liberation and (self-)recognition without being oblivious to the "tender points" that continue to bind it to past and present forms of violence and subjugation?

## Western Literary Forms and their Historical Debt

This interpretive paradigm shift resonates with another shift in contemporary French-language fiction that is less concerned with the stance and mood of "againstness" than with those of "commonality." The works examined in *The Colonial Fortune* show the persistent need for a dialogical approach between Hexagonal and non-Hexagonal literature while accounting for the changes that have intervened since 1980, when Édouard Glissant made the following remarks in *Caribbean Discourse*:

> We see that if Western literatures no longer need a hallowed presence in the world, a useless activity after these serious charges against Western history, an activity that would be qualified as a kind of mediocre nationalism, they have *on the other hand* to reflect on their new relationship with the world, which will be used, not to underline their dominant place in the process of Sameness, but their shared role in cultural diversity. This is what was understood by those French writers who, in the caricatural manner of Loti, the tragic manner of Segalen, the catholic manner of Claudel, the esthetic manner of Malraux, sensed that after so much wandering through the West, it now finally was necessary to undertake the understanding of the East. Today Diversity brings new countries into the open. When I look at literary activity in France at present, I am struck by its inability to understand this phenomenon, this new basis of cultural relationship in the world: that is, ultimately by its lack of generosity. (Glissant 1989, 101–102)[13]

Examples of imbrication of the resistance to and use of Western artistic practices in the colonial era allow for a better understanding of the precarious but enduring mission of literature in carving out a place, a *lieu*, for indigenous forms of expression. In an essay entitled "La 'littérature indigène d'expression française': une histoire pré-postcoloniale," Vincent Debaene focuses on the case of French colonial authors. The context of publication, content selection and critical introductions signed by two heralds of the Négritude movement, Senghor and Damas, of two anthologies from the late 1940s serves to illustrate the moment of emergence and strategies for gaining historical and aesthetic legitimacy by Francophone writers in the wake of the Second World War. After rehearsing the arguments of Pascale Casanova and other scholars about the precarious position of peripheral writers and the indigenous double-bind, Debaene situates the two poetry collections *Les Plus Beaux Écrits de l'Union française et du Maghreb* and *Latitudes française: poètes d'expression française 1900–1945* into what Richard Watts calls the uncomfortable middle ground separating the colonial from the postcolonial (Watts 77). In addition to recognizing the politically, culturally and symbolically transitional nature of these volumes, their inaugural mediation of the visibility and readability of literary texts produced by indigenous colonial writers cannot be overlooked. Two arguments in Debaene's analysis are particularly persuasive. First, he examines the strategies used by Senghor and Damas to shape the reader's expectations by referencing literary awards bestowed upon colonial writers (such as René Maran's Goncourt in 1921) and previous praises received by the work or its writer (from major metropolitan figures such as Anatole France and Paul Claudel). Both authors seek to insert poetic works stemming from the colonies into a larger literary history and, in both cases, Surrealism serves as a historical and aesthetic point of connection allowing them to reconstruct French poetic tradition and expand it beyond its metropolitan boundaries. However, whereas Senghor suggests a "civilizational" (Debaene et al. 290), Herderian model for collecting the writings of Black Africa, Damas seeks to establish "an intercolonial means of expression" (Debaene et al. 294), lacking heretofore, by retracing the dialectics of colonial writers' progressive dis-alienation (epitomized by the tragic figure of the Caribbean writer Étienne Léro). Second, Debaene explains that theoretical rationales generated a new narrative whose devices and classifications shaped the discourse of Francophone scholarship for decades afterwards. Moreover, he draws attention to the fact that, unlike similar literary projects, these anthologies do not aim to provide a definition of poetry nor do they offer an interpretive framework, which allows him to argue that viewing these anthologies as a desire for colonial recognition would be misleading. Their goal is instead to render the texts and their authors readable by making them available and understandable to the French audience, with Senghor and Damas serving as mediators. The generations that followed, from Ahmadou Kourouma, Soni Labou Tansi and Maryse Condé to Patrick Chamoiseau and Calixthe Beyala, and, more recently, Léonora Miano and Rachid Djaïdani, have increasingly shifted from the paradigm of cultural translation to intercultural challenge by practicing, in diverse and singular ways, the poetics of opacity:

> The literary text plays the contradictory role of a producer of opacity. Because the writer, entering the dense mass of his writings, renounces an absolute, his poetic intention, full of self-evidence and sublimity. Writing's relation to that absolute is relative; that is, it actually renders it opaque by realizing it in writing. The text passes from a dreamed-of

transparency to the opacity produced in words. Because the written text opposes anything that might lead a reader to formulate the author's intention differently. At the same time, he can only guess at the shape of this intention. The reader goes, or rather tried to go back, from the produced opacity to the transparency that he read into it. (Glissant 1997, 115)

Such approaches show that the boundaries between colonial (understood as Western or metropolitan) and postcolonial (non-Western) discourses are fluid, shifting and constantly redrawn. Rather than providing definitive answers, they provoke a series of questions about their mutual influences, collisions and collusions, as well as about the new sensible and intelligible forms their encounter may generate. In his "Introduction" to *Culture and Imperialism*, Said argues that "the history of imperialism and its culture can now be studied as neither monolithic nor reductively compartmentalized, separate, distinct" (Said 1994, xx), adding that:

> The great cultural archive [...] is where the intellectual and aesthetic investments in the overseas dominion are made. If you were British or French in the 1860s you saw, and you felt, India and North Africa with a combination of familiarity and distance, but never with a sense of their separate sovereignty. (Said 1994, xxi)

Nineteenth-century literature conveyed the hegemonic discourse and its underlying values by exhibiting the authorial perspective as "an active point of energy that made sense not just of colonizing activities but of exotic geographies and people" (Said 1994, xxi). It is in this context of mutual influence, both revealed and obfuscated in culture, that the author of *Orientalism* situates his new project:

> One of imperialism's achievements was to bring the world closer together, and although in the process the separation between Europeans and natives was an insidious and fundamentally unjust one, most of us should now regard the historical experience of empire as a common one. The task then is to describe it as pertaining to Indians *and* Britishers, Algerians *and* French, Westerners *and* Africans, Asians, Latin Americans, and Australians despite the horrors, the bloodshed, and the vengeful bitterness. (Said 1994, xxi–xxii)

How, then, can one acknowledge the generative power of the common experience of empire without acquiescing to the systemic violence – that is, "the violence inherent in a system: not only direct physical violence, but also the more subtle forms of coercion that sustain relations of domination and exploitation, including the threat of violence" (Žižek 8)

– from which it stemmed? One response has recourse to the "symbolic violence of the language" (Žižek 1) to produce critical readings and counter-readings, forms of "writing back" and hybrid discourses. Another, more ambiguous and even potentially insidious, emphasizes continuity and exults in difference while reminding readers of the exotic strangeness of the new cultural forms born of the colonial or imperial encounter, as does Milan Kundera in his geo-cultural definition of the novel, which draws the boundary between originary and hybrid novelistic forms at the 35th parallel:

> Les romans créés au-dessous du 35ᵉ parallèle, quoique un peu étrangers au goût européen, sont le prolongement de l'histoire du roman européen, de sa forme, de son esprit, et sont même étonnamment proches de ses sources premières: nulle part ailleurs la vieille sève rabelaisienne ne coule aujourd'hui si joyeusement que dans les œuvres de ces non-européens. (Kundera 43–44)

Yet others choose to engage even more deeply with the compatibility between form and subject matter and the compossibility of expression and experience in a physical and symbolic space rent with conflict. In "Reading the South African Landscape," J. M. Coetzee confronts the questions of authenticity and belonging through the issue of representing Africa in a European language: "The questions that trouble white South African poets above all are, as you might expect, whether the land speaks a universal language, whether the African landscape can be articulated in a European language, whether the European can be at home in Africa" (Coetzee 167).

Questions about the geographic origins or cultural essence of the idea and practice of literature, the inherent relation between land and language, and the right to write (who, where, to whom, about what, in what language) are not limited to the postcolonial context. They belong to the group of enduring paracolonial questions born of often-violent intercultural contacts that alter, alienate even, all those involved. In a 2009 lecture entitled "Faire l'histoire, écrire l'histoire," Édouard Glissant finds in William Faulkner's prose the traces of the mutual damnation of slavery: "Il ne peut pas le dire mais toute son œuvre dit que la damnation, c'est l'esclavage, et que le damnant qui est aussi le damné c'est le Blanc. Dit impeccable et si profond" (Perrot-Corpet and Gauvin 35). Even more important than the reasons – be they biographical, psychological or ideological – underlying the inability to tell or write what lies beneath the fragile fabric of a society haunted by its repressed past is the aesthetic generative force stemming from this silence which leads the native of Oxford, Mississippi, to transform writing itself for generations to come: "À partir de cela, Faulkner pratique ce que j'appelle une écriture *différée*. Il dit la malédiction du Sud et son origine sans jamais les dire, tout en les disant toujours" (Perrot-Corpet and Gauvin 35). Contemporary literature emerges in the wake of this event not as an "écriture positive qui affirme, décrit, conduit [...] écriture directe du récit" but as "l'écriture *qui dit, tout en différant de dire, et en disant toujours, pour attendre à l'absolu du dire*. Qui dit la malédiction sans la dire, tout en la disant toujours, et atteint l'absolu du dire qui n'est ni le récit, ni la fiction ni l'histoire" (Perrot-Corpet and Gauvin 35).

A new kind of writing is deployed in the folds of the "dire sans dire, tout en disant toujours," one that struggles with and even moves against or beyond storytelling. It is beholden to the duty of disclosing collective secrets, including the secret of "melancholy attachments" (Aching 91) to the system of subjugation into which one is born or to which one is bonded, and bridges the gaps of official history, a necessary process for which Glissant himself argues in *Caribbean Discourse*.

Éric Méchoulan asks:

> Comment montrer simultanément son respect des contextes toujours particuliers d'écriture, de publication, de lecture et son admiration intangible pour la qualité d'un texte ? Face à tout ce qui nous parle encore au *présent* dans une œuvre, comment la tenir pour une chose du *passé* qui ne nous dirait plus rien ? Bref, peut-on ne pas choisir entre le désuet et l'immédiat ? (Méchoulan 11)

The same question can be asked of the body of works examined here. In spite of their synchronicity, one can hardly overlook the discrepancy between the traditions from which they draw their inspiration and, indeed, their legitimacy, as well as their sense of belonging to a historical and literary period. What is at stake here is literature's duty to remember without memorializing or concealing, without glorifying or trivializing, without erecting monuments to arrest the meaning of the past or casting a veil to shield the present from the horrors of history. Narrative and fiction writing steps into the breach opened by history's own mission as it grapples with two impossible tasks: "L'historiographie suppose qu'il est devenu impossible de croire en cette présence des morts qui a organisé (ou organise) l'expérience de civilisations entières, et qu'il est pourtant impossible de 's'en remettre', d'accepter la perte d'une vivante solidarité avec les disparus, d'entériner une limite irréductible" (de Certeau 12).

Rent with doubt about the continued presence of the past as a living relation with the dead rather than an abstract notion and unwilling to sever the very same relation by drawing boundaries between past and present, history finds itself burdened with an unpayable debt. Éric Méchoulan comments on De Certeau's passage in the following fashion:

> Là où il y avait dette et présence des ancêtres, la dette est désormais perdue comme telle et les anciens sont absents. On pourrait croire que tout va pour le mieux dans le meilleur des mondes possibles, puisque l'on s'est débarrassé d'une encombrante dette, inutile au fond, dans la mesure où l'origine de toute production, y compris celle des dieux, vient de nous. Et pourtant le gain à se décharger de la dette n'a rien d'évident, puisque, du coup, nous voilà hantés par le deuil du passé. Ce 'travail du deuil' auquel nous nous sommes astreints, nous le nommons 'histoire'. Car il s'agit bien d'un travail, d'un lieu de production. Rendre le passé, n'est pas le redonner, encore moins le donner, c'est le produire par la force de travail de l'écriture. Le savoir en est la *plus-value*. (Méchoulan, 40)

The ideal of "producing the past through the force of writing" pervades the pages of novels, short stories and memoirs. Meanwhile, the author's ability to reimagine and illuminate the past is shaped and challenged by personal agendas and public expectations and demands. One intriguing example is provided by the "human rights bestseller" examined by Elizabeth S. Anker through several contemporary English-language novels, such as Salman Rushdie's *Midnight's Children*, Nawal El Saadawi's *Woman at Point Zero*, J. M. Coetzee's *Disgrace* and Arundhati Roy's *The God of Small Things*.

> A genre with both fictional and journalistic instantiations, the "human rights bestseller" [shows] how contemporary narratives of human rights marshal many well-rehearsed conventions of imperialist discourse, along with paternalistic conjectures about the need of the "Third World" for salvation through recourse to the very values that those conventions smuggle in. These apologias for humanitarian intervention are replete with exoticizing, infantilizing, and other demeaning stereotypes, even as they deploy the aesthetic codes of sentimental literature to cultivate sympathy for postcolonial despair. While they thus require that we revisit historically antecedent manifestations of imperialistic discourse, these narratives in addition perform relatively new work in cementing the descriptive authority of the languages of human rights, along with the liberal topographies of selfhood that they imply. (Anker 35)

The narrative of what I call mortified memory, just as the human rights bestseller, presents an example of writerly engagement with the past that makes short work of the debt, or rather perpetuates the aesthetic of exoticism understood as "[l]a totalité de la dette contractée par l'Europe littéraire à l'égard des autres cultures" (Moura 38).

## Liminality and Border Thinking

In colonial fortune writings, the colonial figure – a trope, an event or a scene – appears both peripheral – that is, ex-centric, far from the textual center and the narrative core – and liminal, as a transitional object for the narrator's biographical act and a threshold for the *scriptor*'s entrance into the realm of literature. By emphasizing these moments of transition and contact, these texts also invite readers to reimagine what Walter Mignolo calls "border thinking" or "border gnosis." These expressions refer to specific forms of sensing and knowing acquired by dwelling in imperial/colonial borderlands, which are capable of countering the tendency of occidentalist perspectives to manage, and thus limit, the understanding of the "colonial difference" (Mignolo 5). As a space of transculturation or a contact zone of "shifting and multiple identity," the borderland is "not a comfortable territory to live in [...] Hatred, anger and exploitation are the prominent features of this landscape" (Anzaldúa 1). Whereas Gloria Anzaldúa emphasizes the antagonistic potential of the contact zone, Mignolo argues that its agonism reveals that "a post-Occidental stage is being thought out" (Mignolo 7), which erases "the distinction between the knower and the known, between a 'hybrid' object (the borderland as the known) and a 'pure' disciplinary or interdisciplinary subject (the knower), uncontaminated by the border matters he or she describes" (Mignolo 18). This perspective emerges clearly from the texts I propose to study, which display a similar interest in teasing out the many forms and manifestations of border thinking without doing away with the "contamination" of the border matters. On the contrary, narrative and fiction intensify the frictions, tensions and incompatibilities between the subjects, situations and territories that meet but also collide in these "social spaces where disparate cultures meet, clash and grapple with each other, often in highly asymmetrical relations of domination and subordination – such as colonialism and slavery, or their aftermaths as they are lived out across the globe today" (Pratt 7). They re-enact the colonial drama of the encounter between the sovereign subject and radical strangeness. Such encounters mobilize all forms of knowledge, both *doxa* and *episteme*, philosophy, rhetoric, and science combined or, to use the term that Mignolo borrows from V. Y. Mudimbe, *gnosis* (Mudimbe 23).

The engagements they generate could be described using Carl Schmitt's political model of friend vs. enemy that "denotes the utmost degree of intensity of a union or separation, of an association or dissociation" (Schmitt 26). Schmitt explains:

> The political enemy need not be morally evil or aesthetically ugly, [...] he need not appear as an economic competitor, and it may even be advantageous to engage with him in business transactions. But he is, nevertheless, the other, the stranger; and it is sufficient for his nature that he is, in an especially intense way, existentially something different and alien, so that in the extreme case conflicts with him are possible. (Schmitt 27)

However, unlike the political antagonism, which is primarily positional and collective, circumscribing the sphere of the enemy to the public entity or *hostis*, the colonial antagonism includes both the collective and the individual, *hostis* and *inimicus*, the political other and the ontological other. Even as the process of absorption and displacement is defined as an antagonistic process, it results in new forms of knowledge. The question then becomes whether the antagonistic friend/enemy model that Carl Schmitt uses to describe the absolute negativity that serves as the foundation of the political and can at the same time be viewed as the foundation of the colonial contact (between mutually exclusive groups) may be reworked into an "us/them" agonistic model predicated on the confrontation of equal adversaries. In my analysis of literature's engagement with the "memory wars" over colonial Algeria, I refer to the model provided by Chantal Mouffe, a proposition based on the understanding that "every identity is relational and that the affirmation of a difference is a precondition for the existence of any identity – i.e. the perception of something 'other' which constitutes its 'exterior'" (Mouffe 5). In Mouffe's view, politics is founded on the demarcation between "we" and "they"; however, such a relation need not be antagonistic. Unlike antagonism, which occurs "when the others, who up to now were considered as simply different, start to be perceived as putting into question *our* identity and threatening *our* existence" (Mouffe 5), "agonistic struggle" (Mouffe 7) cultivates conflict, dissent and dialogue between adversaries and not enemies. A similar move from mutual exclusion based on ontological incompatibility to agonistic coexistence could describe the colonial contact, if only in an anachronistic or hypothetical reimagining.

I argue that colonial fortune writing incorporates all these different models without offering a dialectical solution but rather playing up the fault lines, cracks and incongruities of "the space of imperial encounters, the space in which peoples geographically and historically separated come into contact with each other and establish ongoing relations, usually involving conditions of coercion, radical inequality, and intractable conflict" (Pratt 8). Drawing on Glissant's *Poétique de la Relation*, Mignolo writes:

> the imaginary of the modern/colonial world is its self-description, the ways in which it described itself through the discourse of the state, intellectuals, and scholars. [...] By "border thinking" I mean the moments in which the imaginary of the modern world system cracks. "Border thinking" is still within the imaginary of the modern world system, but repressed by the dominance of hermeneutics and epistemology as keywords controlling the conceptualization of knowledge. (Mignolo 23)

In her theorization of the contact zone, Mary Louise Pratt remarks that the expression, borrowed from linguistics, indicates a space where a common language is developed among speakers of different tongues who need to communicate, especially in trade. Such an idiom, she further argues, is considered chaotic, barbarous and lacking in structure. To the European expansionist perspective that inheres in the study of colonialism, the contact zone "shifts the center of gravity and the point of view" and

> foregrounds the interactive, improvisational dimensions of imperial encounters so easily ignored or suppressed by accounts of conquest and domination told from the invader's perspective. A "contact" perspective emphasizes how subjects get constituted in and by their relations to each other. It treats the relations among colonizers and colonized, or travelers and "travelees," not in terms of separateness, but in terms of co-presence, interaction, interlocking understandings and practices, and often within radically asymmetrical relations of power. (Pratt 8)

First, in my view, the borderland or contact zone is not just a common place but also "a common-place" in Glissant's vocabulary of relation: that is, "un lieu-commun (lié d'un trait d'union, par exception à l'usage grammatical autorisé quand l'expression signifie une évidence ou une vérité nue) [...] un lieu où chaque fois une pensée du monde appelle et éclaire une pensée du monde" (Glissant 2009, 25).

Second, as my readings of Le Clézio will show, for instance, this place where the other is encountered, solicited and called upon can be imagined as the non-place of the *khôra*, which oscillates between a logic of exclusion and one of participation (Derrida 1995, 91). Neither being nor non-being, neither a dwelling place nor a void, it "is not that in which is found a subject or an object. It is found in us" (Derrida 1995, 57).

Third, the colonial fortune seeks to "explor[e] a field invested with a particular body of imaginative discourse, marked by both a convergence of themes and a common preoccupation with the modes of address of a new self formulation" (Irele 4), akin to the concept of *African imagination*, defined by Abiola Irele as "a conjunction of impulses that have been given a unified expression in a body of literary texts" (Irele 4).

In the first part of this book, entitled "From Exotic Destinations to Colonial Destinies" and comprised of two chapters, I show that contemporary narratives both exploit and subvert the tropes of finding or making one's fortune in the former colonies or the current neocolonial space (whether it is late nineteenth-century and early twentieth-century Africa or the contemporary avatars of "Françafrique," the early settlements of Mauritius or the slave plantations of Saint Lucia in the eighteenth century) as a plot-starting device, a turning point (a catastrophe, in the Aristotelian sense) or a significant background story. The second part, "Writing as Africans," looks at how narratives of the "colonial fortune" struggle with the loss of the experiential and emotional memory generated by the diversity of colonial life (from rich landowners, poor whites or "Petits Blancs" and various representatives of the colonial administration to native families who share French values, from those who reject oppression and work to overthrow the colonial regime to "métis" children torn between two different cultures or French individuals who imagine themselves living the life of the colonized or subaltern "other"). I therefore argue for a dynamic and transformative interpretation in which colonial encounters can be understood to encompass past and present, taking into account the historical conditions of their occurrence along with their current effects and after-effects. However, these novels also envision the colonial past as an inexhaustible, everlasting and burdensome debt. Thus, in the third part, entitled "Colonial Remanence," I turn to the contested memories of colonial Algeria to investigate whether literature can offer a space of dialogue and civility located between the narratives of nostalgia and reconciliation, on the one hand, and those of anger and melancholia, on the other. I conclude with a series of readings that expound on the idea of "unpayable debt" associated with France's colonial past (in

Haiti, metropolitan France and Africa), while arguing for an approach that pays heed to the paracolonial aesthetics present in colonial fortune writings.

My analysis transitions from the study of natural and vocational tropes in the works of Pierre Michon, Paule Constant, Claude Simon, Tierno Monénembo, J. M. G. Le Clézio and Édouard Glissant, in the first part, to the examination of figures of emotion and self-actualization in Le Clézio, Marie Darrieussecq, Laurent Gaudé, Marie NDiaye and Stéphane Audeguy in the second. I then turn to both fictional reflections of and the literary reflection on the burden of memory and the haunting past in documentary and fictional writing about Algeria, drawing parallels beween several politically motivated texts and the literary works of Leïla Sebbar. I conclude with a perusal of the idea of colonial debt in writings by Lyonel Trouillot, Régis Jauffret and Léonora Miano.

The goal of this book is neither to rehabilitate the colonial perspective or its post- or neocolonial avatars, nor to instrumentalize literature in order to expose, denounce or demystify the overt or covert presence of orientalist nostalgia or postcolonial melancholy. By addressing the topic of the colonial fortune I propose to focus on a shared imaginary space that incorporates symbolic, rhetorical and conceptual aspects of the colonial and postcolonial periods, shaped by past and present discourse, both mimetic and analytical. To attend to the web of colonial references, as they are manifested on the stylistic, narrative or conceptual level, in ways that underscore continuity rather than divergence, adhesion rather than critique, interrelation rather than disconnectedness, does not signal a rejection of the critical stances concerned with the issues of repression, hegemony or mimicry raised by these references. I argue instead for an approach that illuminates both continuities and discontinuities between literary and testimonial texts (fiction, autobiography and essay) that are historically and aesthetically diverse. The core question that emerges from this study is: Can a non-antagonistic reading of colonial scenes, events and tropes reveal something about contemporary French-language writing that is concealed, obfuscated or simply overlooked by other reading models or interpretive configurations? Even as I seek to intervene in the scholarship dedicated to individual authors, I also hope to contribute to recent developments in French and Francophone literary history (McDonald and Suleiman), *littérature-monde* (Hargreaves, Forsdick and Murphy), animal studies (Mackenzie and Posthumus), ecocriticism (Collot; Schoentjes) and memory studies (Rothberg, Sanyal and Silverman). Ultimately, my book can serve as a space of cross-boundary reflection on the disciplinary divisions, ideological preconceptions and intellectual disagreements that characterize the study of French-language literature today.

### Notes

1 "remanence, n." *OED Online*. Oxford University Press, September 2015. Web. December 5, 2015.

2 "para-." *Merriam-Webster.com*. Merriam-Webster, 2015. Web. November 27, 2015.

3 The Winter 2012 issue of *New Literary History* featured two articles by Robert J. C. Young ("Postcolonial Remains") and Dipesh Chakrabarty ("Postcolonial Studies and the Challenge of Climate Change") under the heading "The State of Postcolonial Studies," which sparked a conversation that continued in the following volume with reactions from Bill Bell ("Signs Taken for Wonders: An Anecdote Taken from History"), Simon During ("Empire's Present"), Benita Parry ("What is Left in Postcolonial Studies"), Ato Quayson ("The Sighs of History: Postcolonial Debris and the Question of (Literary) History") and Robert Stam and Ella Shohat ("Whence and Whither Postcolonial Theory?"). This was, of course, one of the more powerful belated iterations of the ongoing debate surrounding the end of postcolonial studies. For an earlier synthesis on the issue, see for instance: *Editor's Column: The End of Postcolonial Theory?* A Roundtable with Sunil Agnani, Fernando Coronil, Gaurav Desai, Mamadou Diouf, Simon Gikandi, Patricia Yaeger and Susie Tharu, *PMLA*, Vol. 122, No. 3 (May, 2007), pp. 633–651.

4 https://www.laits.utexas.edu/africa/ads/1528.html (accessed March 8, 2017). Charles Forsdick finds in Glissant's concept of Relation the same connotations of heterogeneity and compositness that he uses to buttress his argument for an integrative approach to postcolonial studies in French: "I borrow Glissant's term as it reflects the unevenness of these connections to which I have alluded, belying the official and homogenizing rhetoric of any political understanding of la Francophonie and ranging from the neocolonial to more complex processes of transculturation whereby the metropolitan, in a disruption of the entropic logic of globalization, is itself altered, denatured, and sent back in often unrecognizable forms. I am not suggesting that all those in French studies must adopt this approach, or sustain this type of research: in terms of individual specialisms, metropolitan and non-metropolitan focus will often be maintained, although projects will increasingly and inevitably bridge the gap between them, suggesting that these categories are no longer, and perhaps never were, watertight. However, what is required is an awareness of a wider field of operations: issues dubbed 'intercultural' are not only to be addressed by modernists; the objects of 'postcolonial' investigation are not bound by geography or chronology, and must not be defined by a residual

colonial exoticism that denies France's own postcolonial status" (Forsdick 2005, 530).

5 Edward Said, *Representations of the Intellectual: The 1993 Reith Lectures*, London: Vintage, 1994, p. 36, in Forsdick 2005, 530.

6 "La spécificité de notre espèce est qu'elle passe sa vie à jouer sa vie" (Huston 158).

7 See, for instance, Jean Bessière, *Énigmaticité de la littérature*, Paris: PUF, 1993.

8 Roland Barthes, "Réflexions sur un manuel" (1971), *Œuvres complètes*, tome III, p. 949.

9 "En 1971, l'année de la première publication des 'Réflexions sur un manuel' de Barthes, un album de jeunesse écrit par Marguerite Duras, *Ah Ernesto*, présentait un petit garçon refusant d'aller à l'école parce qu'à l'école, le maître veut lui apprendre des choses qu'il ne sait pas. Inquiets, les parents vont voir le maître d'école qui brille par sa stupidité et sa brutalité:

La maman d'Ernesto et Ernesto, eux, regardent le matériel scolaire:
Le pousse-pousse. Le train. La rose. Le papillon. La terre...
... Le Président. Le Nègre. Le Chinois. L'Homme.
– Alors ? conclut encore le maître: on refuse de s'instruire ?...

L'humanisme scolaire sert le colonialisme. Et lorsque Ernesto est prié de dire ce que c'est que 'le papillon orange et bleu épinglé dans sa boîte vitrée', il répond: 'C'est un crime !'. Contre la culture occidentale de fond en comble violente et injuste, le refus de s'instruire d'Ernesto constitue donc un acte de résistance" (Merlin-Kajman 2016, 66).

10 Hélène Merlin-Kajman, *La Langue est-elle fasciste ? Langue, pouvoir, enseignement*, Paris: Seuil, 2003.

11 Stephen Best and Sharon Marcus (eds.), "The Way We Read Now", *Representations*, Vol. 108, No. 1, Fall 2009.

12 See, for instance, the works of Yves Citton, *Mythocratie. Storytelling et imaginaire de gauche*, Paris: Éditions Amsterdam, 2010a and *L'Avenir des humanités*, Paris: Éditions de la Découverte, 2010b.

13 At the time when Beur writers were becoming increasingly visible and vocal, Glissant also had strong words for the ethnocentric "naïveté" of such identitarian discourses that threatened, in his view, to build a "banlieue provisoire" for minority texts and their writings (Glissant, *Le Discours antillais*, 332–333, Folio).

# PART ONE

# From Exotic Destinations to Colonial Destinies

In these chapters I propose to engage with the seminal scene of the departure for and arrival in the colonies, which signify in the eyes of the European colonist the means to a better life or the chance to create a new identity. I analyze the intimate and multifaceted relation between the colonial destination and the modern Western belief in the interconnectedness of individual and historical destiny. For the average Frenchman of the interwar period, when the French empire was at its height, "the colonial image, if any, was that of a grinning black man advertising a sweet chocolate drink: Banania" (Weber 180). The colonies were an inviting, challenging and fascinating place waiting to be discovered, tamed and civilized. Colonial writing exudes a sense of the phenomenon Stanley Cavell calls "to view the world unseen" (Cavell 40), insofar as looking at the colonies from home presents the subject with a triply enticing and challenging, almost cinematic, "elsewhere": it holds the promise of a destiny fulfilled, it is fraught with peril and it represents a black hole for knowledge but a glory hole for the imagination. However, what some experience as a liberating adventure of conquest and self-reinvention others, whom Marguerite Duras calls "les indigènes coloniaux" (Duras and Porte 17), or poor white trash, accept it as a last resort, an exile forced upon them by necessity, poverty and a lack of prospects in the Metropole. The texts in this chapter are born from the encounter of different forms of oppression and human misery blindly mirroring each other.

Jane Bradley Winston draws out an interesting parallel between these two types of colonial writing through the comparison of Richard Wright and Marguerite Duras:

> Where Wright bears witness from the place of the unambiguously oppressed, Duras bears witness from the contradictory position of a figure modeled on her young self – the poor colon daughter. Displaced from the unambiguous subjective witness bearing place of Wright, this position permitted her to disrupt the allegedly 'unified' subject both he and Sartre maintain. Disconnected, passive, *en attente* (in a waiting state), her novel's daughter serves as a relay and a conduit: in and through her (textual place), Duras introduces multiple perspectives on and accounts of colonial oppression, elaborated from various positions of race, culture, and gender. (Winston 27–28)

They center around what Zygmunt Bauman calls the human redundancy of those who are considered to be supernumerary, unneeded or disposable – in other words, "wasted lives" by a modernity stemming from the synergy between capitalism and colonialism: "The production of 'human waste', or more correctly wasted humans (the 'excessive' and 'redundant', that is the populations of those who either could not or were not wished to be recognized or allowed to stay), is an inevitable outcome of modernization, and an inseparable accompaniment of modernity" (Bauman 5). Their narrating or writing subjects bear testimony to the same guilt and self-distrust captured by Marguerite Duras in her sharp statement: "En somme, on part avec une méfiance de soi, avec une culpabilité, on part pour écrire avec des petits bagages de quatre sous, que les autres ont ficelés pour vous, on ne part pas dans la liberté" (Duras and Porte 32).

# CHAPTER ONE

# Departures

## Orphans, Heirs and Adventurers

I will focus on the works of four writers, Paule Constant, Pierre Michon, Claude Simon and Tierno Monénembo, whose scenes of departure (from the characters' native village in the Creuse or Limousin or the cities of Lyon or Paris) and arrival (in Africa or the Americas) are saturated with tropes of yearning and despair that simultaneously conjure up exotic fantasies and deep-seated anxieties of displacement and alienation. The decision to leave for the colonies is often prompted by complex social and economic circumstances. Stripped of their agency and eager to re-establish it, metropolitan subjects undertake the trip to the colonies as a last resort.

Through a series of close readings and comparative analyses I underline the rhetorical and stylistic strategies employed by these four very different writers in their articulation of a similar verbal and ideological connection between the colonial journey, on the one hand, and the sense of individual and collective destiny, on the other. These two diptychs manifest an array of attitudes, positionalities, values and beliefs associated with the liminal moments of the colonial journey, its beginnings and endings. Beyond the obvious reference to Said's theorization of the term "beginnings"[1] as the novelistic production of meaning and cultural difference, the plural signals the constant mirroring and reduplication of the origins in their retrospective, and often belated, narrative framing. Furthermore, I contend that current texts filter the historical past through the subjective perspective of a contemporary individual whose connection to the narrated time and events is at once tenuous and permanent, mediated by an intimate or official memory chain forever imprinted in the subject's own memory. In Pierre Michon and Paule Constant's fiction, the colonial imaginary is a distant mosaic, a literary re-membering of fragmented and shifting family stories, framed by incantatory phrases and magical relics (a bundle of letters, a bag of coffee beans) passed on through generations. These material objects transcend the status of "imported objects" while evincing a similar duality to that of their counterparts in the novels of the nineteenth century: they serve as a "magic" sublimation of money, "but [they act] simultaneously as a reminder that such sublimation is impossible" (Yee 31). For Claude Simon and Tierno Monénembo the colonial experience is a rewriting of an established genre – the historiographic novel – bound by formal conventions, moral codes and value systems.

## Humble Lives and Colonial Transfigurations

In Pierre Michon's *Vies minuscules*, a homodiegetic "biofiction" (Gefen 305), the narrator Pierrot is the erudite but illegitimate offspring of peasants and country teachers, a recurrent figure in contemporary French fiction, from Annie Ernaux and Marie NDiaye to Pierre Bergounioux and Richard Millet. To make sense of his own life, this "transfuge social" must retrace the lives of the people around and before him; thus, his writing has elicited a taxonomical boom, with terms such as "biographical fiction", "pseudobiography" or "oblique autobiography" being used to describe Michon's work as well as that of his peers (Castiglione 2001). Yet, while the provincial themes and the dizzying labyrinth of literary and artistic references have been studied in great detail insofar as they generate a textural fold where an "absolute" style is molded by careful attention to the humble lives of ordinary people, the integral connection between the interweaving of guilt, despair and desire, on the one hand, and the colonial dream, on the other, remains to be elucidated. In an attempt to fill the paternal void and alleviate the mediocrity of his origins, the narrator, a self-avowed Rimbaud imitator and would-be spiritual heir, begins by probing the possibilities of the past in "Vie d'André Dufourneau."

In Paule Constant's heterodiegetical novel *White Spirit* (1989), which received the Grand Prix du Roman de l'Académie Française, the neocolonial dream of fulfillment and legitimacy also stems from the amalgamation of genealogical deficiency and social inadequacy. Orphan and poor, the hero must depart from the place of his humble origins in metropolitan France in order to be reborn in the extension of the national space that is the global postcolony, defined by Achille Mbembe as "a timespace characterized by proliferation and multiplicity [...] an era of dispersed entanglements, the unity of which is produced out of differences [...] an overlapping of different, intersected and entwined threads in tension with one another."[2]

Another striking similarity between the fiction of Constant and Michon lies in the role of the grandmother as both the originator of the journey and keeper of the story; willed into reality by her imagination and imprinted in her memory, the colonial adventure is a fairy tale, albeit one with a bloody ending. The old woman stands in, physically, for absent parents and, fictionally, for a possible future (Constant) or a hypothetical past (Michon).

For Michon, fiction springs from the desire to adorn the paucity of reality with the rich cloth of imagination. As keen as the narrator's questions appear to be on conjuring up a splendid genealogical tree, the answer – or the book itself, which could be construed as a metalepsis of its first paragraph – will persistently thwart the initial scenario – that is, the reconstruction of the narrator's family history. This rhetorical strategy is foreshadowed by the anticlimactic tone of the sentence following the opening paragraph, correcting the reader's assumption by indicating the landlocked, confined and unromantic setting of the story: "La province dont je parle est sans côtes, plages ni récifs; ni Malouin exalté ni hautain Moco n'y entendit l'appel de la mer quand les vents d'ouest la déversent, purgée de sel et venue de loin, sur les châtaigniers" (Michon 9). Narrative patterns collide in Michon's representation of this modern era through a series of elaborate scenes similar to the enlarged details of a painting by Greuze or Le Nain, two recurrent references in his work. The orphan André Dufourneau, a nineteenth-century *alter ego* of the narrator, whose humble destiny is also an anamorphosis of Rimbaud's extraordinary journey from rebel modern poet to African slave trader, offers at first the misleading thread of a rags-to-riches narrative set against the backdrop of French colonial expansion, in what Patrick Crowley calls an "Ivory Coast composed of both the imaginary and the real" (Crowley).[3] In his study of "the French Atlantic's dispersal of 'Frenchness'" (Marshall 301), Bill Marshall underscores the humble origins of French immigrants in the nineteenth century, "such as deserting sailors, those evading military service, indebted shopkeepers, political refugees" (Marshall 264). As a poor young man, Dufourneau's military and academic education provides him with the only prospect of a future outside of the rural setting:

Il voulut étudier, dans la mesure où les servitudes militaires le lui permettaient, et il semble qu'il y parvint, car c'était un bon garçon, capable, disait ma grand-mère. Il toucha des manuels d'arithmétique, de géographie; il les serra dans son paquetage qui sentait le tabac, le jeune homme pauvre; il les ouvrit et connut la détresse de qui ne comprend pas, la révolte qui passe outre, et, au terme d'une alchimie ténébreuse, le pur diamant d'orgueil dont l'entendement éclaire, le temps d'un souffle, l'esprit toujours opaque. Est-ce un homme, un livre, ou, plus poétiquement, une affiche de propagande de la Marsouille, qui lui révéla l'Afrique ? (Michon 13)

The core institution of the Third Republic fulfills its intended mission by becoming the catalyst for the young man's desire to improve his station in life while also contributing to the common good. Furthermore, the two ideals – free education and colonization – promoted by Jules Ferry come together in a passage where schoolbooks, surrounded by an air of mystery and impenetrability, reveal an even greater secret, a more attainable object of desire than knowledge – that is, Africa.

Paule Constant's writing, however, further engages with the postcolonial failure of the ideal. A contemporary Dufourneau seeking his fortune not in the mysterious, yet-to-be-conquered virgin forest of the continent but in the well-oiled machine of the late capitalist trading system, repeatedly described as a "prison," the protagonist of Constant's novel, Victor, has little use for the beauty of language and the symbolic value of its triumph among the formerly colonized. His meeting with the young black teacher Clément demonstrates the discrepancy between the two contradictory legacies of colonialism: materialistic cupidity, on the one hand, and cultural idealism, on the other. This scene of mutual blindness and disappointment draws a parallel with the unrealized encounter between Dufourneau and his future biographer:

Autre espoir déçu, l'instituteur dont il reçut la visite dès la première semaine. Clément était un jeune homme à la mise recherchée et à la langue châtiée, l'exemple parfait de la mission civilisatrice d'une grande culture. Il était méticuleusement soucieux de lui-même, de son aspect, de son langage. Il avait appris par cœur des livres qu'il récitait par chapitres entiers, avec l'aisance d'une brillante improvisation. Par le plus grand des hasards, celui d'une bibliothèque tenue par les jésuites, les livres qui lui donnaient la parole, des ouvrages techniques et scientifiques, dataient du XVIIIᵉ siècle. Sa langue est à la fois abstraite et pleine d'esprit, imagée aussi, mais d'une manière dont on a perdu l'usage. Sans qu'il en eût conscience, ses mots s'imprimaient sur son corps et ses gestes avaient quelque chose de suranné et de dansant, beaucoup de révérence dans les bras et dans la cuisse, une cerise sur la bouche. Clément au village, c'était Bougainville à Tahiti. Version black. (Constant 86)

Whereas the lyrical flow of the tripartite period reinforces the idea of inspirational propaganda in Constant's work, Michon offers the following skeptical interrogation that thwarts any attempt to read this into his text: "Quel hâbleur de sous-préfecture, quel mauvais roman enlisé dans les sables ou perdu en forêt sur d'interminables fleuves, quelle gravure du *Magasin pittoresque* où des hauts-de-forme luisants, noirs comme elles et comme elles surnaturels, passaient triomphalement entre de luisantes faces, fit miroiter à ses yeux le continent sombre ?" (Michon 13–14). The printed and illustrated words of popular magazines and adventure novels become the vector of a Bovarystic desire in which Dufourneau's imagination sinks and gets lost while pursuing the metonymical dream of top hats cutting a triumphant path through rows of shiny faces on the dark continent.[4] Dufourneau – or, more plausibly, his narrator – could have drawn his inspiration not only from popular sources such as magazines and minor colonial writers, but also from a chief literary figure such as Proust himself, who rehearses the leitmotif of exotic travels, both fascinating and potentially fateful or, at least, ultimate as places of no return, in several *loci* of the *Recherche du temps perdu*. The novelist modulates the destination from Algeria to America and then Oceania, making them identical in their fatal power of attraction and interchangeable, devoid of specificity other than a formal, stylistic, perhaps even sonorous distinction/singularity: "Partez donc pour l'Amérique du Sud, me disait à Querqueville M. de Penhoët, vous verrez que vous n'en reviendrez plus," he writes in *Du côté de chez Swann* (Proust I: 659), after crossing off the original "Algeria" (Proust II: 1847), and reprises the phrase later in *À l'ombre des jeunes filles en fleurs* while varying the destination to resonate with his contemporaries' artistic explorations, such as R. L. Stevenson's in Samoa or Gauguin's in Tahiti: "partir pour ces délicieuses îles de l'Océanie, vous verrez que vous n'en reviendrez pas" (Proust II: 31). The extensive use of the preterite in Michon's text signals the contamination of the biographical account by the mediated desire and illusory projection of fiction, further enhanced by the infantile dimension of the colonial dream in which self-affirmation, magical thinking and fantasy combine to form a hybrid mythology of wealth, salvation and masquerade. A ruthless dice-playing god presides over this phantasmatic scene, whose stacked deck and deadly array of symbols ("osselets," "éventrer," "cent têtes," "mille enfants perdus") portends the ancestor's fate:

Sa vocation fut ce pays où les pactes enfantins qu'on passe avec soi-même pouvaient encore, en ce temps-là, espérer d'accomplir d'éblouissantes revanches pourvu que l'on acceptât de s'en remettre au dieu hautain et sommaire de 'tout ou rien'; c'est là-bas qu'Il jouait aux osselets, dispersait les quilles indigènes et éventrait les forêts sous la boule de plomb d'un énorme soleil, misait et perdait cent têtes d'ambitieux couvertes de mouches sur les remparts d'argile des cités sahariennes, sortait avec éclat de Sa manche un brelan de rois blancs et, empochant Ses dés pipés d'ivoire et d'ébène ensachés de buffle, disparaissaient dans les savanes, en pantalon garance et casque blanc, mille enfants perdus dans son sillage. (Michon 14)

With his modest but direct intervention – "j'ose croire" – Michon's "biographer" shifts to another scenario that directly opposes Fortune to fortune, destiny to wealth and ideal to greed. Africa is the place of this bifurcation as a floating signifier, readily available to be filled with meaning:

Sa vocation fut l'Afrique. Et j'ose croire un instant, sachant qu'il n'en fut rien, que ce qui l'y appela fut moins l'appât grossier de la fortune à faire qu'une reddition inconditionnée entre les mains de l'intransitive Fortune; qu'il était trop orphelin, irrémédiablement vulgaire et non né pour faire siennes les dévotes calembredaines que sont l'ascension sociale, la probation par un caractère fort, la réussite acquise qu'on doit au seul mérite; qu'il partit comme jure un ivrogne, émigra comme il tombe. J'ose le croire. Mais parlant de lui, c'est de moi que je parle; et je ne désavouerais pas davantage ce qui fut, j'imagine, le mobile majeur de son départ: l'assurance que là-bas un paysan devenait un Blanc, et, fût-il le dernier des fils mal nés, contrefaits et répudiés de la langue-mère, il était plus près de ses jupes qu'un Peul ou un Baoulé; il la parlerait haut et en lui elle se reconnaîtrait, il l'épouserait 'du côté des jardins de palmes, chez un peuple fort doux' devenu peuple d'esclaves sur qui asseoir ces épousailles; elle lui donnerait, avec tous les autres pouvoirs, le seul pouvoir qui vaille: celui qui noue toutes les voix quand s'élève la voix du Beau Parleur. (Michon 14–15)

The passage weaves a complicated web of social frustration, compensatory ambition and anecdotal geographic and ethnographic references, framed by the literary reimaginings of a distant and improbable heir. Michon writes in a style that is not only steeped in rare terms and literary references but also endowed with an exceptional degree of physicality emanating from complex syntactical constrictions. Additionally, the insertion of nouns, both proper and common, referring to Africa along with the quote from Rimbaud's *Illuminations* creates a sense of present estrangement. The relation between language and power is the lynchpin of Dufourneau's phantasmatic departure. Rather than expansion or escape, his displacement signals, in actuality, a return, by default, to the originary fold, where filiation and wealth coalesce into the ideal of the "belle langue."

The efforts of reaffiliation in Aimé Césaire's *Cahier d'un retour au pays natal* reveal a parallel appropriation of space on the part of the Martinican poet, who retraces Black colonial history on a global scale, from the slave-holding American South to the cell that held Toussaint Louverture prisoner in the Jura mountains: "Virginie. Tennessee. Georgie. Alabama/Putréfactions monstrueuses de révoltes/ inopérantes,/marais de sang putrides/trompettes absurdement bouchées/ Terres rouges, terres sanguines, terres consanguines//Ce qui est à moi aussi: une petite cellule dans le Jura" (Césaire 25).

Thus the elusive ideal of the "belle langue" becomes attainable through the possession of land (metonymically referenced through place phrases such as "là-bas" and "jardin des palmes") and, more importantly, of people. The mediating alterity of natives ("Peules ou Baoulé") enables the ill-educated rural man to rejoin the coveted body of the French language by becoming its missionary among strangers; it is by parting with his native space that André Dufourneau is able to take possession of an elusive, unnamed ideal that could be called Frenchness. In Hannah Arendt's terms, "Only far from home could a citizen of England, Germany, or France be nothing but an Englishman or German or Frenchman" (Arendt 154). However, the reason for his quest is neither national pride nor ideological creed for the offspring of the "nuptials" ("épousailles") between the French colonist and his native tongue, celebrated on the backs of African slaves; it is the gift of speech. The "Beau Parleur" personifies the synthesis between poetics and rhetoric, the art of speaking well in addition to beautifully, the ability to delight as well as persuade.

In Constant's *White Spirit* the symbolic power of the language enhances the reverence for authority in its different forms (economic, religious, cultural). The depth but also the precarity of this relationship in the neocolonial context is highlighted by random and, thus, all the more insidious inconsistencies in the power–knowledge nexus. This discrepancy between the cultural prestige associated with the representatives of the white metropole (Paris and, more generally, France) and the reality of their unpolished language veers to satire when the Jesuit librarian proves himself capable of little else but uttering vulgarities:

Clément attendait que Victor fût, à sa façon, comme un livre, et il ne cacha pas sa déception devant ce jeune homme qui, ne sachant rien, ne savait point parler. Clément avait écouté César, il avait écouté Guastavin, il avait même écouté Ysée, ils ne disaient rien dans les termes qu'il connaissait, seulement quelques phrases hachées et déformées, des mots avalés, recrachés, rien qu'il retrouvât, c'était comme si la langue dans leur bouche était devenue infirme. Il n'avait de cesse que de regagner la biblio-thèque des jésuites, ouvrir un livre pour prendre l'assurance que la langue existait, mais à l'abri. Il refermait le livre soigneusement et le serrait entre les autres pour qu'il n'y eût pas de vide, de peur qu'un peu d'esprit de beauté ne s'échappât. Mais qu'est-ce que tu branles? demandait le jésuite bibliothécaire, qui n'avait pas un très joli langage lui non plus. (Constant 87)

Yet greed ("la convoitise") remains an integral part of this humble colonial adventurer's story. Laurent Dubreuil places "la question de la possession" at the center of the literary experience, reshaping language itself, particularly as literature becomes, throughout the nineteenth century, the vector of colonial expansion:

la littérature se trouve en quelque sorte chargée de dire la possession, qui s'enfuit de plus en plus de la description de la société européenne. [...] La colonie, d'abord lieu de possédés au même titre que certaines campagnes françaises peuplées de sorcières et démons, devient l'endroit géographique où règne l'envoûtement. [...] Pourtant, l'épreuve de la colonisation se présente, dans le langage, comme un coup de possession mené par le soi-disant Occident contre tous les Orients. La colonie doit d'autant plus être possédée de toutes parts qu'elle reçoit la hantise et l'envoûtement sous forme de présent exclusif. (Dubreuil 37)

Possession, both in the sense of the actualization of "convoitise" and the enchanting effect of the colony on the character's psyche, plays a pivotal role in the multiple reimaginings performed by the traveler's relatives. The grandmother's leitmotiv, "'là-bas, il deviendrait riche, ou mourrait'" (Michon 14), which provides the hypotext for the narrator's biographical narrative, testifies to the generative power of Dufourneau's parting scene. In conjuring up pictorial and literary representations, this memorable sentence, reprised in free indirect speech, reveals the surviving storytellers' (the narrator and his grandmother) desire to cast a more dignified light on a mere tale of survival and ambition. Scene, *tableau*, memorable sentence – the artistic lexicon veils under layers of aesthetic varnish the social and economic reality of colonialism. However, Dufourneau's story proves counter-exemplary, departing from the literary framework of colonial adventure, self-fulfillment and, ultimately, sacrifice in two distinct ways.

First, the protagonist and his journey are allowed neither to materialize nor to become the subject matter of a "morality tale" (Gikandi 2001, 4). They appear as distant temporal projections or historical remains of the past in the same phantasmatic way that Africa itself may have appeared to André Dufourneau, and are thus doubly removed from reality. Instead, the missionary fervor, the religious imagery and the sense of destiny that typically inform the colonial fable and are deconstructed by postcolonial writing participate in a reflection on the collusion and collision of literature and the world. Dufourneau's trajectory, as fulfilled by his heir, Michon, presents a reversal and an expansion of Rimbaud's journey. His portrait reflects that of Faulkner, whose physical traits, such as the "ink" moustache or the fury-silencing lips, explicitly evoke his iconic literary persona while indirectly referring to the postplantation American Southern culture of his novels:

> Allons, c'est bien à un écrivain qu'il ressemble: il existe un portrait du jeune Faulkner, qui comme lui était petit, où je reconnais cet air hautain à la fois et ensommeillé, l'œil pesant mais d'une gravité fulgurante et noire, et, sous une moustache d'encre qui jadis déroba la crudité de la lèvre vivante comme le fracas tu sous la parole dit, la même bouche amère et qui préfère sourire. (Michon 17–18)

Moreover, the memorable parting words presented as the origin of the narrator's story and, possibly, of his writerly vocation, are later recast as a sentence willed into reality by the would-be writer himself: "mais c'était moi qui la [*the sentence*] lui [*the grandmother*] demandait, moi qui voulais entendre encore ce poncif de ceux qui partent [...] Je frissonnais alors du même frisson que celui qui me poignait à la lecture des poèmes pleins d'échos et de massacres, des éblouissantes proses" (Michon 16). Therefore, the colonial fable is, in fact, a fable about the ideals and lures of literature informed by the comparison between the tangible yet perilous attraction of a continent and the intangible materiality of writing:

> je ne savais pas que l'écriture était un continent plus ténébreux, plus aguicheur et décevant que l'Afrique, l'écrivain une espèce plus avide de se perdre que l'explorateur; et quoiqu'il explorât la mémoire et les bibliothèques mémorieuses en lieu de dunes et forêts, qu'en revenir cousu de mots comme d'autres le sont d'or ou y mourir plus pauvre que devant – en mourir – était l'alternative offerte aussi au scribe. (Michon 16–17)

As objects of an unquenchable desire, both Africa and literature offer a labyrinthine space of exploration ("la mémoire et les bibliothèques mémorieuses" for the latter, "dunes et forêts" for the former). Their ineffable essence can be rendered only through an oxymoronic web where value and worthlessness, poverty and wealth and materiality and ideality are inextricably connected. Michon thematizes the relation between literature and Africa by exacerbating rather than critiquing several orientalist tropes. His focus on their creative potential confines the story of André Dufourneau to an atmosphere of phantasmagoric realism, rendering it both historically possible and fictionally implausible.

Constant's novel, on the other hand, couples corrosive irony with significant questions about forms of verbal expression, individual identity and communal values, while undermining the rhetoric of pathos associated with them. Victor's encounter with Reine Mab, the one-eyed local competitor to his establishment, casts a burlesque light on the much-debated divide between the spoken and written word. Her pronouncement conjures up the power of allegory to impress upon the young man the superiority of her knowledge, only to be distorted into parody by the narrator's intervention: "Les hommes écrivent quand ils ont perdu LA PAROLE, lui dit-elle: Comprenne qui voudra. Je sais mieux lire que toi-même, ajouta-t-elle, car moi je sais lire L'ÉCRITURE. [...] Il avait offensé la Dignité, blessé la Tradition, lésé le Commerce" (Constant 78). Simon Gikandi's observation that thinking about Africa is intrinsically dilemmatic since its conceptual invention as a site of radical difference is the result of intellectual Eurocentrism exposed but never fully abandoned by recent theories of difference and dissimilarity (Gikandi 2001, 15) also illuminates the continent's fictionalization in the colonial fortune narratives of *Vies minuscules* and *White Spirit*.

The second manner in which Dufourneau's story is counter-exemplary arises from its conclusion that underscores the affective symmetry between two worlds represented by two old women, an African and a French grandmother. While the narrative brings together their distant but mirroring recollections, factual completeness neither brings about fulfillment nor offers a final revelation:

Hier encore peut-être, quelque vieillarde assise sur le pas de sa porte à Grand-Bassam se souvenait du regard d'épouvante d'un Blanc quand miroitèrent les larmes, du peu de poids de son cadavre dont on retira les lames ternies; et morte aussi Élise, qui se souvenait du premier sourire d'un petit garçon quand on lui tendit une pomme bien rouge, vernie sur le tablier; une vie sans conséquences a coulé entre pomme et machette, chaque jour davantage émoussant le goût de l'une et aiguisant le tranchant de l'autre; qui, si je n'en prenais ici acte, se souviendrait d'André Dufourneau, faux noble et paysan perverti, qui fut bon enfant, peut-être un homme cruel, eut de puissants désirs et ne laissa de trace que dans la fiction qu'élabora une vieille paysanne disparue ? (Michon 24)

Instead of a historical tableau or a telling scene or sequence (such as the juxtaposition of memories from the hero's childhood and his tragic death) that captures the meaning of an entire life, the sum of the details is a vanity picture, a private memento of an inconsequential life unfolded "entre pomme et machette." Style and discourse are at odds in this passage. The former is ruled by the Cratylian logic of the poetic word, which, at once meaningful and evocative, can restore the original union of language and the world. A telling example is the juxtaposition of the common yet symbolically rich nouns "pomme" and "machette," a monosyllabic and a bisyllabic noun that both display a double consonant between an open vowel and a silent "e." The latter, however, moves toward dispersal and negativity, burying the overall message – and the very idea of a message – under fragmentation and hypothesis:

Je n'ai jamais rêvé sur ces lettres, au timbre et au cachet rares – Kokombo, Malamalasso, Grand-Lahou –, qui ont disparu; je crois lire ce que je n'ai jamais lu: il y parlait [...] de la saison des pluies et des menaces de guerre, d'une fleur métropolitaine dont il avait réussi la greffe; de la paresse des Noirs, de l'éclat des oiseaux, de la cherté du pain [...]. (Michon 19)

"Vie d'André Dufourneau," just as "Vie d'Antoine Peluchet" in the same volume, provides an exemplary fable of failure and disappointment undermining any colonial illusion or nostalgia. And yet Michon's writing, while fully engaging with the mediated, indirect and therefore creative fascination with the colonial ideation, looks askance, as it were, at any form of explicit commitment or morality, thus mirroring his character's inability to express the indescribable colonial experience. This ineptitude does not arise from a lack of words, however, but rather from their excess.

While the defining tropes of Michon's writing are associated with possession – of gold, language, land, people and destiny – Constant's fiction delves into the imagery of assimilation, through mental incorporation or bodily ingestion. Assimilation – along with its failures – permeates the novel through a web of textual and narrative figures. They affect the facts of everyday life, ideology, economics and politics at the haptic level, as they are woven into the very fabric of the colonial imagination.

References to assimilation are interconnected with images related to the human body (such as physical appearance and demeanor) and language (speech manners and mannerisms, as well as attitudes toward the French idiom). On the narrative level, they delineate a division between that which could or should be shown, incorporated or ingested and by whom. In Constant's novel, Victor, a young working-class man, arrives aboard a boat called *La Volonté de Dieu* in the African "Village-Modèle" near the plantation of Port-Banane, looking to find his fortune and to make a fortune. In this liminal space the neocolonial food counter marks a political frontier: "le comptoir marquait la frontière ultime qu'il ne franchissait pas, il était à la fois prisonnier et gardien" (Constant 85). Through the display of food, consumerist and cultural fetishism reinforce one another and, together, strengthen the (neo) colonial libidinal system:

> LA RESSOURCE DE L'AFRICAIN ressemblait assez à ce que l'on peut imaginer d'une cantine de prison. Peu de choses, et l'utilitaire élevé au rang du luxe. Une savonnette Palmolive présentée sur une étagère comme un flacon de Guerlain et une boîte de sardines Kerbronec mise en valeur comme du Petrossian bleu. (Constant 79)

Michon's fiction exploits the power of relics, such as the pack of coffee beans sent home by Dufourneau never to be consumed by its recipients but only touched, smelled and gazed at. If the epiphenomenality suggests an inability to incorporate this private colonial moment into the family memory, it also indicates the need to maintain its radical difference. It therefore marks the gap between the family memory and the colonial, which, in turn, highlights the significant role played by distance in Constant's fiction. This is first manifested in the use of the familiar direct style that inserts an ironic and often sarcastic tone into the indirect style of the narrative, generating a dissonance or disruption in the flow of discourse, then, through the idiosyncratic use of capital letters that create a typographical contrast between certain words and phrases and the rest of the text, and, finally, through the frequent use of antithesis to contrast the protagonist's beliefs and the reality of the "model-village," colonial ideology and practices and European and indigenous behaviors. The following sentence, harking back to the sentential style of classical moralists and the ethnographic observation of the eighteenth-century philosophers, captures this antithetical worldview: "Ici l'abondance organisait la pénurie. Les indigènes utilisaient l'instinct que leurs ancêtres avaient mis à déjouer les pièges de la forêt originelle pour découvrir ceux que leur montait l'Occident" (Constant 81). Nevertheless, an affective and ethical distance lies at the very core of the story in *White Spirit*; it characterizes not only the perspective of the narrator and her point of view about personal history, but the entire fictional world, with its characters, descriptions and plotlines.

The establishment Victor is brought in to manage on behalf of an import–export company is named "À LA RESSOURCE DE L'AFRICAIN." The narrative thus provides a glimpse into the contemporary consequences of the colonial process defined by Walter Mignolo as "the emergence of a new commercial circuit that had, in the foundation of its imaginary, the formalization of 'purity of blood' and the 'rights of the people'" (Mignolo 38). The author of *Local Histories/Global Designs* explains:

> These two principles were contradictory in their goals: the first was repressive, the second was expansive (in the sense that a new logic and new legal principles were necessary to incorporate unknown people to the imaginary). The principles of "purity of blood" and the "rights of the people" connected the Mediterranean with the Atlantic. A new imaginary configuration was coalescing, one that complemented the transformation of the geopolitical world order brought about by the "discovery" of America: the imaginary of the emerging modern/colonial world system. (Mignolo 38)

Despite the postcolonial setting of the novel, the plantation's dystopian atmosphere highlights the continuity of behaviors, ideas and practices between the colonial period and the era following decolonization. The very name of the food counter harks back to the phraseology of the civilizing mission while simultaneously mimicking the sapiential discourse of African orality. The capitalized name in reality disguises the neocolonial commercial practice of dumping expired and damaged merchandise in Africa, as the text plunges into the maze of material abjection and capitalist perversion that rule European–African trade:

> Ce qu'aurait pu lui apprendre le précédent Directeur de la RESSOURCE DE L'AFRICAIN du VILLAGE-MODÈLE, c'est que la boutique n'obéissait pas, comme on aurait pu le penser, à la loi de l'offre et de la demande, elle dépendait des stocks. La métropole et le monde entier déchargeaient leurs erreurs de fabrication dans la Mégalo. La mégalo, après avoir prélevé ce qu'elle avait trouvé de mieux, se déchargeait du reste sur Port-Banane, et Port-Banane opérait le choix à rebours pour

assurer chaque semaine au VILLAGE-MODÈLE son lot de rebuts. On en avait vu passer, des objets biscornus, de trucs fous, des gadgets bizarres, des bonnes idées de cauchemar, sans compter les reliquats de modes passées, les couleurs qui n'avaient pas pris, les formes obsolètes, les matières interdites, les jouets inflammables, le lait irradié. (Constant 81)

What began with Dufourneau's great dreams of transcending mediocrity through adventure, domination and self-sacrifice ends up in a pile of waste disguised as global goods managed by a Victor whose name belies his fate.

## Obfuscating Archives and the Alternal Novel

In Claude Simon's 1967 novel *Histoire* the colony lives on in material traces, such as the postcards left by the narrator's great-uncle, Henri de Reixach. At the diegetical level it inhabits a young woman's fantasy as the setting of an indefinitely deferred promise of marriage ("les interminables fiançailles"). To the one who impatiently awaits the advent of marital domesticity at home, the postcards project a series of exotic locations in which the immaterial projection of the future husband both eludes and invites possession: "il n'existait déjà pour elle que sous cette forme impalpable et aérienne comme si elles (les fiançailles) avaient en quelque sorte constitué une préfiguration de ce qui l'attendait après l'éblouissante et brève période où elle devait le posséder pour de bon" (Simon 18). The exotic imaginary also permeates the narratorial discourse through the ekphrasis of the traveler's illustrated correspondence:

ce qu'elle aurait ce serait cette conviction à la fois ardente et sereine qu'Il existait dans un quelque part où elle irait un jour le rejoindre un au-delà paradisiaque et vaguement oriental quelque Eden quelque jardin à l'inimaginable végétation tout bruissant du cliquetis des palmes balancées comme celles qu'elle pouvait voir ornant les timbres de ces cartes postales qu'il lui envoyait ne portant le plus souvent au verso dans la partie réservée à la correspondance qu'un simple signature au-dessous d'un nom de ville et d'une date par exemple:

"Colombo 7 / 7 / 08
Henri"
et au recto [...] au recto donc, un port, le palais d'un gouverneur, la salle à manger d'un paquebot, le lac argenté scintillant d'obscurs palmiers au troncs couchés sur l'eau une pirogue, avec, comme légende, Fishing by Moonlight on the Colombo Lake. (Simon 19–20)

If, as D. Viart has argued, epanorthosis is the defining figure of Claude Simon's writing (Viart 231), then how does its corrective drive apply to writing the colony? I contend that in *Histoire* it treads the paradoxical line between archival inscription and corrective obfuscation. The postcards carve out a particular space on the texture of the novel that is neither fully historical – for they do not directly attest to major events such as the world wars that haunt the fiction of the French Nobel prize-winner – nor purely ornamental – since their presence at once enhances the opacity of the style through an excess of substance and dematerializes the subject matter by disseminating its components. Simon's poetics of accumulation relies on the concatenation of different voices belonging to distinct narrative layers that are not separated but, on the contrary, are bound together by nominal sentences and passive verbal forms. The ubiquity of gerundival and participle (present and past) forms generates a confusion of perspectives and abolishes the sense of distance between them:

> ... semblait être non pas la prisonnière ou l'habitante mais, en quelque sorte, à la fois le donjon, les remparts et les fossés, c'est-à-dire non pas retenue par, enfermée dans, mais comme les pierres elles-mêmes, les murailles, défendue par rien d'autre [...] que par une formidable inamovibilité, une formidable capacité d'attente, inaptitude à l'impatience, qui lui faisait (avaient fait) accueillir l'amour ou plutôt l'embrasser [...] les cartes venues d'Asie ou d'Afrique [...] de sorte que les images de femmes laotiennes revenant du marché et celles des villages lacustres se mêlaient avec les vues de la mer de Glace ou de la cathédrale de Bourges pêle-mêle dans la tiroir entassées sans ordre, les années se confondant s'invertissant, la laconique signature calligraphiée avec un soin de comptable au revers de paysages tropicaux, de photographies de prostituées travesties en documents ethnographiques [...]. (Simon 22)

The portrait of the ever-patient fiancée becomes an orientalist impasto devoid of the distance necessary for staging the Other, wherein separate components of the exotic are put on an exhibitionist display shown through a myopic lens that amalgamates the "here" (the Bourges Cathedral) and "there" (Asia and Africa) and passively but ineluctably absorbs the foreign (Laotian women and anonymous prostitutes) and the different (tropical landscapes) into the sameness of the familiar (through their ethnographic distortion). The folds of Simon's vertiginous writing capture and unveil the globe-trotting movements of the absent "Il" who, like a *deus otiosus*, in the eyes of his awe-struck worshipper, becomes indistinguishable from the pictorial projections he conveys.

et onze heures du matin à Zanzibar: Water carriers at the pipe des négresses aux cheveux courts crépus remplissent des bidons de tôle à un robinet placé sur un socle de ciment et derrière elles un mur lépreux décrépi avec deux fenêtres garnies de barreaux les bidons s'entrechoquent avec un bruit creux le soleil tellement violent que l'une des femmes se protège le visage à l'aide d'un bidon vide une autre vêtue d'un tricot moutarde déchiré s'éloigne de la fontaine un bras pendant tiré vers le sol par sa charge le corps penché de l'autre côté pour l'équilibrer le bras libre horizontal en balancier. (Simon 276)

The colonial *ekphrasis* establishes a paradoxical connection between the idly waiting woman whose imagination injects life into these static scenes and the ragged, toiling and abject women represented on the exotic postcards: the former becomes mesmerized by the object of her gaze, the continuum of the bodies of black women, their tattered clothes, the water cans they carry on their backs and their miserable surroundings to the point where she is absorbed (and literally supplanted from the text) into their magnified description.

While Claude Simon's oblique and opaque treatment of the colony stands in contrast with the type of direct investigation offered in Tierno Monénembo's *Le Roi de Kahel* (winner of the Prix Renaudot in 2008), both novelists' poetics favor indirectness as a way of interweaving personal stories and collective history. Monénembo practices a form of historiography that in the Francophone context could be read as a paracolonial answer to what Christopher L. Miller calls the "rather noisy" "African 'silence'" on the continent regarding its inhabitants' responsibility in Western colonization and the establishment of the triangular slave trade (Miller 2008, xiii). The Guinean writer's fiction offers an "alternal" stance on the motivation, process and experience of colonization. In forging the term "alternal," I wish to signal that the narrative combines the internal and the alternative perspectives, as the story is recounted from the point of view of the historical Other, in this case the French colonizer. As I will show in my analyses of Marie Darrieussecq and Stéphane Audeguy's works, they attempt to devise similar narrative strategies with variable results.

Framed as archival fiction by its paratextual devices and bibliographical apparatus, the story of the nineteenth-century Lyon-born explorer of Africa, Aimé Victor Olivier de Sanderval, does nonetheless distance itself from historiographic (meta)fiction, a genre often associated with postcolonial writing. The opening section of the book, which features the author's acknowledgments to Olivier de Sanderval's heirs for granting him access to their forefather's written archives preserved in the city of Caën immediately followed by a racist quotation from the same archives that reads, "Le Créateur les a fait noirs pour que les coups ne se voient pas," adumbrates the poetics of juxtaposition characteristic of the novel. Additionally, it indicates Monénembo's own departure from the literary ideas and practices of moral redress and fictional retribution against the official Western obfuscation of colonial history illustrated by a host of postcolonial writers, from Wole Soyinka to Édouard Glissant and from Salman Rushdie to Patrick Chamoiseau. To call upon an image wrought by Chinua Achebe, this novel could be read as Monénembo's literary *mbari*, a way of reocuppying an imaginary space after a catastrophic devastation and, thereby, a way of reclaiming his colonial inheritance. "To call my colonial experience an inheritance may surprise people," writes the Nigerian author in an essay entitled "African Literature as Restauration of Celebration," "But everything is grist to the mill of the artist" (Achebe 111).

The narrative flows in synchronicity with the frenetic pace of Sanderval's own fantastical idea of searching for the absolute (*L'Absolu* is the title of his ambitious literary, autobiographical and historical work), embodied by the negotiation with the Fulu ("Peul") people over the right to possess land on their territory. This dizzying experience could be rendered in the hyperreal and fantasmatic style of Claude Simon's novel, whose doomsday lexicon (complete with a reference to the plague, perhaps an echo to the "leper" walls in the previous *ekphrasis*) along with the alliteration of the explosive "b" sound presages a prophesy of Biblical proportions:

> comme si quelque chose dans son destin l'avait irrésistiblement vouée à ces multitudes terribles et migratrices tourbillonnant sans fin à la surface de la terre errant de l'orient à l'Occident à travers le temps et l'espace se traînant de lieux saints en lieux saints fanatiques cauchemard-esques avec leurs yeux tordus de colère et leur désespoir le haillonneux troupeau de paralytiques d'affamés de borgnes de boiteux et de bossus se bousculant dans les déserts les défilés les montagnes sauvages les villes pestiférées et vides dans l'espoir d'impossibles miracles se traînant claudiquant véhiculés dans un bruit de béquilles de voitures d'infirmes de carrioles d'autos démantibulées de litanies d'hymnes de sébiles et d'imprécations jaillies pêle-mêle des bouches édentées avec les gluants fragments d'innommables nourritures riz croûtons de pains hosties ou sandwiches Pouvant voir … . (Simon 239–240)

The call of destiny beckons the colonial traveler, a rare visionary – the capital letter of "Pouvant voir" that disrupts Simon's textual continuum underscores the importance of seeing that signals an enhanced ability for the chosen individual – who finds himself propelled toward the multitudes swarming the surface of the earth. Like his fellow near-contemporaries the King of Patagonia, the Gascon Antoine Tounens or the Count Henry de La Vaulx (Gallo 162–163) is first and foremost a dreamer whose imagination models a great individual project in the margins of and against the bureaucracy, prejudices and corruption of the French colonial system. His project closely echoes the unreconciled contrast between the idealism and utopia of the civilizing mission and the scathing criticism of the colonial apparatus exhibited by André Gide in his *Voyage au Congo*. Olivier de Sanderval, who owes his aristocratic title and surname to the belated recognition of his African success by the Portuguese monarchy, is inspired as much by the Romantic ideals of heroism, spiritual conquest and self-fulfillment as he is by the colonial ideas of capital accumulation, geo-political conquest and the civilizing mission. Even though he achieves his goal, becoming Roi de Kahel and the founder of the city of Conakry, he does so at the expense of his national reputation and personal fortune, ultimately cutting a historically tragic figure whose passing away is symbolically obscured by the announcement of the start of the Great War.

Having been bit by the "colonial virus" transmitted through his uncle's stories and the representations offered by popular reviews, such as *L'Illustrateur*, and travel guides, such as *Joanne* and *Murray*, Sanderval is furthermore influenced by famous nineteenth-century explorers such as Mollien, Hecquart, Lambert and, especially, René Caillé, whose travelogues from Tombouctou and Tonkin set the agentic and literary standard for any colonial adventurer. Like an evolved André Dufourneau, whom he surpassed in social setting, family wealth and privileged upbringing, de Sanderval displays an intellectual engagement with the colony absent from Michon's character's conscience. His view of the fabulous world he is about to discover harks back to Claude Simon's vision of "la vaste terre le monde fabuleux fastueux bigarré inépuisable" (Simon 24).

Yet, if Africa's primary function is not to be the source of material fortune for Monénembo's hero, its fantasmatic possession quenches a deeper desire for singular fame and personal glory, without which fortune has little value: "Il irait seul avec ses Nègres, sans bonne, sans valet de chambre, ce ne serait pas un exploit, sinon" (Monénembo 39). His arrival at Fouta-Djalon in 1879 is penned in his *Memoirs* in terms germane to the language of Hugo's orientalist poetry or Balzac's characters: "Me voici, ma vieille Afrique! Me voici!" (Monénembo 21). In Monénembo's *roman d'archives*, the traveler's encounters with the local kings (Lawrence, King of the Nalous in Boulam; the King of Labé; the *almâmi* of Timbo) and princesses (Princess Taïbou who gives him the loving nickname Yémé) read more like a series of *peripeteia* from a picaresque novel imbued with a preexisting wisdom about the natives' *mores* that is supported by the protagonist's ethnographic experience: "Ces gens sont insaisissables aussi bien par la main que par l'esprit. On dirait qu'ils ont tous lu Montaigne ici. Vous ne verrez jamais peuple aussi ondoyant: jamais à la même place, jamais la même parole" (Monénembo 166). Subject to the ups and downs of the traveler's wheel of fortune, sometimes welcomed as an honored guest and sometimes held hostage as a dangerous foreigner, Olivier de Sanderval comes to know the Fula people through the peculiar way in which they practice hospitality. Whether he is cast as witness or victim, friend or foe, the French adventurer achieves his goal through a combination of cunning and audacity: he eventually extracts from the *almâmi* the promise of control over the Kahel plateau. Even as the originality of his peculiar undertaking propels him to the ranks of the geopolitical luminaries of his time, like Jules Charles-Roux, Léon Gambetta or Ferdinand de Lesseps, Monénembo's character fails to attract the same degree of public recognition or to obtain the kind of political support his contemporaries received for some of their failed projects, such as the Panama Canal. Unable to sign treaties with African leaders on behalf of his country that would secure France's influence over areas also coveted by Great Britain or Germany, he must limit his ambitions to the creation of a personal kingdom, only later to be incorporated by France into its expanding empire. Olivier de Sanderval emerges from the fictional world of *Le Roi de Kahel* as a paradoxical colonial visionary. On the one hand, his ideas about the inevitability of colonization in modern times and the contest between European powers to conquer and control new lands in the late nineteenth and early twentieth centuries, though largely ignored during his lifetime, are validated by historical reality; on the other hand, his racialist and racist worldview makes him an exemplary figure of the ultimate failure of the colonial project. As Alice L. Conklin shows, the project

> rested upon certain fundamental assumptions about the superiority of French culture and the perfectibility of humankind. It implied that France's colonial subjects were too primitive to rule themselves but were

capable of being uplifted. It intimated that the French were particularly suited, by temperament and by virtue of both their revolutionary past and their current industrial strength, to carry out this task. Last but not least, it assumed that the Third Republic had a duty and a right to remake "primitive" culture along lines inspired by the cultural, political, and economic development of France. (Conklin 1–2)

Moreover, Monénembo's writing seems to draw on his hero's energy, understood as both the agentic *energeia*, which denotes a constant effort for actualization, and literary *enargeia*, meaning a rhetoric of presence and display and an aesthetic of evidence and imagination, in order to part ways with the postcolonial forms and norms of historiographical fiction.

If Monénembo's aim is to revisit the facts of the past in order to unearth its multiple truths and recreate it as a lived experience, his implied author does not seek to unsettle, demystify, denounce or unwrite the official, popular or hegemonic version of history. The narrative works along the archival grain, to paraphrase Ann Laura Stoler's title, espousing instead of rejecting the "affective mastery" (Stoler 67) at the core of the colonial undertaking and exploiting the "affective knowledge" (Stoler 98) preserved in the colonial archive. By adopting a poetics of juxtaposition rather than antithesis and counter-discourse, Monénembo alternates an internally focalized diegesis with comments that provide a historical and cultural context to the protagonist's actions and thoughts. Despite indicating the moral distance between the narrated past and the present of its recounting, the tone of this authorial commentary remains propitiatory rather than critical:

> Comme par hasard, notre futur roi d'Afrique allait bien avec ce que dit le proverbe bantou: 'On est plus fils de son époque que fils de son père'. C'était le petit du XIXᵉ, tout craché!... *Ordem et progresso!...* Son éducation, son tempérament, tout le préparait à vibrer aux passions de son siècle: les idées, les sciences, les grands voyages. Il avait été pétri avec un mental de pionnier, dans un siècle de pionniers! Sa vie, il l'avait envisagée très tôt comme un escalier raide tendu vers les exploits. Les héros avaient leur légende, sa quête obstinée de la grandeur et de la plénitude aurait son livre. Et ce livre s'appellerait *L'Absolu*, la somme de ses pensées, le point fusionnel de tous les parallèles: l'idée et la vie, le réel et le vide, l'être et le bon Dieu. Commencée à douze ans, cette *Métaphysique* des Temps modernes en était maintenant à sa vingtième version. (Monénembo 38)

With the significant exception of the writer's metafictional signature, incarnated by a character named Tierno who belongs to Sanderval's

African entourage, the narrative remains largely extradiegetic, guided by an authorial discourse that *alternates* between documentary statements and personal commentary indicating various levels of self-distancing through irony and empathy. In one instance, the authorial voice seeks to explain the actions of his protagonist by immersing the reader into the imaginary world of his century rather than offering a critical examination of his personal ambitions and desire for social advancement.

> Né, comme lui, en plein XIX$^e$ siècle, on ne pouvait que devenir poète, savant ou explorateur. La question fut vite réglée en ce qui le concernait, il serait explorateur, c'est-à-dire poète et savant par la même occasion. En ces temps-là, dans les cours de récréation, les colonies revenaient dans les conversations aussi souvent que le jeu de marelle et les billes. Les contes ne parlaient pas d'ogres et de fées, mais de sorciers et de cannibales courant avec leurs sagaies derrière le tout nouveau gibier apparu dans les jungles: les pères blancs et les colons. (Monénembo 17)

This passage introduces readers to the inner life of a child who grows up surrounded by representations of the colonial elsewhere, with its promise of distant lands, horizons and opportunities. This is underscored by emphatic turns of phrase such as "comme lui" and "en ce qui le concernait," and temporal markers such as "en plein XIX$^e$ siècle" and "en ces temps-là," which enhance the allusion to the tale of colonial exploration that has come to epitomize the modern-day fairy-tale. As Jane Bradley Winston notes in *Postcolonial Duras*: "The 1930s discourse of French colonial propaganda cathected French popular desire in the métropole onto an Empire whose contours most ignored" (Winston 14). Monénembo situates his *Bildungsroman* in the perspectival vagueness between a clear historical assessment of Sanderval's actions and a fictional reimagining of his self. In so doing, he transfers the colonial explorer's persona into the knowable yet mysterious and mystifying space previously occupied by the colonies themselves.

The departures of the (neo)colonial adventure – taken both as places of departure for the characters and the places in which colonial adventures leave their readers – mark a gaping hole, a breach, an absence which could be interpreted in three distinct yet interconnected ways: a manifestation of colonial guilt, a supplement of meaning to the meaninglessness of history or an attempt at coping with the inexplicable aspects of life (absence, silence and failure). In engaging with this minor *topos* in French literature, the four writers examined here reclaim imagination while constructing multi-layered, fragmented and diffracted narratives.

Even though the stated (Constant, Monénembo) or implicit (Simon, Michon) purpose of the act of writing is to make sense of the colonial past and its present reverberations, these works of fiction display a keen awareness of the ruse of the colonial story and of history. Therefore, they privilege discontinuity, saturated style and open-ended narratives that accentuate the tension between telling and writing and seek to render the texture of a reimagined life. In so doing, they bring forward the ethical dilemma of contemporary fiction, which makes its political implications critically visible by exhibiting its most visceral aesthetic forms at the risk of reviving and potentially relegitimizing an obsolescent colonial imagination.

### Notes

1 In his book *Beginnings. Intention and Method*, New York: Basic Books, Inc., 1975.

2 Interview with Achille Mbembe, http://www.utexas.edu/conferences/africa/ads/1528.html (accessed February 24, 2017).

3 Patrick Crowley's conference presentation "Empire and Intertext in Pierre Michon's Vie d'André Dufourneau'" compellingly situates Michon's writing in the context of the overlooked *lieux de mémoires* in Pierre Nora's project, at the cross-section of race and class. My gratitude goes to the author for having generously shared his unpublished text with me.

4 The overdetermined representation in foundational texts of modern Western thought by authorities such as Freud and Conrad has been recently studied by Nicholas Harrison in "Metaphorical Memories: Freud, Conrad, and the Dark Continent" (Harrison 2011).

# CHAPTER TWO

# Landscape as Vocation

In what follows, I will further explore the forms of contact and interaction between the metropolitan individual and the foreign environment as they are permeated by colonial fortune tropes, paying particular attention to the subject's immersion into the natural surroundings of the colony, understood and felt by the metropolitan outsider as his or her adoptive land. In the novels of J. M. G. Le Clézio and Édouard Glissant a sense of predestination, destiny, estrangement and belonging defines this ambivalent process. Landscape becomes the imaginary and figurative *locus* of the colonial vocation's duality since "Grands Blancs" and "Petits Blancs" – that is, rich and poor whites – answer the calling to cultivate and exploit the virgin, "savage" land. However, the land, through its climate, conditions and inhabitants, manifests its resistance in forms that are simultaneously "tactical", indirect and "strategic", overt and sometimes violent, according to Glissant's use of Michel de Certeau's terminology, which undermines the colonists' religious, historical and metaphysical mission. Frantz Fanon had already underscored the material and symbolic importance of the land for the anticolonial struggle in a passage from *The Wretched of the Earth* (1961), which links the female colonial subject with a specific, non-idealized form of dignity that precedes and supersedes the abstract principles of the Enlightenment and the French Revolution:

> For the colonized people the most essential value, because the most concrete, its first and foremost the land: the land which will bring them bread and, above all, dignity. But this dignity has nothing to do with the dignity of the "human individual". Such ideal human individual, she has never heard of it. (Fanon 2007, 44)

It is interesting to note the rhetorical commonality between Fanon's passage and Glissant's reference to women in his *Caribbean Discourse*, which elucidates the tactics of ruse and indirectness as ways of dealing with the obscured, camouflaged reality of colonial society, thereby undermining the myth of male heroism. In his discussion of Glissant's treatment of the landscape, Michael J. Dash stresses that "land is central to the process of self-possession" (Dash xxxv). According to Dash, Glissant positions Caribbean writers against European colonialism and suggests that the literary reclaiming of landscape constitutes a means of cultural resistance and a way to rescue histories of which they were denied authorship (Dash 105). Thus, postcolonial writers seek to appropriate what has been taken from them, to stake their claim on something uniquely theirs, particular to their people. Where power dynamics shift, landmasses lend consistency to this moment of political instability. With the land comes the construction of collective memory, an effort once again for recuperation of what seems to have been lost or silenced. Insofar as "landscape is the work of the mind," Simon Schama argues in *Landscape and Memory*, "[i]ts scenery is built up as much from strata of memory as from layers of rock" (Schama 6–7). If landscape is not merely nature but the product of a complex process of human invention, manipulation and censorship that occurs as a result of the combination of memory and nature, then what are the literary uses of this cultural construct in a paracolonial context?

### From the Colonial Landscape to the Paracolonial "Entour"

Current discourses about the concept of community along with their literary instantiations disavow the notions of territory, national belonging and instantly recognizable cultural identity while at the same time conserving and highlighting the importance of geography and of the environment, in particular:

> The ecocritical perspective has always distinguished itself by its interest in how the nonhuman interacts with human culture: how ecological conditions shape cultural expression and, conversely, how culture shapes the perception and uses of natural environments; how cultural communities structure and give meaning to humans' relations with other species; and how risk scenarios, crises, and disasters amplify or reduce sociocultural differences, define community boundaries, and change cultural practices. The question of difference in ecocriticism, in other words, is never purely human. Alterity is always also defined by the nonhuman other. (Heise 638)

Thus, a hybrid fictional discourse emerges, bearing the marks of antagonist forces at play emanating from a new literary consciousness of what ecocritics call, using a term borrowed from science, the "anthropocene" – the human as a geological force. The postcolonial critic is therefore called to think about "two figures of the human simultaneously: the human-human and the nonhuman-human" (Chakrabarty 11) and faced with "the challenge of having to think of human agency over multiple and incommensurable scales at once" (Chakrabarty 1). Graham Huggan and Helen Tiffin draw attention to the dual task of postcolonial ecocriticism: "if the wrongs of colonialism – its legacies of continuing human inequalities, for instance – are to be addressed, still less to be redressed, then the very category of the human, in relation to animals and environment, must also be brought under scrutiny" (Huggan and Tiffin 18). The issue of 'sustainability' occupies a central place in this critical project, which brings with it a healthy dose of skepticism regarding the glorification of indigenous people who epitomize in the postcolonial mainstream discourse the ideal of living locally, in harmony with nature. Instead, ecologically minded literary texts rely on a balance "continually renegotiated by a shifting community of tellers and listeners that is at once profoundly local and inextricably connected to the wider world' (Huggan and Tiffin 70). The postcolonial–ecocritical project acknowledges "the continuing realities of female/environmental/human subjection" and examines how oppression can occur in a "postbodied and post-human" world (Huggan and Tiffin 211). Rather than offering up a corpus of texts representative of this concern, it puts forward a postcolonial–ecocritical "way of reading" (Huggan and Tiffin 13) that challenges "continuing imperialist modes of social and environmental dominance" (Huggan and Tiffin 2) yet preserves "the aesthetic function of the literary text while drawing attention to its social and political usefulness, its capacity to set our symbolic guidelines for the material transformation of the world" (Huggan and Tiffin 14).

In Glissant's writing, as critics such as Carrie Noland and Valérie Loichot have noted, the notion of environment evolves from "paysage," a more traditional, Western idea of the landscape as a natural setting surrounding and, indeed, framing human existence, to "entour," which denotes a contact zone shaped by the constant interaction and exchange between humans and their environment. "*Entour* blurs and even annuls the division between cultural productions and landscape," comments Loichot, who further describes it "as a place of fluidity between the natural and the cultural, the philosophical and the mystic, the human and the vegetal, the dead and the living" (Loichot 2013b, 1016). This perspective affords a better understanding of what Loichot identifies as Glissant's polytheism. I would even call it "opaque polytheism," given the way in which Glissant describes the constant transformation of a landscape that incorporates humanity even as it is shaped by it while ultimately eluding any sole, monotheistic explanation. In so doing he parts with the centuries-old tradition spanning from Lucretius's "suave magni maro" to Romantic thought and its modern reverberations predicated on the contrast and comparison between humanity and nature for the sake of philosophical reflection. Although one could identify in the Martinican writer's reflection a form of "thinking of the environment as a connected network of flows of death feeding life" (Loichot 2013b, 1025), this goes beyond the mere articulation of a philosophical discourse on the circularity of life and death.

In reading them together, I would like to argue that Glissant and Le Clézio's works offer more than an abstract argument on the interconnectedness of humanity and its environment stemming from their shared affinity for Pre-Socratic philosophy; they furthermore imagine a fluid yet discontinuous space where history and memory are dissolved and disseminated into a myriad of affective and corporeal manifestations. This contrasts with the colonial "landscripting" defined by Marie-Paule Ha as a descriptive practice that "often coincides with the imperial vision of the Other" (Ha 31). Moreover, I contend that the affordances made possible by fiction writing provide the lynchpin between the theoretical construction of the relation between human and non-human, on the one hand, and the lived experience of this relation, on the other. I propose to examine how these conceptual tensions are addressed, configured or obfuscated in two novels, both published in 2003 (in the same "collection blanche" by Gallimard): Édouard Glissant's *Ormerod* and J. M. G. Le Clézio's *Révolutions*. The two writers' fictional works exhibit striking similarities in their engagement with themes such as errantry on a global and even cosmic scale, genealogy and communal memory as it unveils the hidden relations between the precolonial past, the colonial present and the postcolonial future past. In their novels, the importance of a non-territorial geography emphasizing the connection between human and non-human natural forces that make up the environment can also be connected to Kwame A. Appiah's idea of a "rooted cosmopolitanism" (Appiah 2005, 213). Grounded as they are in the colonial period, they feature multidirectional narrative temporalities, with the past appearing as an illusory safe haven from the tragedy of colonization and the future being imagined by its tragic consciousness.

## Novel Spaces

In Carlos Fuentes' view, the novel is both a utopian form of resistance against the close-minded identitarian stance prevalent in today's world and a mode of expression that offers the possibility of a contemporary universalism (Fuentes 24–25). Thus it re-creates the Republic of Letters' cosmopolitan humanist environment. Endowed with the multiple qualities of encyclopedic knowledge and philosophical investigation, moral questioning and poetic invention, the contemporary novel builds a transfrontier community whose members share the responsibility of constructing a conception of the world – indeed, of worldmaking that generates a new affective and intellectual entity called "la nación de la novela" (Fuentes 23). The Mexican writer's idea of the novel as a utopian, transnational and anti-identitarian community (one might say a deterritorialized imagined community) resonates with Édouard Glissant and Patrick Chamoiseau's joint reflection on the dichotomy of globalization and identity politics. The conclusion formed by their contemplation draws attention to the transformative force of imagination that enables the world community to unmake the monolithic notion of the "world-market" and to conceive instead of a multitude of singular, non-territorial, yet interconnected "places":

> Les arts, les littératures, les murs et les chants fraternisent par des voies d'imaginaires qui ne connaissent plus rien aux seules géographies nationales ou aux langues orgueilleuses de leur à-part. Dans la Mondialité (qui est là – tout autre que nous avons à la fonder), nous n'appartenons pas en exclusivité à des "patries", à des "nations" et pas du tout à des "territoires", mais désormais à des "Lieux", des intempéries linguistiques, des dieux libres qui ne réclament pas d'être adorés, des terres natales que nous aurons décidées, des langues que nous aurons désirées, ces géographies tissues de terres et de visions que nous aurons forgées. Et ces "Lieux", devenus incontournables, entrent en relation avec tous les Lieux du monde. C'est le chatoiement de tous ces Lieux qui ouvre à l'insurrection infinie des imaginaires libres: à la Mondialité. (Glissant and Chamoiseau 16–17)

Three rhetorical and stylistic gestures are worth pondering in this fragment, which contains many elements of the hybridization of poetry and philosophy that has come to define Édouard Glissant's essayistic writing. The first of these gestures leads to a transformation of the meaning of belonging, which, although maintained as a relevant concept, no longer refers to a univocal connection between an individual and a clearly circumscribed space such as "motherland," "nation" or "territory." Instead, belonging is reascribed an antithetical definition – that is, a relationship of detachment or multiple associations not with any particular language but with "lingustic storms," not with one single god but with "free gods who not require adoration," and not with one homeland but with a plurality of lands. The second rhetorical feature, the tripartite repetition of the adjectival past participles "decided," "desired" and "forged," indicates a reversal of the hierarchical order of identity. To counter the idea of national predetermination through land and language and the nineteenth-century phantasmatic conception of autochtony as the unique and inseparable bond between man and native soil, Glissant and Chamoiseau propose the liberating project of a hybrid agency, both human and non-human, manifested through will and desire, reason and vision. Finally, the sense of the homeland as an ever-changing and even moving space, constantly shaped by human imagination and action, is further reinforced by the sea metaphor of "chatoiement" used in reference to the myriad places that make up the world. In so doing, they perform a defining ecocritical gesture, which is to "[bring] a distinctly spatial imagination to bear on the question of alterity. Place in its varying material and symbolic significations figures centrally in comparative ecocriticism as a way of mapping relations between culture and nature" (Heise 639).

Echoing the rich tradition of theoretical reflection and literary expression centered on the image of the sea as a cradle to the many Caribbean cultures as well as a witness to the darkest moments of colonial history, such as the genocide of local populations by the first waves of colonists, the triangular slave trade and the countless acts of resistance to oppression, expressed in Derek Walcott's 1986 poem "The Sea is History," in Kamau Brathwaite's idea of "seametrics" or "tidalectics" (Brathwaite xiii) and in Michelle Cliff's reflections on the region's "history under the sunken sea" (Cliff 14), Glissant articulates his understanding of contemporary relation. This is embodied by the process of creolization as "a new and original dimension allowing each person to be there and elsewhere, rooted and open, lost in the mountains and free beneath the sea, in harmony and in errantry" (Glissant 1997, 34). Moreover, inasmuch as they rely on a poetics of opacity and test the limits of stylistic intelligibility, Glissant's novels eschew the criticism Richard Price and Sally Price direct against the writers of the creolization movement, such as Patrick Chamoiseau:

> In our view, there is a tendency for the literary works of the créolistes to be complicitous with the celebration of a museumfied Martinique, a diorama'd Martinique, a picturesque and "pastified" Martinique that promotes a "feel-good" nostalgia for people who are otherwise busy adjusting to the complexities of a modernizing lifestyle. (Price and Price 138)

At times, though, certain themes in *Ormerod* dovetail with the dark romance genre that has become an integral, if disputed, part of the postcolonial canon. Summoning memories of *Jane Eyre* and *Wuthering Heights*, the name of the plantation where the character of Flore Gaillard endures the yoke of slavery is Lovenblade, and its spectacular burning by vengeful rebels is sealed with the incantatory words "*Épiphanie, messié! Parol palé! Love n'blade! Dormez tous, dormez tous!...*" (Glissant 2003, 30). Additionally, Flore Gaillard's magical powers, her talent in seducing men and animals alike and the use of socio-cultural commonplaces further reinforce this impression of intertextuality.

Nevertheless, questions about generational attitudes and gender roles arise both from Fuentes' post-Hegelian and post-Sartrian effort to elevate the novel to a postcolonial universal form where individual expression meets communal responsibility and from Glissant and Chamoiseau's attempts to reinscribe the relation between the individual and the environment in a setting defined by seemingly opposing notions of human agency and an ethical surrender to the "chaos-monde."

### Fictions of Vocation

In what I will call Glissant and Le Clézio's fiction of vocation, characters receive and respond to a momentous historical call that strongly implies an element of destiny. Even as vocation is stripped out of the strict theological dimension without forsaking its messianic overtones, landscape becomes the spatial vector of an existential quest manifested through errantry and insurgency. Both novels offer transhistoric, multigenerational narratives retracing the consequences of a profane messianic event, absurdly tragic yet motivated by destiny. In the last section of *Révolutions*, the ancestor's departure for the colonies finds its most poignant elucidation following a long description of Brittany's lost battle against the French army in the fifteenth century:

> Trois cents ans plus tard, quand Jean Eudes Marro marche à travers la campagne pour rejoindre l'armée révolutionnaire, au même moment à quelques années près l'Anglais Young écrit sa relation de voyage, où il dépeint la région de Rennes et de Mordelles comme la plus pauvre qui soit, enfants en haillons courant pieds nus le long des chemins pour mendier une croûte de pain, vieillards mourant de faim. C'est ce pays que les Bretons fuient au but du monde pour tenter de survivre. (Le Clézio 2003, 537–638)

The intimate imbrication and the mutual concealment of the colonial event and the *longue durée* of human history are powerfully transfigured in the first chapter of *Ormerod*, "Le Piton Flore," in which several open-ended paragraphs characterized by a hybrid style, both poetic and abstract, and sparse punctuation retrace the world history of the colonial conquest. Unlike Le Clézio's narrative, which maintains the focus on the colonial traveler, Glissant's pendulum-like perspective shifts the attention from the native to the "Intrus" (Le Clézio 2003, 56):

> Ces plages frémissantes de brûlures et d'aveuglements dessinaient à la fin un immense champ-flot où il chassait et guerroyait saison après saison, se cachant avec sa famille maintenant que les envahisseurs étaient là [...] à ce moment où il abattit le premier marin qui avait relié d'une enjambée décisive les univers qu'ils appelleraient, sans qu'il le sût jamais, l'Ancien et le Nouveau monde, le premier conquistador à poser le pied sur le sable, mais celui-là serait oublié pour toujours, comme s'il n'avait jamais existé, car bien sûr les arrivants reconstituèrent sans lui la parade du débarquement de Cristóbal Colón, Christoforo Colombo, après avoir bien nettoyé les abords de la plage, et peut-être comme d'autres marins le firent sans doute souvenez-vous pour le retour télévisé du général MacArthur en Asie [...]. (Glissant 2003, 51–52)

Both novels work fictionally and discursively through the aforementioned issues raised by postcolonial ecocriticism. In addition, my analysis will address an issue of foremost concern, which is that

> literature, with its traditional emphasis on plot, character and psychological states, has been seen perforce as being focused on individuals or groups of humans, or at least anthropomorphised animals, even in genres such as traditional pastoral or romantic elegy where human interaction with, and apparent concern for, the natural world come to the fore. (Huggan and Tiffin 16)

In J. M. G. Le Clézio's *Révolutions*, the polysemic title delineates a space where myth and history, individual progress and cosmic cycles, belonging and errantry constantly clash and merge with each other. The similarity with his first book, *Le Procès-verbal*, enables critics to suggest that the 2003 novel is a return to the imaginary space of his 1963 work and, possibly, its rewriting. Within the more recent novel's plot, the reference to political revolutions as historical events seems to provide an obvious correlation with the title and to prompt a series of counterpuntal readings. Either juxtaposed or interwoven, three main plotlines create a hybrid, labyrinthine narrative landscape stretching from the middle of the twentieth century, when Jean Marro's life begins, surrounded by the wars in Indochina and Algeria, back to the period following the 1789 Revolution that witnesses the life and colonial exodus of his ancestor, Jean Eudes, and then into the nineteenth century, recounting Kiambé's story of the 1822 slave rebellion on Isle de France. The multiplication of references to world-changing historical events operates both in a centrifugal way, insofar as they prevent the novel from crystallizing along a single story line by providing instead several fictional possibilities, and in a centripetal one, by holding together at the symbolic level the multitude of stories that crisscross the novel. Furthermore, the structure of the narrative lies somewhere between a constellation of singular historical events and a mythical circle of repeating human and cosmic occurrences. The effects of history on individual and collective lives are intimately related to this repetitive regime; the transhistoric inevitability of disappointment, exile, trauma and death creates a cycle that resists any linear or teleological interpretation of human destiny. Le Clézio's novel reveals an imagined landscape shaped by the encounter between concrete and specific geographic and cultural conditions, on the one hand, and the subject's desire to overcome the symbolic separation between past and present, absence and presence, in order to recreate, in Lacanian terms, the originary unity of the real, on the other. The most subtle yet powerful *loci* of negotiation for the constant state of revolution that implies its own negation, whether it be psychological, political or planetary, appear in scenes of intimacy between lovers, friends or close family members, in which the sense of emotional and spatial confinement creates an implosion of imagined possibilities, an openness to the world or availability to others:

> C'était comme d'attendre, comme s'il y avait un bombardement aérien ou quelque chose en surface, et quand on sortirait de cette cave, tout serait détruit alentour.

Mais Jean aimait bien ces moments-là, où il avait le sentiment de toucher aux racines de plusieurs mondes. (Le Clézio 2003, 313)

The tension between a cyclical, mythical understanding of human existence and a historical, perfectible notion of the world is further enhanced by the reference to progress as represented by the industrial revolution and modern technology. Catherine Marro's neighborhood in Nice bears the traces of this process, which leads to its transformation from a suburban, semi-rural environment to an urban setting where "… les bâtiments de cinq étages et mansardes avaient remplacé les jardinets et les cabanons des fermiers" (Le Clézio 2003: 13). As the process intensifies, Jean Marro observes that the familiar streets of his childhood have grown more impersonal under the alienating effect of technology, losing their specific look and sound: "Les bruits surtout étaient différents. Non pas le silence, au contraire, il y avait davantage de bruit qu'auparavant. Jean avait pensé à la mort du serin" (Le Clézio 2003: 102). The narrator frequently remarks on the passage of time as it becomes apparent in the changes undergone by the old building on the rue Reine-Jeanne: "pendant des mois, Jean s'était absenté, le monde avait tourné, La Kataviva avait subi des dommages irréversibles" (Le Clézio 2003, 101); "Tout glissait à la ruine" (Le Clézio 2003, 158). The sense of an irrevocable transformation imprinted on the subject's surroundings, visibly externalized rather than internally felt, accompanies the young Jean throughout his travels away from places such as his aunt's neighborhood and his hometown. While finishing his medical studies in London, he experiences a similar feeling in reaction to a change in the environment to which he had become accustomed: "À la mi-juin, après les examens, Jean est allé revoir le pavillon … tous, ils avaient disparu. Même les aides-soignantes avaient changé" (Le Clézio 2003, 338).

Even as the young man finds himself at the center of his own imaginary landscape, his sense of being in the world is defined by several key figures. Chief among them is his aunt, Catherine Marro, the blind keeper of the family's memory, whose character evokes a recurring figure in Le Clézio's novels: the evanescent woman who nonetheless maintains the family's or the group's spiritual continuity (Lionnet 2015, 308). Her stories are torn between her desire to depict Mauritius as a lost paradise and her awareness of the fundamentally unsustainable nature of colonial life, betrayed by the many failures and transgressions of mostly male family members that led to their ruin. Her blindness invites mythological interpretations of justice, as she unwittingly informs Jean's sense of ethics, or, equally, the idea of prophesy, as she bemoans the loss of past wealth, happiness and security while condemning the move away from a colonial setting and toward independence. The prophetic dimension unites, albeit latently, the three Marro generations, represented by the first settler, Jean Eudes, who dedicates himself to the practice of nauscopy, or the art of predicting the arrival of the ships based on atmospheric observation, then by the witness to the squandering of his legacy, Catherine, and finally by the belated heir of the family memory, Jean Marro, who travels the world in a universal quest for meaning. In the old aunt's personal utterance of the consent to hegemony the most intimate and irreducible connection with the family legacy meets the general and objective law of atavism, manifested in both land and blood ties: "N'oublie pas, tu es Marro, de Rozilis, comme moi, tu descends du Marro qui a tout quitté pour s'installer à Maurice, tu es du même sang, tu es lui [...] C'est lui qui est en toi, qui est revenu pour vivre en toi, dans ta vie, dans ta pensée" (Le Clézio 2003, 53–54). The reference to sanguinity and atavism harkens back to the blood metaphor that appears both as a racialist *topos*, exploited since Gobineau's mid-nineteenth-century study on the inequality of races[1] and maintained through early twentieth-century colonial writing, and as an image of anticolonial struggle and discursive resistance in Césaire: "Que de sang dans ma mémoire! Dans ma mémoire sont des lagunes. Elles sont couvertes de têtes de morts [...]. Ma mémoire est entourée de sang. Ma mémoire a sa ceinture de cadavres!" (Césaire 35).

Then comes the tragic figure of Aurore de Sommerville, the "deaf and dumb" woman born in Hanoi of uncertain origin brought to France by the General de Sommerville, her putative father, who is reduced to a servile condition and haunts the Kataviva house as a floating signifier of the colonial past. Jean's father is another phantomatic character whose service in the British army has left him physically, mentally and also morally traumatized. In his rare utterances he expresses a similar loathing of colonialism – "La colonie, c'est la plus grande honte de notre époque" – and *"communist terrorists"* (Le Clézio 2003, 36), whom he blames for his downfall after having suffered a defeat at their hands in Malaysia.

Standing out among the people of his generation who see their lives as irremediably changed or curbed by the Algerian experience is the character of Santos Balas. Santos's disappearance begets the death of intelligibility, of reason itself, under the unremitting assault of heterogeneous factors such as the natural elements (the heat-generating sun that kills geraniums in their pots) and human constructs (borders and war), whose combined forces unleash an unfathomable violence:

> Que voulait dire le "soleil" d'Héraclite? Le "fleuve"? Que signifiaient "il est" ou "il n'est pas"? [...] Est-ce qu'il y avait une destination pour ces mots, ces sentences, ces brisures, devant la ligne électrifiée qui barrait le nord de l'Afrique entre un pays appelé Algérie et un autre appelé Maroc? Est-ce qu'il y avait un sens à ces pensées défuntes quand chaque jour les hommes mouraient sur la terre sèche, de l'autre côté de cette même mer? (Le Clézio 2003, 199–200)

As his strange friend and mentor, whose dark and brooding appearance of "Andalou marocain" betrays an exotic and unsavory family story featuring a Middle-Eastern mother and a rich but absent father, Santos tutors Jean on philosophical matters according to the guiding idea that: "La philo, c'est être accordé au temps céleste, comprendre le cours des astres" (Le Clézio 2003, 99). The lack of pretension in Santos's language denotes his great familiarity with the texts of pre-Socratic thinkers, from Heraclitus and Democritus to Anaxagoras and Parmenides. Faced with the crisis of the great metaphysical systems, the two young men find new meanings in the fragmentary, poetic and pluralistic ideas of ancient philosophy, which foreground the importance of the natural elements in the understanding of the world and human life: "*Car depuis que toutes choses ont été nommées lumière et nuit, et que ces choses existent selon l'un ou l'autre de ces pouvoirs, tout est plein de lumière et de nuit aveugle également, car en elles le néant ne se divise pas*" (Le Clézio 2003, 99, italics in the original). Jean populates his own notebook with quotes from aphoristic philosophy, collecting "crystals" from the pre-Socratics to Pascal and Nietzsche; moreover, his style of writing, which juxtaposes and intermingles serious reflections and media headlines, popular culture trivia and war bulletins, models itself after the Parmenidian fusion of being and thinking, thus acting as a hypotext for the entire novel. Adding to the sense of inseparability between life and thought, and between myth as the essence of life and history as its narrativized unfolding, these philosophical conversations take place in the "jardin des Oliviers," a site in the city of Nice called the "Olive Garden" that the aptly named Santos reveals to his less experienced friend, surrounded by the elemental forces of nature – the sea, the wind, the sky – all of which contribute to a feeling of eternity. The idea of the eternal return takes on somber overtones as Santos utters his last pronouncement – "*Et pour moi c'est tout un là où je commence, car je retournerai*" (Le Clézio 2003, 100, italics in the original) – before failing his philosophy examination for the baccalauréat and, having therefore lost his right to a reprieval from the military draft, being dispatched without delay to the Algerian front, never to be seen again.

Also addressing individual positionality in the revolutions of time, the novel's title could be read as a philosophical or ideological revolution that places Jean into communion with classical thinkers. This marks a departure from the binary nature–culture stance that characterizes the early works of the French–Mauritian writer, most notably embodied by the protagonist of *Le Procès-verbal*, Adam Pollo, who "fuit les idées, les concepts et les systèmes abstraits qui conditionnent la vie moderne pour renouer contact avec le milieu naturel et la réalité matérielle qui nous entoure" (Thibault 40). Upon Santos' departure, Jean is left behind in an empty, anguish-ridden city and seeks to eschew its Camusian atmosphere by fleeing into the sea and the promise of future journeys that the sea holds out to him:

> Il pensait: je vais voyager. Je vais continuer, nager vers l'horizon, si loin que je ne pourrai plus revenir en arrière. Un instant, il avait pensé cela, non pas mourir, mais partir. Mais quelque chose l'en avait empêché. Le soleil s'était immobilisé, il s'était durci. Sous le corps de Jean, la mer était devenue profonde, froide, effrayante. (Le Clézio 2003, 101)

Whereas, in that moment, the young man catches a glimpse of his future as a world-wanderer (an illumination that underscores his bond with his forefathers), he is also stunned by the deadly immensity of his potential encounter with the world. Around him, the aquatic world turns menacing under the influence of a polysemic "something," an empty signifier that can be interpreted as a manifestation of the Freudian uncanny, an ethical reminder of man's insignificance in the natural world or even a fictional elucidation of the Deriddian idea of hospitality applied to the level of the anthropocene. The young man's escapist and suicidal impulse is reinscribed into a lesson on the stages of life – from the "élan vital" to the survival instinct, fear and the corporeal understanding of the flow of life.

However, as Jean Marro's story continues, he finds himself again in the proximity of aphoristic philosophy, this time illustrated by one of Pascal's thoughts: *"L'immortalité de l'âme est une chose qui nous importe si fort, qui nous touche si profondément qu'il faut avoir perdu tout sentiment pour être dans l'indifférence de savoir ce qu'il en est"* (Le Clézio 2003, 403, italics in the original). On this occasion, philosophy re-enters Jean's life thanks to Miriam, his Algerian Kabyle companion and soulmate, who passes her baccalaureat exam by successfully answering the implicit questions raised by the seventeenth-century Christian thinker and exemplary stylist. He is simultaneously undergoing, on behalf of his aunt Catherine, a process of reparative immersion into his surroundings in an effort to compensate for the loss of the family home in Mauritius: "C'était pour elle, pour compenser la perte de Rozilis, qu'il s'imprégnait de ce coin isolé, protégé des regards de la ville, où il pouvait se croire revenu au pléistocène, à l'ère où régnait sans conteste les oies et les baleines, quand le monde n'avait pas encore vraiment commencé" (Le Clézio 2003, 403). To overcome the family trauma of being uprooted and having his legacy squandered, Jean makes himself available as a conduit between past and present, yet he neither clings to the phantasmatic workings of nostalgia nor embraces the stagnation of mourning and melancholia. Instead, he allows himself to be impregnated not by a metaphysical spirit of the place but by the place itself. This creates the possibility for a Leclézian "geography of difference," an expression coined by Rob Nixon in *Slow Violence and the Environmentalism of the Poor*, and an "ethics of place" (Heise 639) mindful of the fact that in colonial and postcolonial contexts "'[p]lace is displacement'" and [...] engages with processes of dislocation, migration, and hybridization rather than with the conventional ecocritical tropes of dwelling and inhabitation" (Heise 639). The narrator uses the phrase "this corner of the world" hidden away from the "gaze of the city" – that is, from the transformative agency of humanity grown increasingly pervasive and destructive in the age of the anthropocene, to designate a space where one could still project oneself into the prehistoric past. The object of Jean's search is a secret that precedes individual and community alike; a prehistoric secret: "un secret d'avant les guerres, de très loin en arrière" (Le Clézio 2003, 48). In Le Clézio's writing, grasping this secret is the task of literature and of a certain philosophy that embraces the world's irreducible opacity. These philosophers, too, make up an important part of Jean's origin, as they do for the common origin of human thought. This is especially salient considering the universal, humanistic ideas Jean associates with these thinkers, as a revolution not of new thinking but of rethinking the old. It is the figurative iteration of a pendulum or of a revolving clock that turns and returns in a great human narrative.

Narrative operates as a form of survival to combat the relentless assault from the forces of time at both individual and universal levels.

In the merciless environment of the boys' school, the young Jean learns the most basic skills to protect himself from routine humiliations, while also imbuing himself with the duty for preserving the memory of the past: "Au cours d'histoire, Jean essayait de suivre. Il découvrait que son attention était décuplée dans le noir. Il guettait chaque mot du prof [...] ça s'inscrivait au fond de sa mémoire" (Le Clézio 2003, 34–35). Years later, the absurd violence raging in North Africa, to which the character is a distant but anguished witness, will resonate in his memory, coupled with the fear and fright brought on by the absurd violence of the schoolyard: "Kernès avait une voix grave, un peu étouffée. Jean ne pouvait pas s'empêcher de se remémorer quand il était debout tout seul dans la cour du lycée, et qu'il pleurait parce que les enfants l'attaquaient comme une meute de chiens sauvages déchirant un buffle, tournant un peu sur lui-même [...]" (Le Clézio 2003, 197).

A sense of duty enables the individual to transcend the narrowness of his own environment and construct with his words and actions a communal space; thus, when answering the call to join the revolutionary army, Jean Eudes calls himself a philosopher–soldier: "voilà que je vais devenir un vrai soldat-philosophe" (Le Clézio 2003, 59). Jean Eudes Marro inscribes in his war diary (later to become a travelog incorporated gradually into the body of the novel under the title *Nauscopies*) the hopelessness that overcomes men and landscape as revolutionary France finds itself under the occupation of invading foreign armies.

The Britton's note on the generalized violence brought on by conflict, "Il y avait une violence vraiment exceptionnelle dans cette ville en ce temps-là" (Le Clézio 2003, 205), foreshadows the detailed and gruesome stories from colonial war fronts 200 years later, when his eponymous relative "voyait la violence partout" (Le Clézio 2003, 199). The battle of Dien Biên Phu has reduced young Jean's father, Charles Marro, to a state of heartbreak and silent neurosis; on the rare occasions when he expresses himself, the former soldier situates the origin of his illness in a borderland both geographical and symbolic: "En quelques jours, en quelques heures, sur cette frontière, nous étions devenus d'autres hommes" (Le Clézio 2003, 126). Moreover, Jean's father is not able to detach himself from this interstitial space where war begets war, the conflict in Algeria having followed on the heels of the defeat in Indochina: "La guerre faisant horreur à ce vieux soldat. Depuis la Malaisie, son retour forcé en France, son corps n'avait pas cessé de trembler. Il écoutait les nouvelles à la radio anglaise avec une indignation muette" (Le Clézio 2003, 206).

Echoing Jean Eudes' "nauscopic" narrative, which etymologically describes the ability to detect the movement of approaching ships based on the study of atmospheric phenomena, Jean Marro's storyline contains two types of extradiegetic sources of information concerning the ongoing "events," as French officials have for a long time persisted in calling the colonial war in North Africa. First, press headlines are directly inserted into the narrative discourse:

*Attentat FLN à Alger (bombe)*
*1 mort, 22 blessés.*
*De Gaulle à Batna: 'Une seule France de 55 millions de Français de Dunkerke à Tamanrasset! Tous unis!'* (Le Clézio 2003, 264–265)

These quotes, or "crystals" collected by Jean in his "black handbook," break the stylistic and emotional unity of the narrative by introducing either the impersonal sound of colonial propaganda or voices alternative to those of the narrator or the story's characters. The world as worded and ordered by the media tears up the fabric of the text, creating an impression of estrangement; yet, by setting the headlines apart in a special section almost five pages long, typed in italics, in a vertical list bearing a formal resemblance with poetry, the *scriptor* succeeds in reincorporating the "crystals" into the geology of the book. The second source of information is the testimonials that Jean elicits or simply records from his friends and acquaintances who participated in the Algerian conflict. Recounted in a direct, raw manner, they provide a fragmented and sensorial glimpse into the experience of modern war: "Tu vois cette Renault là-bas? Avec un bazooka je pourrais la foutre en l'air sans problème" (Le Clézio 2003, 197). Its insidious nature is revealed through the permeation not only of the colonial landscape it destroys but also the metropolitan landscape, thus negating the imaginary security its people seemingly enjoy behind the shield of colonial ideology and the veil of media propaganda. The young man's desire to escape is manifest in his relentless search for his family's past, expressed metaphorically in his finding refuge from reality in the garden of the idealized past: "D'une certaine façon, il comprenait que cette époque-là était révolue. Pourtant, ce jardin était le seul coin qui échappait à la violence..." (Le Clézio 2003, 142).

In the mirroring stories of the two Jeans, the French and Algerian revolutions mark two experiences that shape the characters' understanding of their environment and profoundly influence the ways in which they interact with it. Going beyond the political act of opposition, they reveal the revolutionary (or cyclical) nature of the human experience: "C'étaient les temps nouveaux. C'était indifférent. Ça n'avait pas d'importance. Pour Jean, seuls les temps anciens pouvaient resurgir, comme des fantômes personnels. La tante Catherine le disait bien: 'La roue tourne, ce qui est mort est mort'" (Le Clézio 2003, 105). Yet the circularity of life and death does not negate the importance of a historical consciousness, something that is particularly evident in the relaying of memories between generations. Even as La Kataviva, "l'immeuble décadent," operates as a metaphorical reminder of loss and destruction, relegated to solitude and poverty, prisoner of its own disillusionment, as the comparison with M$^{lle}$ Picot's caged bird attests, it also metonymically contains an entire world frozen in time, a house where "le temps s'était arrêté" (Le Clézio 2003, 20). The subject's own identity is shaped by the vacillation between the constant metamorphosis of the subject's environment and the feeling of permanence emanating from it.

In the aftermath of the 1789 revolution Jean Eudes writes about his own metamorphosis on the battlefield:

> Comme un temps que je n'avais pas vécu, mais qu'on m'avait raconté, un temps qui avait commencé loin avant moi, dans la mémoire d'un autre (…) J'y étais. (…) Mais j'étais devenu quelqu'un d'autre, j'avais perdu sur le champ de bataille une partie de moi-même, mon enfance, ma jeunesse, et sans doute mon avenir. (Le Clézio 2003, 61)

As the Enlightenment's promise for a better world fails to materialize, he sets sail for "the end of the world" and travels "jusqu'à Maurice, sur la Rozilis" (Le Clézio 2003, 112). The ship will become the cradle of his new life and give its name to the settler's new home. The resulting triple erasure is at work in this process, which alienates the traveler from his native country while stripping the local land of its previous name and compelling generations of Marros settled on Isle de France or Mauritius increasingly to adopt the colonial behavior their ancestors used to despise (Le Clézio 2003, 228–232). Sharing these memories is pivotal in the novels because remembering and hearing about different experiences allow characters to relate to each other. Jean feels a connection to his similarly named ancestor because he can relate to his aunt's retelling of Jean the elder's experiences: "Maintenant c'est à Jean de parler, la mémoire de Catherine est en lui. Tout ce qu'elle a vécu, tout ce qu'elle a connu est passé dans son cœur…" (Le Clézio 2003, 359). The cyclical nature of human experience necessitates an understanding of time that is equally cyclical. The characters separated by historical time do not relate to one another across a teleological, historicist understanding of human progress, but rather operate under an individual understanding of temporal relationships in which time is more fluid, circular instead of linear. It is Jean's personal understanding of and interaction with his own history and the history of his ancestors that puts him in the position to experience a connection with his origins. He is temporally constituted, but he is also able to connect to the revolving nature of time. Moreover, having been forced to abandon their estate in Mauritius and return to France dishonored and destitute, to retrace their forebearer's steps backwards, as it were, Jean Marro's family members identify as "errants" or, to risk a pseudo-etymological interpretation, "marrons". The singularity and simplicity of the tombstone, marked only by the capital name "MARRO," serve as a counterpoint to the absence, erasure and dereliction that have affected all other native places where Jean pursues his pilgrimage. Bringing his life of errantry to a close, if only for the sake of revisiting the phantasmatic dwelling place of Rozilis, proves a daunting task. Even though the last section of the novel, "Retour à Ébène," holds the promise of a return to the native island, the hypothetical linearity of the movement it announces is disrupted by the multiplication of voices indicative of a divergence of meanings.

In his historical and literary analysis of the Atlantic slave trade, Christopher L. Miller contrasts the impossibility of the slave's return with the multiple metropolitan returns by juxtaposing the semiosis of the term in Aimé Césaire's *Cahier d'un retour au pays natal* with the plural French form *retours*, a word not only used to describe "the journey home to France" but also "used constantly to indicate the merchandise brought back from the islands; the 'returns' on the original investment made by the *armateurs* months or even years earlier" (Miller 2008, 55). In Le Clézio's novel, leaving behind the colonial fortune is achieved through a spatial "trialogue" (Miller 2008, 92) between London as the bleak but neutral place where Jean Marro takes refuge from the war in Algeria, France as the ambivalent homeland of return and resentment, and the colonial paradise, the true home forever lost. The indifference of the Londonian landscape appears as a metonymical foreshadowing of Jean's reaction to the news of the Evian treaty, which marks the conclusion of France's last great colonial war and its reluctant but definitive acceptance of decolonization.

The free indirect narrative focused on Jean's consciousness as he travels to Brittany in 1968 and then to Mauritius in 1969 is interspersed with excerpts from aunt Catherine's diary that recount the family's last days in Rozilis in 1909 and the first-person story of Balkis, the granddaughter of Kiambé, a twentieth-century descendant of a long line of Kiambés and Balkis. As Jean sets foot on Jean Eudes' native soil of Brittany, the turmoil of history, with its revolutions, wars and struggles, clashes with and ultimately surrenders to the impassivity of nature, a recurrent theme throughout the novel. His repeated discovery of "the place" – first in the war-torn Britton landmark of Saint-Aubin-du-Cormier and then in the Mauritian cemetery of Cassis – both fulfills and negates the expectations of an ultimate revelation:

> Sorti du village à pied, passé une boucle, soudain Jean découvre le lieu.
>
> C'est une pente boisée en pins et en chênes, ouverte sur une vaste clairière qui descend jusqu'au marécage de la lande d'Ouée. Une étendue absolument vide, un pâtis, mais on devine qu'autrefois cette pente nue devait être semblable aux autres landes, mangée d'ajoncs gris, de buissons d'épines, avec de loin en loin un bosquet de chênes et de sureaux. Alentour, au nord et à l'est, la forêt d'Usel est sombre, si dense que la lumière du soleil y entre à peine. Une forêt pleine de secrets et de maléfices, comme la forêt de Brocéliande. Mais ici c'est l'histoire qui est le seul maléfice. (Le Clézio 2003, 535–536)

From the fifteenth-century battle that decided Brittany's loss and its eventual subservience to France to the eighteenth-century war fought by Jean's ancestor under the impetus of dire poverty, famine and widespread misery that had plagued the region for centuries, the landscape provides a paradoxical page to the writer of the family saga. On the one hand, nature bears the imprint of past struggles, irrevocably transformed by the blood spilled and the bones left on the battlefield; on the other hand, its constant renewal obscures any traces of the past, leaving the present solely visible. As a continually rewritten palimpsest, the place – and, to an even greater extent, the place of origins – lends itself to multiple readings, in the synchronicity of competing contemporaries or chronologically, as subsequent generations review, revise and reincorporate the facts of past (people, dates and spaces) into their perception of the real. Nowhere is the interpretive dissonance or internal dysrhythmia of space more salient than in Jean and Mariam's trip to Maurice. Preferred to Oran, Algeria is a more "neutral" honeymoon destination for the couple since Jean's Algerian wife "n'est pas prête à regarder son passé en face" (Le Clézio 2003, 540), the Indian Ocean island appears to be "easier" place to (re)visit. The language describing their choice is slightly euphemistic and ingratiating, as though to ward off any misgivings about the return to the lost colonial possession. The absence of any material reality representing the Marros on the island, save for their name inscribed in official archives and on a tombstone, outlines along with its peaceful decolonization a preferable scenario to France's bloody separation from its North African colony. Furthermore, the key to overcoming historical trauma lies in the healing power of nature, as represented by the sun's ability to melt away the ghosts of the past and provide nutrients to the luxuriant vegetation that overruns the old colonial haunts: "Maurice, c'était plus facile. C'est neutre. Il n'y reste plus personne du nom de Marro. Juste des fantômes, mais le soleil, l'éclat des plantes et l'indépendance toute neuve doivent bien venir à bout des fantômes" (Le Clézio 2003, 540). The litany about the loss of the family dwelling place (a colonial estate owing its name to the ship that had brought Jean Eudes, Marie Anne and their daughter, Jeanne Eugénie, to Mauritius) – "Rozilis a disparu" (Le Clézio 2003, 542) – verbalizes the contemporary character's freedom from his burdensome past, supported by the phrase "la végétation [l']a envahi" (Le Clézio 2003, 542).

The primal scene of colonialism can never exist in isolation. There are always already two or more scenes that co-exist, either juxtaposed or overlapping, in awareness or in ignorance of one another. In fact, each generation constructs its own scene, which is then folded into the familial or communal narrative. Jean Eudes' anxious yet hopeful arrival in Mauritius is mirrored by Catherine's desolate departure from the family home, which effectively and affectively hyphenates her life, forever condemning it to a "before" and "after" Rozilis: "Ce jour fatal du 1er janvier 1910, quand avec sa famille elle a été chassée du paradis" (Le Clézio 2003, 543–544). The messianic parenthesis in the Marros' genealogical destiny is closed. What is left is the choice between a mournful re-enactment of the past, as exemplified by Catherine and Charles Marro's lives in France, or an immersion into the present reality of the family's former natural and human landscape in order to overcome its hold over the individuals' existence. In a *descensus ad inferos* scene, Jean plunges into the geological depth of his Mauritian ancestor's abode (along the bed of the Terre Rouge river) in an attempt to relive their experience:

> Au fond du ravin la chaleur est étouffante. C'est un lieu perdu, séparé de la Maurice actuelle, si différent, Jean a le sentiment de voir avec les yeux de son aïeul ce qu'il a regardé il y a cent cinquante ans quand il est venu ici à la recherche du lieu de sa thébaïde. Un monde encore intact, où il pouvait oublier avec Marie Anne et ses enfants la vindicte et la

médiocrité, et sans doute son échec à faire fortune avec la course. Loin de la mer, loin de la guerre, au cœur de la nature." (Le Clézio 2003, 543)

The scene ties together two strands of the colonial vocation narrative in one iconic moment. As the contemporary heir strives to immerse himself into the past by offering his own body as a vessel for the reincarnation of those who went before him, the text itself is imbued with the metaphorical technique of "setting things before the eyes" (*pro ommaton poiein*) (Aristotle 1410b 34). The vivid, quasi-experiential effect thus generated increases both the persuasive force and the emotional appeal of the text. Established as an enduring Western *topos* by Virgil's scene of *regere imperio*, in which Aeneas' departed father Anchise foretells the foundation of a great people, the *katabasis* will also become in Césaire's *Cahier* a "trope for a visit to a land, not of the living, but of underworld shades" (Davis 2011, 196) as well as a point of origin for a new life through the symbolism of the "sang neuf" and for new forms of expression generated by his stylistic innovations, the epitome of which is his signature word "verrition" (Césaire 65).

The irruption of Kiambé's story in the later part of the novel strengthens the sense of an immediate past. The nineteenth-century African woman's first-person account not only draws a vivid picture of her capture, enslavement and rebellion but also enlists the persuasive powers of storytelling in order to project another side of the colonial vocation. Kiambé's story is an exemplary one, illuminating through an individual experience the global process by which "the Atlantic triangle (along with the Eastern slave trade) stimulated the slave market in Africa, which in turn spread the social mayhem of war, kidnapping, and depopulation ever deeper into the continent" (Miller 2008, 61). From her capture and sale by a local leader, the "Mwarabu," through the horrifying sea crossing on a slave boat ridden with disease and death under the authority of the "bad white man," or "Mzungumbaya," to the alienating experience of the plantation, where she is first stripped of her name and, later, of her intimacy, when she is married off against her will as a punishment, Kiambé performs her own infernal descent. She, too, is summoned by colonialism, yet, as an enslaved being deprived of identity and agency, her answer is silenced. In the absence of official records and family notebooks, which serve as material traces of the history of the European Marros, Kiambé's vocation – etymologically, calling or mission – is to voice out her story and those of her companions. Le Clézio's choice to insert her first-person account (echoed later by that of her great-great-granddaughter, Balkis) might be construed as a recognition of her singular status. Such a unique structural feature could indicate a need for fictional reparation of the colonial phenomenon Édouard Glissant describes as "non-history" or the "erasure of collective memory" ("le raturage de la mémoire collective") (Glissant 1997, 224). Although the lack of a recorded past condemns the slaves and their descendants to a "suffered history" ("histoire subie"; Glissant 1997, 22), it nonetheless enables them to avoid the exogenous ideas and tools of recording the past (chronologies, archives and official historical truths) in order to devise different forms and techniques of memorialization. The folktale and its modern avatar, the novel, can construct a "prophetic vision of the past" (Glissant 1997, 227) capable of delving into the trauma of colonial "dispossession", uncovering its hidden connections with the present and imagining new futures. Just as the physical and symbolic violence of colonization and slavery have led to an erasure of history, so does the novel recreate this obscurity not only on the textual plane but also on a rhythmic and affective level. For its refusal of unicity and transparency, the folktale, a paramount artform in African and Creole cultures, stands in ontological and axiological opposition with the Western myth. Glissant writes:

> Myth, which is mysterious, opens up the full range of the unknown; the tale, which is straightforward, sees this as inadequate.
>
> The tale has crossed this primordial forest; but it does not emerge with a line of action (*n'ouvre pas sur une filiation*), it increases the darkness in the tortured consciousness. The Caribbean folktale zeroes in on our absence of history: it is the site of the deactivated word. Yet is says it all. Where myth explores the known-unknown and emerges with an absolute view of history through a systematic process, the tale animates ordinary symbols in order to proceed to approximation, by going back and forth. The Caribbean tale outlines a landscape that is not possessed: it is anti-History. (Glissant 1989, 84–85)

In myth, form operates as a simplifier of meaning, reducing it to a formula or "absolute filiation" in Glissant's terms, such as Oresteia's lesson of vengeance in Glissant's *Ormerod* and Thebes' bloody fate in Le Clézio's *Révolutions*. According to Barthes's iconic example of the colonial photograph depicting a Black soldier looking at the French flag, form reduces meaning without cancelling it out entirely and instrumentalizes reality while continuing to represent it:

> le nègre reste là, le concept a besoin de lui: on l'ampute à moitié, on lui enlève la mémoire, non l'existence: il est à la fois têtu, silencieusement

enraciné, et bavard, parole disponible tout entière au service du concept. Le concept, à la lettre, déforme mais n'abolit pas le sens: un mot rendra compte de cette contradiction: il l'aliène. (Barthes 1957, 231)

Myth is thus a "stolen language": the Black man in the picture is confiscated from his personal history and incorporated into a larger, dominating concept. This gesture "abolit la complexité des actes humains, leur donne la simplicité des essences, [...] supprime toute dialectique, toute remontée au-delà du visible immédiat" (Barthes 1957, 240) and projects a binary image of the world while at the same time offering a reassuring impression of "une clarté heureuse; les choses ont l'air de signifier toutes seules" (Barthes 1957, 240). In Le Clézio and Glissant's writing, fiction works both to unravel the obscurity at the heart of the myth and to dismantle the clarity of its message-making machine. Whereas the myth is "un mode de signification [...] une forme" that "ne se définit pas par l'objet de son message, mais par la façon dont il profère: il y a des limites formelles au mythe, il n'y en a pas de substantielles" (Barthes 1957, 225), the novel tarries with the historical substance and the lived experience from which it was born. Whereas the myth is "un système de communication, [...] un message" (Barthes 1957, 225), the novel eludes explanation and dwells in the interstitial space between the known and the unknowable where, in Glissant's terms, it works to reconcile "l'écriture du mythe et l'écriture du conte, le souvenir de la Genèse et la prescience de la Relation" (Glissant 1995, 48).

One narrative device stands out in *Révolutions*, incorporating the features of the Caribbean folktale into the account of a Mozambican woman brought to Mauritius to become a slave. It is the leitmotif of Kiambé's self-naming; each and every one of the interspersed sections of her story presents an *incipit* that describes her identity. As her story devolves into alienation before evolving into a newfound freedom of resistance and rebellion, this formulaic section changes content and style, from the proud affirmation of Kiambé's African genealogy to the acceptance of her slave name, Balkis, the name of the Queen of Sheba in Arabic literature reduced by the white slave owner's whim to a phenotypic commonplace, and ultimately to a renewed sense of self, from "Je suis Kiambé. Je ne suis pas Balkis" (Le Clézio 2003, 455) to "Mon nom est Kiambé, celle qui est créée, fille du guerrier Askari, fille de Malaika. J'ai retrouvé mon nom, et les noms de tous ceux qui sont en moi et que je croyais morts" (Le Clézio 2003, 504).

Defined, one after another, by "tous ces noms, tous ces lieux" (Le Clézio 2003, 423), names of people and places, at first familiar and reassuring, the names of her kin and kith, then strange and alienating, words learned in fear and under the lash, Kiambé's relation to the world is one of sensorial discovery. After being captured by Africans and sold to white slaver traders she relies on her perception to make sense of her new surroundings. In the port city before departing for the colony, she sees the rain and sea for the first time in her life and projects the landscape of her captivity into the setting of her homeland, likening the ocean to a lake: "je regardais cette surface lisse qui brillait, et je pensais que c'était le grand lac près de notre village, dans la province d'Arusha" (Le Clézio 2003, 425). The first encounter with the white man leaves her feeling a foreboding "frisson," a cold sensation that alerts her to her future torment; later on, her meeting with the rebel leader, Ratsitatane, a Malgasy prince fallen victim to a family fight for succession, will fill her with "chaleur," a warmth both physical and spiritual.

The gendered distribution of narrative roles in Kiambé's story, between the men who act in order to enslave or liberate and the women who are the object of their action, highlights the latter's indirect, oblique involvement with history in *Révolutions*. As exemplified by the characters of Kiambé, Catherine Marro and Mariam Charifa, their primary roles appear to be as witness to memorable events as well as catalyst or conduit to men's actions (fighting, writing, traveling and fathering). Is this oblique, indirect or mediated participation in history a sign of female passivity? In this respect, Kiambé's character seems merely reactive to others' agency, such as her captor's, her master's and her liberator's decisions and desires, a trait further confirmed by her malleable identity, which is rhetorically emphasized by the formulaic beginnings of each section of her story. Yet Kiambé's own "revolution" leads her to the reappropriation and reinvention of her alienated self. The key to her rebirth in the land of her captivity is her organic connection with the surrounding landscape, from which she draws her strength to withstand the violence of human action and in which she recognizes the omens of future threats and finds a protective space against human aggression. As a house slave, her initially hesitant and then increasingly bold exploration of the plantation evolves from a soft, tactical form of disobedience of the master's rules into an instinctive yet determined gesture of resistance that eventually leads her to freedom. The space of her displacement and uprootedness is transformed into a familiar landscape by her nightly wanderings as Kiambé increasingly takes possession of it, colonizing it with the smells, sounds and sensations of her homeland:

Les chiens aboyaient, ils m'avaient flairée, et ils m'entendaient marcher
dans les herbes, c'étaient les chiens du maître dressés pour chasser les
marrons. Il faisait chaud et lourd, la terre était trempée par la rosée.
Je respirais l'odeur de cette terre de mon enfance, après que la pluie
est tombée. Je regardais le ciel où la pleine lune mangeait les nuages.
Je ne savais pas pourquoi je marchais à travers les champs, mais j'étais
heureuse, je retrouvais tous les noms que j'avais connus autrefois, ils
revenaient dans ma tête et se cognaient dans ma poitrine, dans mon
ventre. (Le Clézio 2003, 451)

Certain moments reveal an even deeper, more mysterious bond
between the young woman and the natural elements, as, for instance,
when she briefly mentions the fate that befalls her former mistress, who
had Kiambé brutally punished and then married by force to a violent
man: "Je n'ai jamais revu mademoiselle Alix. Mais j'ai su par une
servante qu'elle avait pleuré. Et, la même année, un ouragan est venu
et a détruit la guildiverie, et mademoiselle Alix est partie avec sa mère
pour aller vivre en France" (Le Clézio 2003, 452). After reimagining the
colonial island as a homeland, the young woman takes a second step
toward *marronage* by seeking out, first, the community of plantation
slaves and, later, the rebels hidden in the mountain. A near-death
experience following her escape from the plantation marks a crucial
stage in her metamorphosis:

J'ai couru sans m'arrêter à travers champs, jusqu'à ce que je sois dans les
cailloux de la montagne, et j'avais les pieds en sang. Il s'est mis à pleuvoir,
et j'ai remonté le lit du torrent vers les nuages, pour que les chiens des
miliciens ne suivent pas la trace de mon sang. Pendant deux jours je
me suis cachée dans la forêt, en m'abritant dans une grotte. (Le Clézio
2003, 454)

Frightened and exhausted, her body bruised and bloodied, she finds
refuge in a cave where she undergoes a rebirth. Through this process,
she rediscovers her original survival skills, the familiar gestures of
hunting and food-gathering and the sensations of her childhood: "j'ai
dans la bouche le goût de la boule de manioc qu'elle [Malaika, la mère]
me donnait, en me disant des mots très doux, *kidege kisuri*, joli oiseau,
*ua mangu*, ma fleur, des noms comme du sucre" (Le Clézio 2003, 455).
In this instance, the narrative moves from the past tense to the present,
signaling both a recovery of her identity, as the term "redevenue" might
indicate, and the possibility of a true agency, as she performs herself the
gestures and actions that used to belong to the realm of others (father,

mother, elders, masters): "Je suis Kiambé. Je ne suis pas Balkis. Je suis redevenue celle que j'étais" (Le Clézio 2003, 455).

The character's progression is underpinned by the semantics of traversing the land, especially on foot, by walking or running. Charles Forsdick explores the potential of travel literature centered around the trope of walking for offering new perspectives on travel in general and analyzes the ways in which the body and the senses are represented in "walking" literature. He points out that there has recently been renewed scholarly and non-specialist interest in travelogues, in particular in the travelogues published long ago that had largely been neglected by the reading public. While the rediscovery of old travel texts can be partly explained by a feeling of imperial nostalgia, it equally suggests a certain "exhaustion of contemporary discourses of travel" (Forsdick 2001, 48) and the need to explore new possibilities.

Contemporary traveling is increasingly altered by the activity of racing and speed, described by Paul Virilio under the term "dromology" as participating in the dematerialization of the real: "We now have the aesthetics of the disappearance of a numerical, unstable image of fleeting nature, whose persistence is exclusively retinal" (Virilio 1991, 36). Faced with these challenges, walking literature, as Forsdick calls it, becomes fertile ground for a discussion of the consequences of the acceleration of the world and offers a new and refreshing perspective on the question of traveling: "In the light of these shifts, it is the element of deceleration that becomes central to walking's potential as an alternative means of travel and insight" (Forsdick 2001, 54). Walking is a fundamental human activity that implicates the body and the mind. As compared to other – faster – means of transportation, walking is characterized by slowness, which causes a shift of focus in walking literature from space to time. It activates all the senses and allows the traveler to experience the world in its complexity and with its nuances "rather than as a disjointed series of objects and individuals" (Forsdick 2001, 51). This aspect takes on a particular importance for colonial fortune narratives; although walking can lend itself to superficial exoticism, it more often than not becomes a privileged terrain for examining the interrelation between the walking body and the exterior world: "Because of the bodily nature of walking and the bombardment of the senses it entails, the walker actively engages with the world and relies on perception to negotiate a passage through it" (Forsdick 2001, 51). At the same time, the acceleration of the postmodern world contributes to the perception of the walker as marginal or even dangerous, and most certainly somewhat redundant:

"[t]he normalization of speed has made the body seem weak, fragile and anachronistic" (Forsdick 2001, 52).

The aesthetics of separation, dominant in travel accounts that use conventional modes of transport, is replaced in walking travelogues with "an esthetics of proximity" (Forsdick 2001, 55). Owing to its propensity to inspire attention not just to the outside world but also to people, walking "becomes an activity with an anthropological as well as an ethical dimension" (Forsdick 2001, 55).

Physicality is an essential quality of walking and walking travelogues, since the walker actively participates in travel rather than experiencing it passively: "Rhythmic, repeated contact with the ground wears away the body and the walk becomes a process whereby the walker discovers the limits of his or her own physicality" (Forsdick 2001, 57).

Walking journeys further "undermine the sovereignty of the gaze, the hypertrophy of the eye associated with mechanized travel" (Forsdick 2001, 58). Finally, there is a crucial link between walking and memory. Forsdick notes that many walking journeys do not focus on immediate experiences but rather tend to privilege memories, to the extent that "walking seems to become a means of reactivating or recovering the past" (Forsdick 2001, 59). Forsdick once again explains this by the involvement of the body in the process of walking and the fact that going by foot is slow in comparison with other means of travel: "it triggers processes of memory and allows access to layers of space that are eroded and often lost in accelerated journeys" (Forsdick 2001, 58).

The peripatetic motion of Kiambé and Jean Eudes creates a subtle correspondence between their colonial accounts and connects both of them with the feverish movement of Jean Marro, searching for his family's memory and his own place in the world while wandering the streets of Nice: "C'était une sorte de fièvre, marcher sans arrêt, sans but, sans remède" (Le Clézio 2003, 93). Although the French man and the Mozambican woman's plotlines remain separate, the two characters' imaginary paths may have crossed, as different circumstances brought them to the same island in the same era. Their steps criss-cross on the soil of the Isle of France just as their meandering life stories do on the textual surface of Le Clézio's novel, mapping out singular but overlapping areas of experience and memory. Walking though the island in the company of his trusted friend awakens in Jean Eudes a renewed sense of adventure; the colonial surroundings enhance his proprioceptive quality thanks to which he situates himself in space but also in historical time: "je retrouve le goût de la marche et de l'aventure, que jc n'avais connu depuis la guerre contre la Prusse" (Le Clézio 2003, 233). Jean Eudes' travelogue of his arrival on "Isle de France" in 1798 combines a Montesquieu-inspired interest in social and moral ideas with a Rousseau-like sensibility to the transformative influence of nature on the individual. His writings reveal his dislike for colonial *mores* through both the criticism he directs against French settlers who exhibit excessive luxury in order to erase their humble origins and employ violence against their slaves to better establish their authority, on the one hand, and his initially successful efforts to implement Enlightenment's revolutionary ideals of social progress through education in founding a school for non-white children, on the other. However, his peripatetic notes are teeming with enthusiastic yet contradictory representations of the locale:

> C'est une nature vraiment sublime, que Bernardin de Saint-Pierre n'a pas exagérée. Lorsqu'on remonte de la côte vers l'intérieur, on entre dans une forêt épaisse composée d'essences rares telles que bois colophane, bois noir, ébénier. On avance au fond de gorges où cascadent les rivières, dans un décor de lianes et de fleurs multicolores. Et toute cette nature n'est habitée par aucun animal malfaisant, ni serpent ni bête de proie d'aucune sorte. Le seul danger provient des bandes de marrons qui occupent les montagnes. Aussi sommes-nous armés de fusils, et nous ne nous écartons jamais du chemin. (Le Clézio 2003, 233)

The travelogue is saturated with Western tropes of the sublime and literary references to a phantasmatic paradise where humanity can return to an originary relation with nature, reflected in all activities, such as love, religion and work. The message of social meliorism is underscored by Jean Eudes and Marie Anne's constant efforts to care for the poor indigenous and black people of the island. The two project an unsentimental, non-Bovarystic[2] replica of Paul and Virginie, whose story, described by Françoise Lionnet as the foundational fiction of Mauritius that has eclipsed other narratives of endurance and survival (Lionnet 2012, 32), serves as an explicit model for the travelogue. Nonetheless, Jean Eudes does not refrain from casting a utilitarian gaze on this paradisiacal nature by signaling the capital or potential market value held by its rare natural resources ("colophane, bois noir, ébénier"), just as he does not hesitate to employ the classic orientalist trope of opposition between the goodness of nature and the human danger embodied by the fugitive slaves ("marrons") hiding in the mountains. Such scenes stand in subtle contrast with the Leclézian ecopoetics manifest in Kiambé's story and articulated in his essays

*L'Extase matérielle* and *Terra Amata*. Insofar as the paracolonial gaze is constitutive of the modern historical subject, its presence in Le Clézio's fiction challenges an ecocentric reading of his work:

> For Le Clézio, humanity does not have the right to exercise absolute dominion over the rest of the universe without reflecting upon the greater consequences of our actions for other life forms. Affirming that the worth of these trees in the garden and the species that depend upon these resources for survival is not utilitarian in terms of the value that humans place upon them [as he does in Terra Amata], Le Clézio's worldview clearly reflects what the sustainability researcher Don Clifton refers to as an "ecocentric approach." (Moser 2013, 114)

While concurring with Moser's interpretation of Le Clézio's literary stance as a "concerned global citizen," it is in this discursive site of dissonance, where the anthropocentric gaze conveying political anxiety belies the ecopoetic project, that I would like to situate the story of Flore Gaillard, which provides the narrative and figurative core of Édouard Glissant's novel *Ormerod*. I contend that the account of the octoroon slave's transformation into the leader of a slave rebellion fills a lacuna in Kiambé's story, which thus becomes a pre-text to *Ormerod*. Conversely, Flore Gaillard's story can be read as a buried tectonic plate (what Glissant terms "une plaque d'en dessous") in Le Clézio's *Révolutions*. The brief opening section of Glissant's book, entitled "Deux prétextes," invites an intertextual reading in that it establishes the organic connection between its content and the rhizomatic as well as dynamic configuration of the Caribbean archipelago. The movement of skipping from one rock to another, from one island to another, from one period to another is both explicitly thematized and suggested through the movement of his writing style:

> Ce souffle haletant donne mesure à la cadence du conteur, à la parole qu'il profère d'une fois entre deux respirations, comme entre les battements d'un tambour des Mornes mis en tourmente par la vieille lune, et ainsi d'un souffle à l'autre poussé haut il exhale sa divagation, criant le cri du monde. Qu'y a-t-il de commun entre le souffle, quand même il serait saccadé, sur le point de finir, et le bêtes et le vent, un vonvon, un manicou, un colibri, et Flore Gaillard à Sainte-Lucie, et la tragédie de Grenade en 1983, et un taureau exaspéré? (Glissant 2003, 13)

Gesturing toward the ideas of origin and reason, the first pretext addresses the reader, who becomes at once interlocutor and audience, a mark of oral storytelling that also imprints Kiambé's first-person narrative. While announcing the narrative threads spun and interwoven in *Ormerod*'s fabric – an eighteenth-century slave rebellion in the island colony of Saint-Lucia, the 1983 US invasion of the island of Grenada and the contemporary voices of the humble social security employee Nestor'o Sourde-fontaine, conceivably an ironic throwback to Glissant's own criticism of the neocolonial welfare politics that render Martinique systemically dependent on France, and his poet-friend Apocal – these inaugural passages impart at the same time a fictional language that overcomes the separation between subject and object, between the word and the world. As it revisits the tragic history of the West Indies by placing the focus on moments of utopian irruption,[3] Glissant's novel acknowledges that "our thinking about ourselves now stretches our capacity for interpretive understanding" (Chakrabarty 13) and heeds the call for "non-ontological ways of thinking the human" (Chakrabarty 13). Although history provides the narrative pretext, the agentic power of humanity is absorbed into a decentered elementality governed by force, dynamism and relation, so that humanity itself "has melted away in the Woods": "Là où la mer et la forêt se joignent, au haut de Sainte-Lucie, vous rencontrez Flore Gaillard l'insurgée de cette année 1793, vous vous étonnez. N'apparaît-il pas que son humanité a fondu dans les Bois?" (Glissant 2003, 14).

The second pretext takes a step further in collapsing the distinction between human and non-human entities by overcoming the bifurcation of mind and nature, which Le Clézio designates as the "genesis myth":[4]

> Il est dit, *de science et prophétie certaines*, que bientôt, demain, un monstrueux raclement des plaques d'en dessous provoque – comme une écriture cassée concassée qui d'elle-même s'emporte et se meurtrit – l'apocalypse qui engloutit ces terres et submerge la mer elle-même, dans une furie d'eau sans dimension ni intention, et de vent sans direction. (Glissant 2003, 16)

The passage points to an apocalyptic writing wherein different discourses, epistemologies, visions and sensibilities converge to render a chaotic, primordial and elemental movement. As Michael J. Dash points out, Glissant's text unfolds as an awe-inspiring forest that forces readers to adjust to a deficit of intelligibility caused by a scriptural reflection of the confusion and uncertainty that characterize the Caribbean identity: "Here the forest of interwoven relationships, fragmented time and constantly shifting landscape makes easy penetration impossible. The ultimate response is awe at its daunting luxuriance" (Dash 80).

In *Ormerod*, the human/non-human separation is obscured by the constant oscillation between, first, humanity and a sentient universe "sans dimension ni intention," and, second, the anthropomorphic commitment of literature in general, in particular postcolonial writing, and an ecopoetics of the chaos-monde.

Thus the description of Flore's battered body offers a paradoxical manifestation of her will and affirmation of her leadership: "Les tapis de feuilles de cacos sauvages brûlaient sous les pieds, Flore Gaillard roulait son corps dans cette fournaise, pour reprendre force" (Glissant 2003, 19). She submits herself and "her" soldiers, a group of ragged, mud-covered former male plantation slaves, to this harsh treatment. Born on the Lovenblade plantation and raised by a protective master, Bellac, "un demi-Anglais demi-Français" (Glissant 2003, 28), who reveals his true intentions by raping her, Flore welcomes this turn in her destiny and joins the slaves in the cane fields as an equal to the strongest males: "Ma sueur est aussi bonne que celle d'un congo…" (Glissant 2003, 20). In so doing, she affirms her independence in the manner of "Batoutoo" women, an imaginary people introduced by Glissant in his 2011 novel, *Sartorius*, signaling that her freedom from slavery begins with freedom from male domination:

> attentive maintenant à échapper à ceux de ces nègres de houe qui eurent connaissance du caprice du patron et crurent pouvoir profiter à leur tour du corps de cette fille à peine fille mais bien debout, qui ne reconnaissait personne de son entourage qui pût la défendre et ne se réclamait d'aucun attachement. (Glissant 2003, 20)

Under the tidal wave of the French revolution, Flore asserts herself as a charismatic and unifying military leader: "Les nègres la suivirent, accompagnés ou précédés des femmes qui ne la jalousaient pas, au contraire" (Glissant 2003, 23).

However, her victories are confiscated by official history, which credits her male companion as the brains behind her military exploits. Colonial reports of slave rebellions appear in both *Révolutions* and *Ormerod*, offering a counterpuntal view of the capture and punishment of the rebels. In Le Clézio's novel the account provided by a British army clerk, William Stone, whose name forms a dispersed stratum from the ashes used by Kiambé to alert Ratsitatane to the danger and Jean Marro's memorializing crystals, foreshadows the defeat of the rebels with a scene of victory against nature. In Glissant's book, also belonging to the process of lithification and crystallization, reminiscent of volcanic eruption, where history and geology meet are Flore Gaillard's dust ashes, inhaled by the audience witnessing her execution by fire: "Vous aurez pu entasser dans cette poussière tout l'amas des histoires mêlées insoup-çonnées qui avaient poussé dans la terre de Sainte-Lucie" (Glissant 2003, 302). In Glissant's novel, the ashes of the fallen rebel are not scattered away or reduced to the dust of her mortal body, a notion predicated on the religious dichotomy between the transient corporeality and the eternal life of the soul, but join a universal materiality that spans not only modern times but all of history, and not only Saint-Lucia but all of the Antilles.

French and British troops join forces to stifle the Saint-Lucia rebellion and, thus, thwart another Haitian revolution. The environment is utilized, resisted or dominated following the needs of military strategy, and the successful repossession of the rebel-harboring mountain signals the victory of the colonial operation. In *Révolutions*, first, the troops conduct an exploratory mission to check the terrain and ascertain the position of the rebels; then they must climb the mountain up to the point where it becomes nearly impassable: "*À cet endroit il n'y avait plus de chemin, et nous devions grimper aux rochers en nous servant des pieds et des mains comme les singes*" (Le Clézio 2003, 460, italics in the original). By physically lowering themselves to the level of animals, they seek to capture their bestial enemy in his "*repaire*" (italics in the original) ("lair"). In keeping with the culture vs. nature logic sketched out in Jean Eudes' walk through the same landscape, Ratsitatane is found "*au fond d'un ravin de la rivière Cascades*," tied up as a beast captured by hunters, "*attaché à un arbre les jambes en sang car les chasseurs l'avaient frappé à coup de pierres*" (Le Clézio 2003, 461, italics in the original). Yet at this point the British clerk's narrative deviates, somewhat destabilized by Ratsitatane's enduring humanity. The colonial witness confesses his surprise that, despite his trials and concealment in the mountains, the Malgasy prince continues to hold himself up proudly and defiantly, like "*un homme qui n'a jamais cessé d'être libre*" (Le Clézio 2003, 461, italics in the original).

The question of confiscated and falsified official history could also be raised in relation to *Ormerod*'s narrative discourse, which emphasizes Flore Gaillard's seductive powers over men and her bewitching use of words, demonstrated by her plurilingual use of an incantatory expression that draws men to her growing army: "*Viens avec moi*," "*Vini épi moin*," "*vini ek moin*," "*vini with mo*" (italics in the original). However, in Glissant's novel, Flore Gaillard's story is told from an internal perspective, through the communal yet individuated voice of an I/eye-witness, an anonymous but fully invested participant in the events recounted: "je comprends que j'étais dans ces ils qui allaient dévaler, je tremblais comme feuille corossol, tremblade et résistance en même moment, oui tous ces ils c'était Flore Gaillard" (Glissant 2003, 26).

Whereas Kiambé's story centers on her unfulfilled dream of returning to the "Grand-Terre" of Madagascar and spending her life with her idealized male companion, whose name "résonnait comme un tambour de guerre" in the palace of King Radama (Le Clézio 2003, 457), Flore Gaillard embodies, as her hybrid, androgynous name indicates, the masculine image of a strong ("gaillard") and brave leader, while still conserving her feminine powers of seduction and empathy ("flore"). The Mozambican woman credits Ratsitatane with restoring her old identity and calls him the liberating master of Black people ("notre maître," Le Clézio 2003, 455). Owing her life to him, Ratsitatane rescues her from the cave whence she emerges as a newborn "nue à cause des buissons qui avaient déchiré ma robe et mes pieds [...] en sang" (Le Clézio 2003, 456). Kiambé revels in his soft words that, albeit foreign, are reassuring, an impression further confirmed by his warming touch, sensorially contrasted with the cold touch of the white slaver. He thus becomes her first true husband who shows her kindness and respect, calling her by her real name without abusing her like the Kilwa slaves or her plantation husband. However, Kiambé's story, despite revolving around the figure of Ratsitatane, does register the latter's flaw: that is, his disconnect from his natural surroundings. At the crucial moment of the uprising he does not understand the warning Kiambé provides him by sprinkling ashes over his food to alert him to the arrival of a traitor in their midst (Le Clézio 2003, 457). This scene brings to light the abstract, even hieratic nature of his character; in spite of the frequent references to his physical power, he never quite inhabits – or relates to – the place he occupies. Ultimately, Ratsitatane is an abstract character in both the etymological sense of being withdrawn from the world and the proper sense of being an idealized projection of African male corporeality, for, depicted as strong and protective, he stands for a benign version of the law of the father as well as a projection of African nostalgia insofar as, unable to relate to the land of his slavery, he constantly hearkens back to the lost homeland. This duality is captured in the ritual performed by an African priest to ensure the uprising's success and their subsequent return to Madagascar. While offering an animal sacrifice to summon the power of the elements, the officiant explains the meaning of his gestures: the mix of blood and land shall bring about the clouds and the wind to conceal and protect the rebels from the incoming white soldiers and ensure their safe passage back to the homeland, while the drawing of a star shall protect the leader and see his enemies defeated. Yet, Ratsitatane witnesses the ritual with sadness, aware of the betrayal perpetrated against him. His last act of kindness for his wife is to share with her his magic necklace "avec les coquillages et le bois noir, pour que j'aie la protection du Dieu de la Grand-Terre" (Le Clézio 2003, 458). The token will indeed protect Kiambé throughout her imprisonment in an asylum and the birth of Ratsitatane's daughter, but instead of auguring their return to Africa it is passed on through several generations and resurfaces in the contemporary story of Balkis, great-granddaughter of Kiambé, whose name signals a hybrid identity shaped both by the family dream of a return to the native land and her individual dreams for the future: "je peux," she affirms, in bringing the "Kilwa" storyline to closure, "deviner l'avenir dans mes rêves" (Le Clézio 2003, 552).

Glissant's heroine, who does not cultivate the nostalgic dream of Africa, enters into a living dialogue with her Caribbean surroundings. Schooling herself in the ways in which the elements of the biosphere coexist, communicate and thrive, Flore learns various fighting strategies in the midst of the "Bois" and becomes a skilled eco-hermeneut:

> Elle a parfois la chance de voir les nuages dans une trouée des branches et elle les suit quand ils se déplacent, examinant et analysant les choses et les pays qu'ils forment dans le ciel. [...] Elle tente de deviner les tactiques, et qui parmi elles décide de contourner un obstacle ou passer dessus. (Glissant 2003, 31)

After the failure of her rebellion, Flore's execution extends even further the deanthropomorphization of the character whose physical body, burned at the stake, is literally consumed by the vegetal matter ("bois") that makes up the forest ("Bois") she used to roam. The transformation of her humanity into the organic matter of the forest simultaneously fulfills the promise of her given name, which takes precedence over the male symbolism of her second, and offers a reimagining of the disjunctive incommensurability on which postcolonial thinking is predicated. Alongside the opposition drawn by Chakrabarty between human and non-human, the binaries of male/female, agency/passivity and death/birth are transcended in the protagonist's fusion with the natural surroundings through a series of chemical processes such as calcination and evaporation.

C'est alors que ces hommes dehors versèrent du bitume liquide, de la poix et de la résine, déjà chauds, sur le bûcher et sur Flore Gaillard, qu'ils laissèrent pénétrer dans les détails des bois entassés et dans les échancrures des vêtements. Puis ils y portèrent le feu, qui brûla lentement. Flore Gaillard éclatait en hurlements, quand elle sentit sur tout son corps cette bouffée calcinée, la chaleur bourrée d'odeurs de la forêt elle-même, comme elle l'avait sentie une fois dans la solitude de cette guerre, et qui s'étendait sur elle et la protégeait contre les brûlures et les arrachements de sa chair et de ses organes, un linge de naissance plutôt qu'un voile des morts, qui prit soin d'elle et la fit entrer enfin dans les Bois où son esprit s'évapora, tant que dura ce feu sur son corps. (Glissant 2003, 301–302)

Glissant's writing stylistically mirrors the character's diegetic evolution in the novel. This homology is ostensible in several key passages from *Ormerod* in which the grammaticality and legibility of language are undermined from within. The novel tests the limits of verbal articulation, discursive reason and aesthetic expression, rendering visible and audible the apocalypse of the "écriture cassée-concassée" announced in its "Deux prétextes." Rather than following a propositional logic by conveying fully formed thoughts and ideas, the writing surrenders to the chaotic sensoriality of nature:

Imaginez la terre comme elle est, comme elle nous paraît, grouillis de boues verminées de cribos affamés de pieds prostrés en pourriture de bras arrachés de docteurs-feuilles épuisées la tête entre leur mains rougies de corps éventrés sous les roches de ventres qui coulent à vue de charpies empuanties de morts-vivants dévorant des racines à peine déterrées amères empoisonnées de morts-vivants titubants sous le vent impatient la pluie ne nettoie aucune de ces innommables crasses elle a beau couler en rivière au long des lianes trop lourdes ravager les frondrières de roches s'engouffrer dans les fonds la putréfaction est universelle. (Glissant 2003, 90)

The imperative "imaginez" that sets the passage in motion, morphologically devoid of an explicit subject, opens up the cascade of nominal phrases connected by gerundival and participial verbs. In the absence of active verbs, with the exception of the impersonal "paraît" and "coulent," which describes the oxymoric image of "flowing rocks," this fragment suggests the natural world's primacy over human subjectivity. The environment is not passive, static, modeled or controlled by the agentic force of man; it is, rather, a force that absorbs the human and non-human in a continuous cycle of regeneration and decay.

The trials of the African woman of Mauritius as well as those of the octoroon slave of Saint-Lucia are strikingly similar: reduced to a life of captivity by birth or by force, they are subjected to physical and sexual violence and humiliated and dispossessed of their identity, before rising up to take part in an insurrection of fugitive slaves. Yet these structural resemblances generate very different narrative outcomes. Kiambé's story revolves, like Penelope's patient web, around another's dream of return to the native land. "Grand-Terre," or Madagascar, is the native land of Ratsitatane, the rebellion leader who figures as Kiambé's companion and freely chosen "master" to whom she owes her life, her freedom and her new identity. In Glissant's book, Flore Gaillard is the heroine of a legend recounted by the many voices of witnesses and heirs of her exploits as an insurgent slave and charismatic leader. The hybrid symbolism of her name, which combines female sensititvity with male strength, signals the organic relationship between her and the island's nature. Flore learns about war and strategy by immersing herself into the life of the primordial "Bois," where she studies the movement of the ants, the flight of the birds and the cloud formations. By contrast, Ratsitatane is an abstract being in the etymological sense of *ab-straho* (to be drawn away): drawn away from his native land, he remains separated from the island of his enslavement. He also embodies the proper sense of the word, for he is cast as the idealized African male whose archetypal dignity is matched by a superhuman physical strength. Insofar as he is a fictional incarnation of the law of the pre-colonial Father, Le Clézio's character fulfills the role of the heroic traveler who instills meaning and order into the narrative of a woman tasked with perpetuating his bloodline and his legend. In a telling contrast, Glissant's novel recounts the tragic story of a female rebel who impregnates the memory of the Creole storyteller and his modern heir, the scribe.

## Notes

1 "The existing races constitute separate branches of one or many primitive stocks. These stocks have now vanished. They are not known in historical times at all, and we cannot form even the most general idea of their qualities. They differed from each other in the shape and proportions of the limbs, the structure of the skull, the internal conformation of the body, the nature of the capillary system, the color of the skin, and the like; and they never succeeded in losing their characteristic features except under powerful influence of the crossing blood" (Joseph-Arthur de Gobineau, *The Inequality of Human Races*, tr. Adrian Collins, New York: H. Fertig, 1967 [1853–1855], 133).

2  "Elle avait lu *Paul et Virginie* et elle avait rêvé la maisonnette de bambous, le nègre Domingo, le chien Fidèle, mais surtout l'amitié douce de quelque bon petit frère, qui va chercher pour vous des fruits rouges dans des grands arbres plus hauts que des clochers, ou qui court pieds nus sur le sable, vous apportant un nid d'oiseau" (Gustave Flaubert, *Madame Bovary*, Paris: Gallimard, Folio classique, 2001, 84).

3  Bronwen Martin offers an interesting analysis of Le Clézio's *Révolutions* as a quest for utopia (Martin 109–179).

4  Quoted in Keith Moser's monograph, the "genesis myth" according to Le Clézio is the belief that "nature is given to man so he can use it" (Moser 2013, 101). One finds a similar phrasing in Glissant's *Caribbean Discourse*: "The control of nature, and of one's nature, by culture was the ideal of the Western mind, just as to broaden one's culture to the cosmic dimensions of one's nature, and all nature, was perhaps the dream of the Oriental mind" (Glissant 1989, 73).

PART TWO

# Writing as Africans

In this chapter I propose to look at how encounters born from crossing boundaries between territories, cultures, languages and memories can either amplify or mitigate relations of antagonism, domination or rivalry. Stemming from different engagements with the colonial past and its postcolonial avatars, and presenting contrasting views of the colonial fortune, these relations lay bare the imperfections, frictions and jagged edges of contemporary identity construction. I will consider "the dialectic of self and the other than self" in contemporary narratives in French inasmuch as it is predicated on but also opposed to an idea of collective or national identity. In *Oneself as Another*, Paul Ricœur posits the distinction between two distinct meanings of identity that arise from the Latin terms *ipse* and *idem*. *Idem*-identity stresses the permanence and continuity of the self, its sameness as opposed to concepts like "'other,' 'contrary,' 'distinct,' 'diverse,' 'unequal,' 'inverse'" (Ricœur 1992, 3). *Ipse*-identity opens itself to difference and otherness since it "involves a dialectic complementary to that of selfhood and sameness, namely the dialectic of self and the other than self" (Ricœur 1992, 3).

As Ricœur notes with regard to what he calls "the most harmful ideologies of 'national identity'":

It will be the task of a reflection on narrative identity to balance, on one side, the immutable traits which this identity owes to the anchoring of the history of a life in a character and, on the other, those traits which tend to separate the identity of the self from the sameness of character. (Ricœur 1992, 123)

In the postcolonial context, contrasting narratives of historical and identitarian anchoring and the rejection of stereotypical sameness are equally precipitated by transcultural, global and transfrontier encounters, which Mireille Rosello has dubbed "performative." Such phenomena "[coincide] with the creation of new subject-positions rather than treating preexisiting (pre-imagined) identities as the reason for, and justification of, the protocol of encounter – whether it is one of violence or trust, respect or hostility" (Rosello 1). While these encounters are a necessary exercise in cultural self-questioning and can provide a welcome threshold for engaging with or indeed opening up to difference, called by Jean-Luc Nancy "la pensée de l'altérité ouverte par et exposée hors de la mêmeté" (Nancy 2005, 41), they can also be the source of self-serving and self-aggrandizing ventures. The impulse to move toward the colonial other is constantly faced with the risk of delusion; the experiential dimension underlining the first attitude is always haunted by the possibility that it might lead to the second.

# CHAPTER THREE

# Distant Empathy

J'ai joué avec les statues d'ébène, avec les sonnettes de bronze, j'ai utilisé les cauris en guise d'osselets. Pour moi, ces objets, ces bois sculptés et ces masques accrochés aux murs n'étaient pas du tout exotiques. Ils étaient ma part africaine, ils prolongeaient ma vie et, d'une certaine façon, ils l'expliquaient. Et avant ma vie, ils parlaient du temps que mon père et ma mère avaient vécu là-bas, dans cet autre monde où ils avaient été heureux. Comment dire? J'ai ressenti de l'étonnement, et même de l'indignation, lorsque j'ai découvert, longtemps après, que de tels objets pouvaient être achetés et exposés par des gens qui n'avaient rien, et même pis, pour qui ces masques, ces statues et ces trônes n'étaient pas des choses vivantes, mais la peau morte qu'on appelle souvent "l'art."

(Le Clézio 2004, 65)

This passage is lodged at the heart of an autobiographical book entitled *L'Africain*, by the 2008 Nobel Prize-winner Jean-Marie Gustave Le Clézio. By undertaking a rather common literary project among writers at the zenith of their career, the author, whose family history stretches back to the plantation society of the Mauritius island, extends as far as Guyana and spans the English Channel to encompass French and English languages, cultures and histories, casts a retrospective look at his father's life as a way of reflecting on his own. The story is thus doubly significant. On the one hand, it allows Le Clézio, the son, to understand and forgive his father's cold demeanor and aggressive behavior by retracing his life path, from his arrival in Europe as a young man after his own father, J. M. G. Le Clézio's grandfather, ruined and disgraced, is forced to leave his colonial property in Mauritius and settle for a life of relative poverty in England to his years in medical school, where his study of tropical diseases foreshadows his entire career as a doctor, at first in British Guyana and then, for decades, in Africa, from Ghana and the Congo to Cameroon and Nigeria. On the other hand, this oblique autobiography, a literary form in which the author recounts his own existence through the prism of someone else's, provides the writer with an opportunity to ponder the foundational values of his work, to reflect on his own choices, while rationalizing his father's actions insofar as they hold a mirror to his own. Le Clézio has often professed his belief in a world without a center and in literature's freedom from the constraints of national identity. Nonetheless, instead of rejecting the concept of identity, he shifts it from the bio-political to the cultural paradigm: "Identity is absolutely essential, and it is linked to language. Identity does not necessarily mean a link with a notion or a piece of land, but mostly with a modern culture or an ancient culture" (Le Clézio 2009).

In this chapter I will engage with the ethical contradictions between empathic *ethos* and orientalist tropes associated with the momentous departure for Africa as well as the depiction of the continent that incites fascination in fictional works by three French-language writers: J. M. G. Le Clézio, Marie Darrieussecq and Laurent Gaudé. This could be construed as an attempt to probe Christopher L. Miller's assertion that, when it comes to theorizing and – I would add – more generally, narrating Africa, Africans and the African experience, there can be *"no real ethics without ethnicity"* (italics in the original). In *Theories of Africans*, Miller states that in the postcolonial context – and I would again expand this imperative to paracolonial writing – one cannot begin to construct an ethical discourse "without the disquieting, untidy presence of the other. The relation to the other is the relation of ethnicity; it is also the relation between any theoretical discourse and Africa; claiming an ethical imperative does not exempt the Western critic from a relation of difference" (Miller 1990, 63–64). First, I will examine Le Clézio's autobiographical text *L'Africain* in order to uncover the narrative sites that display this tension. I will then read Le Clézio's writing against the works of Laurent Gaudé, a self-professed "Mediterranean," "traveling" writer, and against Marie Darrieussecq's novel *Il faut beacoup aimer les hommes*. Finally, I will return to Le Clézio and his novel *Désert*, while raising several questions inspired by Simon Gikandi's analysis of the affective approach to literature.

## African Subjects

In Le Clézio's autobiographical text the "African part" lies at the center of the father–son relationship as well as at the point of overlap between other distinct identities. While Africa plays a different role in shaping each of their destinies, both the writer and his remembered father share similar attitudes of closeness and distance, familiarity and estrangement, practical necessity and elective affinity with, as his mother puts it, "ce continent à la fois si neuf et si malmené par le monde moderne" (Le Clézio 2004, 60). These terms indicate a series of contradictions that permeate Le Clézio's "little book" and characterize empathic writing about Africa. Three examples illustrate this textual and ethical tension.

The first moment of tension consists of the narrator's recantation of his father's momentuous decision to leave Europe behind in order to seek meaning and fulfillment in areas of the world where the individual is not hemmed in by social strictures and appearances, where a man is worth more than his business card.[1] The first time this is mentioned in *L'Africain*, the emphasis is placed on the deliberate, existential and ethical choice of the young doctor:

> Il avait choisi autre chose. Par orgueil sans doute, pour fuir la médiocrité de la société anglaise, par goût de l'aventure aussi. Et cette autre chose n'était pas gratuite. Cela vous plongeait dans un autre monde, vous emportait vers une autre vie. Cela vous exilait au moment de la guerre, vous faisait perdre votre femme et vos enfants, vous rendait, d'une certaine façon, inéluctablement étranger. (Le Clézio 2004, 43)

The almost Sartrian situation in which the father is cast, a narrative of responsibility and sacrifice, contrasts with the brief comments made in the historical present just a few pages later, which shed a new light on the father's colonial departure by revealing that it stemmed from circumstances beyond his control (his family's destitute state): "Il fait une spécialité de médecine tropicale. Il sait déjà qu'il n'aura pas les moyens de s'installer comme médecin privé. L'épisode de la carte de visite exigée par le médecin-chef de l'hôpital de Southampton ne sera que le prétexte à rompre avec la société européenne" (Le Clézio 2004, 50). What at first appears to be a deliberate act, a symbolic rejection of British and European values, is later exposed as a pre-determined path, a literary trope Le Clézio's narrative shares with a host of other French writers, from Louis-Ferdinand Céline to Claude Simon and Pierre Michon and from Marguerite Duras to Paule Constant and Frédérique Clémençon.

The second contradiction is triggered by the direct contact with the empire, which prompts several strong disavowals of the diverse facets of colonialism: political, administrative, social and philosophical. The memoirist emphasizes the difference between his own childhood memories of Africa in the 1940s and the world described by colonial English novelists such as Joyce Cary and William Boyd:

> Nous n'avons rien connu de ce qui a pu fabriquer l'identité un peu carica-turale des enfants élevés aux "colonies." [...] Je ne sais rien de ce qu'il décrit, cette lourdeur coloniale, les ridicules de la société blanche en exil sur la côte, toutes les mesquineries auxquelles les enfants sont particu-lièrement attentifs, le dédain pour les indigènes, dont ils ne connaissent que la fraction des domestiques qui doivent s'incliner devant les caprices des enfants de leurs maîtres, et surtout cette sorte de coterie dans laquelle les enfants de même sang sont à la fois réunis et divisés, où ils perçoivent un reflet ironique de leurs défauts et de leurs mascarades, et qui forme en quelque sorte l'école de la conscience raciale qui supplée pour eux à l'apprentissage de la conscience humaine – je puis dire que, Dieu merci, tout cela m'a été complètement étranger. (Le Clézio 2004, 19)

The interjection "thank God, all that was foreign to me" is one of several rhetorical devices (explicative digression, emphatic repetition, hyperbolic refutation) used to highlight the difference between the narrator's father's (and, by extension, his own) meaningful presence in colonial Africa, on the one hand, and the senseless and arrogant behavior of the amorphous mass of colonial officers, agents, businessmen and families, on the other. Another statement – "J'étais seulement un enfant, la puissance de l'empire m'indifférait assez" (Le Clézio 2004, 24) – nuances this exceptionality by underscoring a lack of colonial awareness on the part of the narrator and his brother, fully immersed as they are in the experience of a new home, a new family life and the constant discovery of a new world. However, a textual tension arises when the narrator gives free rein to his evocative imagination. For the young narrator and his brother, running free through the savannah, reveling in their freedom and communing with nature also brings about feelings of domination over the space they inhabit, of mastery and control of their environment:

> Alors nous, nous étions sauvages comme de jeunes colons, sûrs de notre liberté, de notre impunité, sans responsabilité et sans aînés. [...] Ces journées à courir dans les hautes herbes à Ogoja, c'était notre première liberté [...] Je crois que je n'ai jamais senti un tel élan depuis ce temps-là. Un tel besoin de me mesurer, de dominer. (Le Clézio 2004, 28–29)

The third contradiction stems from the narrator's questions concerning the role Africa played in shaping his father's personality. By the time the family is reunited in the wake of World War II, the trials of the mother and her young sons in occupied France and the bitter disappointment of the father, confined to his post in Ogoja after a failed attempt to help them escape through Algeria, have severely altered the family dynamic. Pondering over the reasons for his father's transformation into an angry, bitter and distant man, the writer grapples with two entities – one might even say entelechies – that is, two vital forces that affect a person's destiny: "Était-ce la guerre, cet interminable silence, qui avait fait de mon père cette homme pessimiste et ombrageux, autoritaire, que nous avons appris à craindre plutôt qu'à aimer? Était-ce l'Afrique? Alors, quelle Afrique?" (Le Clézio 2004, 41). These questions try to find the key that would unlock the mystery of the paternal behavior between the war as a human catastrophe, a man-made tragedy and a continent. Lydie Moudileno has established the connection between the use of the colonial stereotype and the attempt to generate a "contre-récit de filiation postcoloniale" (Moudileno 2011, 70). In the parallel between the two entities, Africa can take on a plurality of meanings – as a chronotope, a social melting pot, a cultural conglomerate – yet it is also contaminated by the same ominous connotations, conjuring up the image of a natural calamity or a hybrid natural and human catastrophe.

> L'Afrique avait mis en lui une marque qui se confondait avec les traces laissées par l'éducation spartiate de sa famille à Maurice. L'habit à l'occidentale qu'il endossait chaque matin pour aller au marché devait lui peser. Dès qu'il rentrait chez lui, il enfilait une large chemise bleue à la manière des tuniques des Haoussas du Cameroun, qu'il gardait jusqu'à l'heure de se coucher. C'est ainsi que je le vois à la fin de sa vie. Non plus l'aventurier ni le militaire inflexible. Mais un vieil homme dépaysé, exilé de sa vie et de sa passion, un survivant. (Le Clézio 2004, 57)

The irreconcilable duality of Africa, depicted both as a transformative space, a catalyst for a deeper connection with one's own emotions and surroundings, and as an overwhelming and indifferent universe, a geographic and cultural embodiment of the Kantian "sublime," is a recurring trope in contemporary writing. Laurent Gaudé's novel *Eldorado* (2006) utilizes the trope of Africa's duality in an explicit and dramatic way by thematizing the realization of the continent's crushing greatness through a road accident that puts an end to the hero's life. One can read into this final, cathartic act a personification endowing Africa with an agency and subjectivity often obfuscated by other colonial or postcolonial works that paint it as a political, social and economic wasteland: "Il ne restait plus que la vaste nuit d'Afrique, indifférente aux hommes et à leur souffrance, soucieuse du seul cri des oiseaux qui fait frissonner les arbres centenaires. Salvatore Piracci gisait près de cette route sèche, le corps disloqué. Il ne laissait rien derrière lui. [...] Le choc l'avait brisé" (Gaudé 2006, 238).

In this ending, one can hear echoes of a more memorable text, Albert Camus's "La Femme adultère," whose female protagonist breaks free from her isolation and alienation by stepping away from the human world and into the Algerian desert. A climactic experience is brought about by the French woman's self-abandonment to the natural elements in a place previously felt as foreign (Camus's writing emphasizes the strange sights, smells, sounds and people in the places through which she and her husband, Marcel, have to move). The passage teems with terms that suggest the immersion of the protagonist's subjectivity into the landscape: like a plant, she senses the sap rising from her roots; she feels as though she were submerged under water while tears spring from her eyes, and she ends up lying on the ground, her inner obscurity suddenly illuminated by the stars around her. But this elemental dissolution of humanity also points to a self-affirming transformation, an entelechy or an actualization of her latent powers, perhaps mirroring that of the country itself, an interpretation supported by Camus's frequent use of marital imagery to describe the relationship between France and Algeria or the Pieds-noirs and Arabs:[2]

> Après tant d'années où, fuyant devant la peur, elle avait couru follement, sans but, elle s'arrêtait enfin. En même temps, il lui semblait retrouver ses racines, la sève montait à nouveau dans son corps qui ne tremblait plus. Pressée de tout son ventre contre le parapet, tendue vers le ciel en mouvement, elle attendait seulement que son cœur encore bouleversé s'apaisât à son tour et que le silence se fît en elle. Les dernières étoiles des constellations laissèrent tomber leurs grappes un peu plus bas sur l'horizon du désert, et s'immobilisèrent. Alors, avec une douceur insupportable, l'eau de la nuit commença d'emplir Janine, submergea le froid, monta peu à peu du centre obscur de son être et déborda en flots ininterrompus jusqu'à sa bouche pleine de gémissements. L'instant d'après, le ciel entier s'étendait au-dessus d'elle, renversée sur la terre froide. (Camus 1957, 27–28)

It is with this text that E. Said chooses to illustrate his reading of "Camus's fiction as an element in France's methodically constructed political geography of Algeria, which took many generations to complete, the better to see it as providing an arresting account of the political and interpretive contest to represent, inhabit and possess the territory itself" (Said 1994, 176). Said develops his argument against the symbolic reading of colonial writers through the prism of "Western consciousness," which he calls "a receptacle emptied of all but its capacity for sentience and reflection" (Said 1994, 174). Instead, the author of *Orientalism* suggests the need for a "restorative interpretation," capable of peeling off the layers of geographical concealment, historical bias and hermeneutical shortsightedness in order to show, *"contrapuntally"* (Said 1994, 178, italics in the original), that "Camus's writing is informed by an extraordinarily belated, in some ways incapacitated colonial sensibility, which enacts an imperial gesture within and by means of a form, the realistic novel, well past its greatest achievements in Europe" (Said 1994, 176). Ultimately, the title character's "specific history as a Frenchwoman in Algeria does not matter, for she has achieved a superveningly immediate and direct access to that particular earth and sky" (Said 1994, 177).

I would argue that a similar belated and unexamined colonial sensibility resurfaces in the novels of Laurent Gaudé, winner of the Goncourt prize in 2004 for the Mediterranean-inspired family saga *Le Soleil des Scorta*, which vacillate between melancholy and "presentism" (Hartog 2003) as their narratives attempt to establish a delicate balance between the empathic re-enactment of the past, in its material and affective manifestations, and the critical scrutiny of its social and political underpinnings. On his blog, Gaudé details his sources of inspiration: the journey "to faraway lands" or "remote past eras," the shout ("le cri") "or those who passed on without being able to voice it," Antiquity and the Mediterranean. Combining empathy and sympathy, these categories relate to the concept of *Einfühlung*, or "feeling into," described as an embodied (emotional and physical) response to an image, a space, an object or a built environment (Keen 209).

The writer's mention of the shout ("le cri") is strikingly reminiscent of the central idea of the Négritude movement, yet this reference remains unacknowledged by Gaudé. What might appear to be an ambiguous, if not unethical, use of an important intellectual contribution by African and Antillean French-language writers could by the same token be construed, in the light of the paradigmatic shift away from what Simon Gikandi calls "theories of difference" (Gikandi 2001, 5) to what Stuart Hall calls "the politics of articulation" (Hall 1986), as a new manner of integrating Senghor, Césaire and Damas's thinking into the mainstream cultural vocabulary without indexing their difference and intellectual contribution. To test this hypothesis, we can turn our attention to three of Gaudé's novels: *Cris* (*Shouts*), *Eldorado* and *La Mort du roi Tsongor* (*The Death of King Tsongor*). Each of them relies on the fictionalization of Africa, in an explicit or allusive manner, whether as a central theme or a secondary narrative feature, such as a character or a backdrop. Furthermore, since the texts are replete with intertextual echoes they also echo the concerns and themes of a host of very diverse books: *Il deserto dei Tartari* by the Italian Dino Buzzati, *Waiting for the Barbarians* by the South African J. M. Coetzee, *Ségou* by the Guadeloupian Maryse Condé and the trio of *Les Contes d'Amadou Koumba* by Birago Diop, *Douceur du bercail* by Aminata Sow Fall and *Le Cavalier et son ombre* by Boubacar Boris Diop, all three Senegalese authors writing in French and belonging to different political and literary generations.

The first of Gaudé's novels, *Cris* (2001), is a short narrative featuring fictional testimonies of soldiers who fought in World War I, called in France "the Great War" because of the unprecedented impact it had on the country and its people materially and, more importantly, psychologically. In addition to inspiring countless literary works in the postwar era, the traumatic memories of those who took part in the conflict generated a pseudo-literary genre called "paroles de poilus" ("words from our braves"). Laurent Gaudé draws on this tradition while imagining the inner thoughts of different participants in the war, from lowborn, uneducated infantry soldiers to middle-class professionals such as doctors and aristocratic officers, all facing the horror of the trenches and the prospect of certain death. After an attack with mustard gas, a new character emerges in *Cris*, absent from the majority of World War I narratives – a regiment of "Senegalese sharpshooters": "Un régiment d'Africains est venu en renfort. Nous avons vu arriver cette aide improbable et nous sommes restés bouche bée devant ces hommes venus de nulle part qui avaient encore la force de se battre, qui avaient encore la force de plonger dans la tourmente pour aller chercher nos blessés" (Gaudé 2001, 114–115). At first, "these people who came from nowhere" appear as an indistinct, collective entity whose depiction parallels an array of stereotypical representations, from Jacques Cartier's noble savage to Joseph Conrad's mysterious beings dissimulated in "the stillness of an implacable force brooding over an inscrutable intention" (Conrad 60). Soon thereafter, out of this nameless, faceless, enigmatic but providential group, only one man is endowed with narrative agency insofar as he is given a name and a voice. M'Bossolo is one of the "men of the night," in the words of Ripoll, the French lieutenant, ready to sacrifice his own life to save his brother in arms. As the only character who does not express any fear or criticism of the war, the African's sole focus is his rescue mission, which he sees as not only a military but a human duty, carried out in the name of the "common blood" that unites all men. Camaraderie and humanity echo back and forth in the dialogue between the rescued and the rescuer. M'Bossolo's lines exhibit an almost biblical, chant-like tenor, abounding in enigmatic, lyrical and prophetic statements: "Laissez-moi le porter, mes frères. [...] Le sang nous est compté" (Gaudé 2001, 113), and "Tu me demandes où tu vas et qui te parle. Je suis M'Bossolo, camarade. Tu reviens à toi. Je sens ton corps qui s'agite sur moi. C'est bien. Accroche-toi. [...] Tu es mon frère, camarade. Je te ramènerai à toi" (Gaudé 2001, 114). This poetic tone influences Ripoll's previously more realistic and sober style to the extent that the wounded Frenchman's voice becomes stylistically indistinguishable from that of M'Bossolo:

> Je sens parfois un de tes compagnons qui te propose de te remplacer mais tu ne veux pas. Tu veux aller jusqu'au bout. Me porter jusqu'au bout. Nous avançons. Je n'ai pas la force de te dire merci. Mais nous sommes frères, M'Bossolo. [...] Pauvre humanité en marche qui porte ses blessés comme des divinités de bois. Laissez passer la procession des morts. Laissez passer M'Bossolo qui se tord sous mon poids. Laissez passer les hommes au visage noirci d'effroi. (Gaudé 2001, 115–116)

However, despite this verbal coming-together that mirrors the narrative solidarity of the two soldiers, the substance of their monologues indicates subtle nuances and ambivalent values. Unlike the other characters, M'Bossolo never gives any indication about his personal history or past; his subjectivity is purely relational and his actions entirely dedicated to the rescue mission and his duty to win the war. He is a colonial Saint-Christopher, carrying on his back the Christ-like Ripoll. This sacrificial interpretation is supported by the French officer's references to the "poor humanity carrying the wounded on its back like wood-made divinities" (reminiscent, in an intertextually discordant way, of Ousmane Sembène's famous novel *God's Bits of Wood*) and to "M'Bossolo twisted under [his] weight" as well as the African's description of Ripoll's body "like an open wound," whose heavy burden he promises to carry to safety. Aside from the religious connotations, the political significance of this scene cannot be overstated. The impassionate monologue delivered by M'Bossolo reads like a metaphorical manifesto of the civilizing mission, the cornerstone of French colonial ideology:

Je te porterai jusqu'au bout. Tu n'as pas de crainte à avoir. Mon corps a mis du temps à s'habituer à ton poids mais il n'y a plus de fatigue maintenant. [...] Je t'emmène à l'abri. Au- delà des tranchées et du champ de bataille. Il n'y a pas de pays qui soit trop vaste pour moi. Il n'y a pas de fleuve que je ne puisse enjamber ni d'océan où je n'ai pied. Je te porterai jusqu'à chez moi. Bien au-delà de la guerre. Je ne te poserai que lorsque nous aurons atteint la terre de mes ancêtres [...] des pays que tu ne peux imaginer [...] des lieux sûrs où aucun ennemi ne pourra t'atteindre. La guerre, une fois là-bas, te semblera une douce rumeur. [...] Tu seras bercé par le cri des singes hurleurs de mon enfance. [...] Et lorsque je t'aurai confié à mon vieux continent, lorsque je me serai assuré que tu es sain et sauf, je reviendrai sur mes pas et je finirai ce qui doit être achevé. Le combat m'attend. Il nous reste encore à vaincre. T'avoir mis en lieu sûr me rendra indestructible. Je retrouverai sans trembler la pluie des tranchées et l'horreur des mêlées. [...] Je me fraierai un passage parmi nos ennemis. Plus rien, alors, ne pourra me stopper dans ma charge. Je ne dormirai plus. Je ne mangerais plus. [...] Je serai un ogre. Et j'achèverai la guerre d'un coup de poing plongé au plus profond de la terre. (Gaudé 2001, 123–124)

The African's words mirror an idealized version of the colonial message as it was re-evaluated and developed through the major crises that shook Europe in the twentieth century: World War I, the Great Depression and World War II. First, the "dark continent" is portrayed as an oasis of peace and happiness where humanity, and Western humanity in particular, can return to its natural state to find renewed strength and purpose. Second, the African's vow to resume the fight and win the war while displaying a superhuman, ogre-like might and determination fulfils the French expectations that their African colonies can provide the resources for winning the two wars in which the country became embroiled. This reluctance to question old values and truly engage with the colonial imagination, even while constructing narratives that seek to fill gaps in the collective memory or shed a new perspective on topics obfuscated or ignored by the mainstream neocolonial discourse, is equally as apparent in Gaudé's *Eldorado* (2006). The novel's timely theme, clandestine immigration, is treated from the point of view of a European border patrol officer who becomes an immigrant himself, retracing the journey of the hungry masses of Africans in search of the Western "Eldorado," backwards, as it were, from Europe to Africa:

L'Eldorado. Il ne pensait plus qu'à cela. Il savait bien qu'il allait à contre-courant du fleuve des émigrants. Qu'il allait au-devant du pays où la terre se craquelle de faim. Mais il y avait l'Eldorado tout de même et il ne pouvait pas s'empêcher d'y rêver. La vie qui l'attendait ne lui offrirait ni or ni prospérité. Il le savait. Ce n'est pas cela qu'il cherchait. Il voulait autre chose. Il voulait que ses yeux brillent de cet éclat de volonté qu'il avait souvent vu avec envie dans le regard de ceux qu'il interceptait. (Gaudé 2006, 147).

Salvatore Piracci, the traveling hero of Gaudé's novel, suffers – or, in a more Camusian vein, is contaminated by – a profound melancholy caused by his daily encounters with "ces hommes qui ont le regard fixé sur l'horizon avec impatience et appétit" (Gaudé 2006, 147). On the border, a site of encounter and hospitality but also of exclusion and domination, the Other's hungry gaze feeds the individual's sense of inadequacy to the point where it grows into a form of jealousy. One could see in this a contemporary manifestation of the Western man's postcolonial guilt were the character's feelings not to develop into an all-consuming lust for the Other's drive, despair and desire, a more acute manifestation of the repetition compulsion detected by Roland Barthes in Pierre Loti's fiction: "Le résident est en somme un touriste qui répète son désir de rester" (Barthes 1972, 175). Since Piracci sets out to walk in the illegal immigrants' shoes, his behavior can be construed as empathy, an affective and effective understanding of their experience. This narrative situation calls to mind Nadine Gordimer's post-apartheid novel *The Pick-up* (2001), featuring a similar journey by Julie Summers, a white South African woman whose relationship with an immigrant forced to return to his home country leads her to discover her home among a community of foreigners. Commenting on the meaning of this movement against the grain of the mainstream migratory discourse, Julián Jiménez Heffernan observes:

> This passage articulates a tripartite dialectic: relocation as taking possession of new land (or new mines), relocation as taking possession of oneself, and relocation as immigratory transfer to a new place. The three phases are embodied in the new class of global conservationists, in Julie and in Ahmad. Whatever the relocated subject newly possesses (land, herself or a new network), in truth, it involves renegotiating the new societal determinants. (Heffernan 106)

If Gordimer's novel illustrates the post-apartheid stage of her literary career, inaugurated by the 1994 elections that prompted the writer's statement: "I am no longer a colonial" (Gordimer 134), one could wonder whether Gaudé, despite France's decolonization dating back to the 1960s, can say the same about himself. As Elizabeth Anker points out in her study *Fictions of Dignity*:

Such a question becomes especially pressing in light of the extent to which a deconstructive hermeneutic has regulated postcolonial literary analysis, leading critics to prefer texts that can be seen to dramatize the plea of radical Otherness for inclusion or recognition. Indeed, this concentration on alterity has at times produced a fetishization of that condition and a sublime fascination with victimization that inadvertently covers over rather than encourages critical scrutiny of the material disparities that generate such failures of justice as well as law in the first place. (Anker 12)

Laurent Gaudé's fiction dwells on the unstable border between postcolonial stance and colonial style; as the narrative frame points to an open transfrontier ethical auctorial intention, the substance of his writing is laden with references to traditional colonial dichotomies and representations. His works challenge our own critical perspective, requiring a special attention to distinguish between texts born of good intentions, whose admirable political or moral objectives are unmoored by their inability to bring anything new to our understanding of the world, on the one hand, and morally or politically ambiguous texts that challenge, surprise and force us to think, on the other.

## Ill-fated Love and Racial Disintegrations

When discussing the relation between the cognitive and aesthetic value of books, from Proust and Barthes to Ngugi wa Thiong'o and Gayatri Spivak, the literary *doxa* often distinguishes between books that come with reading directions, with a label providing a "solution" or *legenda*, and books that leave us wondering "How should we read this?", requiring that we revisit and revise our own reading practices.

Marie Darrieussecq's 2012 novel *Il faut beaucoup aimer les hommes* presents readers with precisely such a challenge by offering a hyperbolic parody of the contemporary racial imaginary. The title recovers a sentence used by Marguerite Duras in *La Vie matérielle*[3] and, in my view, exacerbates its meaning by casting it into a narrative of obsession where Stendhal's "amour-passion" meets Fanon's "dual narcissism," born of the identitarian principle according to which "The white man is sealed in his whiteness. The black man in his blackness" (Fanon 1967, 10). The writer's own literary and political situation, as a white French woman from the Basque region, further complicates the status of this fictional account of bi-racial love. Situated in the jet-setting world of Hollywood, Darrieussecq's story focuses on Solange, the returning heroine from her previous novel, *Clèves*, a white French starlet of Basque origin who falls madly in love with a charismatic and elusive black actor named Kouhouesso. Devoured by her passion for the Cameroonian-born Canadian actor, himself engrossed in the project of adapting Conrad's *Heart of Darkness* into a movie to be set in Africa, Solange experiences the solitude her name's popular etymology (which she rejects in favor of the Latin meaning of "solemn") foreshadows as well as contamination by the black man's absence and pulverization by the destructive power of his magnetic force: "Un champ de forces irradiait de lui, palpable, éblouissant, le souffle d'une explosion fixe. Elle était traversée par une onde qui la désintégrait. Ses atomes étaient pulvérisés. Elle était suspendue et déjà elle voulait ça: la désintégration" (Darrieussecq 17). By the writer's own admission, the novel falls within a sub-category of her work called "romans de l'absence."[4] The French woman's first contact with the object of her affection occurs through the gaze that reveals his striking, yet otherworldly presence: "Dans le contre-jour des lanternes ses cheveux longs lui creusaient une profonde capuche et sa silhouette longiligne avait quelque chose de monacal" (Darrieussecq 18). His body, highly eroticized later in the narrative, emerges as an unattainable, monacal, ghost-like figure that does not return her gaze: he "ne la regardait pas" (Darrieussecq 18). Kouhouesso's functional and psychological role in the narrative is to delineate "a zone of nonbeing, an extraordinarily sterile and arid region, an utterly naked declivity where an authentic upheaval can be born" (Fanon 1967, 8), which Frantz Fanon defines as the imaginary locus of the black man in white psychopathology.

The erotic vocabulary's racial semantics further highlights the ambivalence of this second-degree bi-racial love story, which Darrieussecq sets out to exploit facetiously through the complex interplay of a triple symbolism of cannibalism, contamination and nothingness. Fatally drawn into her dark lover's forcefield, Solange is at first enveloped by his loving body, described as "grand, enveloppant, la bouche sur ses seins, les doigts dans ses cheveux, ses hanches aux siennes" (Darrieussecq 37), a body whose materiality is intoxicating and undeniable while remaining ungraspable and phantasmatic: "un homme qu'elle perdait de vue, un homme comme inventé [...] comme si le corps de cet homme, quand elle le tenait dans ses bras, était de la texture du temps, et fatalement fugitif" (Darrieussecq 89). She soons develops symptoms of a sickness diagnosed by a Congolese woman as "Jungle fever [...] ce qu'on dit quand une Blanche veut un homme noir" (Darrieussecq 256). This so-called "maladie chronique" (Darrieussecq 89) manifests itself as the desire to be fully consumed by this black Chronos, father of the Greek gods whose defining *mythème* is cannibalism, who inhabits her thoughts despite his physical absence: "'Mange-moi', songea-t-elle. Une prière, une supplique au cannibale. Mange-moi. Qu'on en finisse. Qu'il la mange à jamais" (Darrieussecq 265). Echos of christic communion and anthropophagy converge in the besotted woman's plea while her psychological condition takes on the physical aspect of a mysterious skin disease, caused by contact with the pearls adorning her African lover's tentacle-like dreadlocks. An endless, Penelope-like wait and a feverish longing for "reinfection" mark the next stage of the woman's suffering. Solange's surrender to cannibalism and contamination leads to the purging of her own self. The hollowness of her brain and her memory thus threatens the cognitive core of her identity: "son cerveau est vide quand elle est près de lui" (Darrieussecq 94), as evidenced by her amnesia when attempting to remember past holidays she used to celebrate with her family in Clèves. Furthermore, her very name becomes meaningless unless uttered by Kouhouesso, described as "son expliqueur, son déplieur, son royal agenceur du monde" (Darrieussecq 239), a performative act that brings her back into being: "'Solange'. Il l'appelait. [...] Elle existait [...] 'Solange'!" (Darrieussecq 168). Finally, the woman's body becomes a site of gradual (a)void(ance): the tears falling from her eyes turn her into a small pile of white powder ("un petit tas de poudre, blanche," Darrieussecq 214), foreshadowing her final disappearance during the screening of Conrad's adaption, when her lover cuts all of her scenes out of the film: "Elle n'apparaissait pas. La forme blanche qu'elle aurait dû être. 'Ce loquace fantôme.' Le fantôme, personne. Sa voix, perdue" (Darrieussecq 305). Having stared into the African nothingness, the contemporary Hollywoodian female counterpart to Conrad's nineteenth-century Kurtz finds herself dispossessed of her name, body, emotions and agency, therefore exchanging places symbolically with Fanon's Black man and coming to experience his political and existential "nothingness."

Nevertheless, such a conclusion drawn from a seemingly naïve surface reading of Darrieussecq's *Il faut beaucoup aimer les hommes* can hardly account for the writer's multilayered and alternal poetics that relies on intertextuality, parody, pastiche, shifting focalization and the confusion of points of view in order to revisit deeply entrenched cultural and political stereotypes. What I have called Solange's journey of (a)void(ance) combines stock images of love narratives shaped by a centuries-long tradition extending from the twelfth-century *Érec et Énide* to Proust through M^me de Lafayette and Stendhal, and colonial–exotic tropes wrought by early twentieth-century writers such as Paul Morand and Pierre Loti, to generate a highly ambiguous dynamic of possession cast as dispossession, centrality cast as marginality and phantasmatic domination cast as submission. At first, the synergy of opposites creates a peculiar effect by underscoring the stereotypes that shape the heroine's perspective. Thus, her all-consuming passion translates into a pantheistic desire to become the world gazed upon by her lover: "Un regard sur la mer et elle voudrait être la mer. Un regard sur les vagues et elle voudrait être les vagues" (Darrieussecq 45). As the text unfolds, Solange comes close to experiencing a phantom limb illusion by projecting herself as a part of Kouhouesso's body (his eyes, his neck, his head, his voice): "Comment avait-elle fait, sans son descriptif inlassable? C'était comme être privée de ses propres yeux. De ses propres mains, songeait-elle en les prenant dans les siennes. De sa propre tête sur son propre cou. De sa propre voix douce et mouillée" (Darrieussecq 239). If these instances seem to point to a form of passionate dispossession, almost self-sacrificial in nature, they are nonetheless tempered by another rhetorical segment that asserts the woman's desire to inhabit the man's coveted body:

> Elle voudrait être le vide, elle voudrait être l'ailleurs, elle voudrait être la chanson qu'il a dans la tête et elle voudrait qu'il la chante, elle, qu'il dérive, oui, mais vers elle; elle voudrait être cette pensée évasive et déserteuse, cet en dehors du film d'il y a trois ou quatre ans. (Darrieussecq 45)

Ultimately, the novel's discourse is characterized by a series of rhetorical and stylistic slippages indicating a reversal of the initial couple dynamic. The traditional male–female role distribution in which the woman willingly consents to occupying the periphery, as reflected in Darrieussecq's phrase "Si elle dessinait leur amour sous forme de cercles, il occuperait tout le centre de son moi; et elle, elle serait à la périphérie de lui" (Darrieussecq 177), is also a counter-image to Kouhouesso engulfing Solange's body during their intimate encounters. The woman's unstated or understated power to contain her lover, albeit phantasmatically, gains further salience from her cinematic transformation into a vampire-like creature at the hands of her filmmaking: "[…] elle s'était peut-être entrevue…le halo cendré…le teint vampirique [...] On percevait peut-être une lueur blanche" (Darrieussecq 306). Eventually cast as Kurtz's fiancée, whose faith in the nobility of his

colonial adventure sways Marlowe's determination to recount solely
the truth, Solange's ghost-like screen presence – as the white trace of
a white actress playing the role of a far-away white fictional character
– not only mirrors Kouhouesso's but can be said to absorb it. The
Conrad-inspired role as the European intended to become a colonial
explorer creates a *mise en abyme* of Solange's pathos-filled role as
the waiting woman who uses her soft power to weave a captivating,
inescapable narrative. In the end, her Cameroonian lover is relegated
to a narrative of return to his native land: "dans son film, tout à son
montage, dans son fleuve, là-bas" (Darrieussecq 299). Framed by a
grammatical and stylistic configuration predicated on conditionals,
hypotheticals (if- clauses) and comparisons ("comme si"), the text
avoids both metaphorical escapism and direct engagement with the
contemporary discourses of race and power while simultaneously
exploiting their literary and media representations.

## The Phenomenology of the Subaltern Spirit

J. M. G. Le Clézio's 1980 novel *Désert* offers another travel narrative
connecting Africa and Europe, one that focuses on the circular journey
of a young African woman, Lalla Hawa, as she flees her modest
home in the "Project," made up of shacks in the West African desert,
for the French cities of Marseille and Paris. Read alongside Gaudé
and Gordimer, Le Clézio's novel strongly resonates with Heffernan's
question: "is desertbound singularity a solution available to a rural
Muslim young woman engaged in a process of emancipatory subjec-
tivation?" (Heffernan 106). After experiencing the jobless, homeless
and hopeless life shared by thousands of immigrants on the streets
of Europe's metropoleis, Lalla is discovered by a photographer who
transforms her into a celebrity that is the object of interest and desire
for the same crowds who ignored her when she was just another faceless,
poverty-stricken woman. Her story concludes with a pregnant Lalla
returning home as anonymously as she had left to give birth to her baby,
"Hawa, daughter of Lalla," in the same dunes and at the foot of the
same fig tree where her mother had brought her into the world. Lalla's
modern narrative is framed by and interwoven with the late nineteenth-
century story of the great sheik Ma al-Aïnine, whose religious and
military leadership over the people of the Saguiet al-Hamra valley
is challenged and ultimately defeated by the French colonial army

after Governor Coppolani's assassination in the early 1900s. First, the connecting thread between the two narratives is Lalla's family relation to Al-Azraq, the Blue Man, a former warrior of the desert who listens to God's call and becomes a saint. Ma al-Aïnine, "Water of the Eyes," is one of his disciples, who reverses Al-Azraq's path by shifting from religious enlightenment to military command. Second, the circularity of the two men's life paths is mirrored and amplified by Lalla's own cyclical journey. Third, both Lalla and her forerunners' geographic and symbolic trajectories stand in contrast with the linear, all-conquering movement of the French army and its leaders, generals consumed by the desire to put an end to the "fanatical" sheik and his followers. Reversed life paths, circular travels and linear progression – the titles of the three parts that compose the novel seem to echo the feelings conveyed by these different types of movement, "Desert" recounting the legend of al-Aïnine from the point of view of a young boy named Nour, "Happiness" dedicated to Lalla's childhood, and "Life with the Slaves," the last part, narrating Lalla's time in France interwoven with fragments about the final tragic confrontation between the French colonial armies and the people of the desert. This fictional distribution of ethical and affective values may have seemed overly simplistic if not for the layers of contrasting, tension-laden images teeming throughout the book. While living in the Project, the young girl passes her time contemplating the immensity of the desert, gazing at the birds in the sky but also singing one fascinating word taken from a French song:

> Elle joint ses mains autour de ses genoux, elle se balance un peu d'avant en arrière, puis sur les côtés, en chantonnant une chanson en français, une chanson qui dit seulement:
> "Méditerra-né-é…"
> Lalla ne sait pas ce que cela veut dire. C'est une chanson qu'elle a entendue à la radio, un jour, et elle n'a retenu que ce mot-là, mais c'est un mot qui lui plaît bien. Alors de temps en temps, quand elle se sent bien, qu'elle n'a rien à faire, ou quand elle est au contraire un peu triste sans savoir pourquoi, elle chante ce mot, quelquefois à vois basse pour elle, si doucement qu'elle s'entend à peine, ou bien très fort, presque à tue-tête, pour réveiller les échos et pour faire partir la peur. (Le Clézio 1980, 72–73)

In the same way, she likes to chant the names of several Spanish cities that possess a special significance for Old Naman, a grandfatherly figure who shares with her and the other children of the shacks stories from his time as a young man living in Europe "before the war." The visual manipulation of the text makes them appear as a poem, but the other youngsters care only about their practical meaning: "they want to know serious things, not names to dream about. They ask Naman about the money that can be earned, the work to be had, how much clothes cost, food, the price of a car, if there are a lot of movie theaters" (Le Clézio 2009, 74).

Afterwards, when Old Naman falls sick with the "wind of ill fortune," Lalla completes the cycle of memory by offering back to him the soothing incantation of city names and the mythical world they create:

> "Algésiras"
> "Granada"
> "Sevilla"
> "Madrid" (Le Clézio 1980, 95)

> Elle lui raconte ce qu'il a lui-même conté autrefois, à propos de ses voyages dans les villes de l'Espagne et de la France [...] Elle lui parle des rues de toutes ces villes, comme si elle y avait marché, Sevilla, Córdoba, Granada, Almadén, Toledo, Aranjuez, et de la ville si grande qu'elle pourrait s'y perdre pendant des jours, Madris, où les gens viennent de tous les coins de la terre. (Le Clézio 1980, 184–185).

Lalla's poetic and the boys' practical use of city names represent two instances of positive exoticization of the European signifier, albeit for entirely different reasons. For Lalla, however, the meaning will evolve from a purely sonorous, imaginative one to an intentional act of resistance. When the prospect of an arranged marriage threatens her peaceful, dream-filled life, the young girl conjures up the imaginary power of European names in order to find the strength to set off on her own:

> ces villes d'Espagne aux noms magiques, Algésiras, Malaga, Granada, Teruel, Saragoza, et de ces ports d'où partent les navires grands comme des villes, des routes où les autos vont vers le nord, des trains qui s'en vont, des avions. [...] ces montagnes enneigées, [...] ces tunnels, [...] des fleuves qui sont grands comme la mer, des plaines couvertes de blé, des forêts immenses, et surtout [...] ces villes parfumées, où sont les palais blancs, les églises, les fontaines, les magasins rutilants de lumière. Paris, Marseille, et toutes ces rues, les maisons si hautes qu'on voit à peine le ciel, les jardins, les cafés, les hôtels, et les carrefours où l'on rencontre des gens venus de tous les côtés de la terre. (Le Clézio 1980, 182)

The repetitive accumulation of names saturates the descriptions and, along with the rich imagery Lalla's mind weaves around the foreign words, turns Europe into a fairy-tale universe. Her decision is, however, not without apprehension, as "elle frissonne un peu d'inquiétude," before being quickly overcome by her desire "d'être dans ce chemin de fer, de ville en ville, vers les lieux inconnus, vers ces pays où l'on ne sait plus rien de la poussière et des chiens affamés, ni des cabanes de planches où entre le vent du desert" (Le Clézio 1980, 96). The happiness announced in the second chapter's title is clearly fraught with conflict, and the somewhat odd use of the verb "être" rather than "aller" in the above quote signals that at stake is the very nature of her being. Lalla's strong sense of belonging to her community and the space it inhabits as well as her profound attachment to her friend, the Hartani, a mysterious deaf and mute shepherd boy who teaches her how to live in perfect communion with nature, are challenged by her desire to break free of poverty and social constraints (such as being forced to work in a sweatshop and to marry an older man who buys her from her aunt) in order to discover – or to be in – the world.

Yet, her act of rebellion and personal liberation places her in a stereotypical situation strongly reminiscent of Gaudé's fiction. As a poor immigrant in Marseille, Lalla occupies, from a narrative, stylistic and symbolic viewpoint, an unproductive, repetitive space. Unlike the poetic profusion of the names in the previous chapter, the objective, realistic descriptions of Western cities are intentionally flat, devoid of metaphorical depth. The sterile and unfeeling reality of the city itself belies the fertile, empathic promise of its name:

> C'est un pays étrange, cette ville, avec tous ces gens, parce qu'ils ne font pas réellement attention à vous si vous ne vous montrez pas. Lalla a appris à glisser sliencieusement le long des murs, dans les escaliers. Elle connaît tous les endroits d'où l'on peut voir sans être vu, les cachettes derrière les arbres, dans les grands parkings pleins de voitures, dans les coins des portes, dans les terrains vagues. Même au milieu des avenues très droites où il y a un flot continu d'hommes et d'autos qui avance, qui descend, Lalla sait qu'elle peut devenir invisible. (Le Clézio 1980, 251)

Lalla completes her transformation by changing her physical appearance to reflect this new diminished, emotionally flat state. She cuts her black curly hair, "full of sparkling sunshine," short, allowing it to become dull, almost gray; her skin turns pale and gray, and she wears a brown, saggy coat, an invisible cloak of sorts that, after her short foray into the vertiginous world of instant celebrity, becomes a metonymy for her return to the homeland and her own rebirth accomplished through the birth of her child.

Lalla's gaze searches the urban landscape, attempting to understand and find connections between its disparate components. Through the lens of her consciousness, focused on the obscure, hidden and forgotten aspects of life, the similarities between Europe and Africa are highlighted; yet, while the latter allows for a cohesive, organic and empathic explanation, the former exhibits one unifying principle: fear.

> Elle ne savait pas ce qu'était la peur, parce que là-bas, chez le Hartani, il n'y avait que des serpents et des scorpions, à la rigueur les mauvais esprits qui font des gestes d'ombre dans la nuit; mais ici c'est la peur du vide, de la détresse, de la faim, la peur qui n'a pas de nom et qui semble sourdre des vasistas entrouverts sur les sous-sols affreux, puants, qui semble monter des cours obscures, entrer dans les chambres froides comme des tombes [...]. (Le Clézio 1980, 262)

Le Clézio's phenomenological prose grazes the surface of things and progresses in a slow, "shadowy" motion, much like Lalla's gaze, unfolding one by one the layers of life in the city and exposing their interplay to create a new reality that is neither European nor African, but one in which the anguished opaqueness of the first is read through the lens of the second. In semiotic terms, the language of Africa is the *interpretant* that answers the solicitation of the European *interpretandum*, allowing its "unnamed fear" to be expressed not only by antagonism but also by synthesis. The reference to the "evil wind" that bursts, so to speak, in the middle of the Marseille description ties together the two stages and landscapes of Lalla's journey. In another scene, she "searches the darkness," conjuring up the desert with its familiar faces of "Naman, les filles de la fontaine, le Soussi, les fils d'Aamma, et lui surtout, le Hartani [et] celui qu'elle appelait Es Ser, le Secret, celui dont le regard venait de loin et l'enveloppait, la pénétrait comme la lumière du ciel" (Le Clézio 1980, 269). Bringing the African desert's light into the European desert's darkness can be construed as the second leg of a chiasmic pattern initiated by Lalla's dream of the light-filled cities illuminating the African desert. The chiasmus appears to be the signature trope of Le Clézio's African (and world) writing in *L'Africain* and *Désert*, as well as in his other novels, such as *Onitsha* (published in 1991 and foreshadowing, in fictional form, the father's biography) or *Révolutions* (2003). Its logic of transferring meanings and bodies as well as crossing borders and boundaries informs every level of the book, from the spatial and emotional evolution of its main character to the symbolic unfolding of the story.

Expressed in the free indirect speech that fuses together Lalla's and the narrator's consciousness, one question captures the perils and paradoxes of Le Clézio's empathetic writing: "Mais peuvent-ils venir jusqu'ici, de l'autre côté de la mer, de l'autre côté de tout?" (Le Clézio 1980, 270). Such a question is hardly surprising of an author whose Nobel Prize acceptance speech was entitled "In the forest of paradoxes" and who champions the crucial place of literature in today's world thanks to its ability to "create interculturality through imagination." This notion could be otherwise rendered by an expression that Spivak borrows from Derrida when she states that literature's power – and moral dilemma – lies in its "teleopoesis," which has nothing to do with an utilitarian or philanthropic "'learning about other cultures'" but rather with "imagining yourself, really letting yourself be imagined (experience that impossibility) without guarantees, by and in another culture, perhaps" (Spivak 2004, 52).

Laurent Gaudé, Marie Darrieussecq and J. M. G. Le Clézio raise similar questions, both in their fictional utterance and in their authorial stance, when they set out to write not only *about* but *as* Africans. They adopt their point of view, borrow their voices and, ultimately, in a post-Fanonian twist, place fictional black masks over white skin. While both literary projects signal similar attempts at imagining ethics as "the experience of the impossible" (Spivak 1996, 196), and even of what I would call the *impossible other*, the vastly different aesthetic choices made by these writers lead Gaudé to fall back on orientalist positions and thus participate in the "manufacture of otherness" (Appiah 1993, 156), Darrieussecq to position herself in an in-between space of empathy and irony, and Le Clézio to construct a decidedly empathic and multipolar perspective.

In an article entitled "This Thing Called Literature ... What Work Does It Do?", Simon Gikandi contrasts his own literary education, influenced by Sartre's view of literature as a "universe of meanings" and focused exclusively on the writer's responsibility to signify, with his students' approach, centered on reading as an experience that not only allows but invites the "mystical," wondrous and emotional side of literature. Referring to the affective turn in criticism during the 1990s, he then asks,

> Why did a poetics of wonder and a phenomenology of enchantment powerfully challenge the semantics of literature? For one, they called attention to the ability of works of art to affirm their pure, almost wordless presence; instead of processing the literary experience through

the sieve of thought, affective approaches took objects out of the realm of meaning and the conduit of practice. (Gikandi 2012, 14)

Even though Gikandi limits his discussion to how Western reading practices are shaped by the encounter with "difficult" postcolonial books that deal with war, genocide and exploitation, particularly in Africa, the scope of his investigation could be expanded to include Western writers. They are, first and foremost, readers, and their decision to engage with topics that were traditionally considered the concern of "postcolonial" or "Francophone" writers may be construed as a way of reclaiming the freedom of their imagination without forsaking the Sartrian responsibility to create meaning. Empathic writing, as the works by Le Clézio, Darrieussecq and Gaudé show, originates or disintegrates in this encounter.

## Notes

1   "C'est cette image que mon père a détestée. Lui qui avait rompu avec Maurice et son passé colonial, et se moquait des planteurs et de leurs airs de grandeur, lui qui avait fui le conformisme de la société anglaise, pour laquelle un homme ne valait que par sa carte de visite, lui qui avait parcouru les fleuves sauvages de Guyane, qui avait pansé, recousu, soigné les chercheurs de diamants et les Indiens sous-alimentés; cet homme ne pouvait pas ne pas vomir le monde colonial et son injustice outrecuidante, ses cocktail parties et ses golfeurs en tenue, sa domesticité, ses maîtresses d'ébène prostituées de quinze ans introduites par la porte de service [...]" (Le Clézio 2004, 58–59).

2   "On dirait que des fous, enflammés de fureur, conscients du mariage forcé dont ils ne peuvent se délivrer, ont décidé d'en faire une étreinte mortelle. Forcés de vivre ensemble, et incapables de s'unir, ils décident au moins de mourir ensemble" ("*Lettre à un militant algérien*", first published in October 1955 in Camus 1958, 128). "[L]e choix en Algérie n'est pas entre la démission ou la reconquête, mais entre le mariage de convenances ou le mariage à mort de deux xénophobies" ("L'Algérie déchirée", Camus 1958, 146).

3   Paris: POL, 1987.

4   R. Solé, "L'ecriture physique de Marie Darrieussecq", *Le Monde des Livres*, http://www.lemonde.fr/livres/article/2010/05/20/l-ecriture-physique-de-marie-darrieussecq_1360601_3260.html (accessed February 20, 2017).

# CHAPTER FOUR

# Maps of Frenchness

## Between Self-Invention and Delusion

*Mon cœur à l'étroit* (2007), by Marie NDiaye, features a martyrology of mediocrity focused on a middle-class character whose actions, thoughts and relationships are ruled by the principle: "Il faut bien endurer." The narrator and her husband, like many of the fictional beings created by the writer, are compelled by external circumstances rather than an internal motivation to embark on a labyrinthine and often fantastic search for a truth that is neither fully revealed nor ever entirely ignored. Nadia and Ange are schoolteachers in their fifties, living in Bordeaux, whose quiet life and peaceful conscience are surreptitiously undermined by an unknown malaise, a sickening and incomprehensible feeling of guilt and an unnamable yet indisputable doubt. The woman's self-portrait offers a mixture of delusion and lucidity, affirming stereotypes and revealing bitter insights: "Je suis maintenant une bourgeoise respectable, toujours très soigneusement habillée, coiffée, maquillée, et je parle sur un débit rapide, un ton légèrement haut, en ne ménageant que très peu d'espace entre mes phrases" (NDiaye 2007, 178) or "je suis là, protégée par mon argent [...] – je suis là, bien maquillée et coiffée dignement, et certes bien trop grosse et quelque peu suante" (NDiaye 2007, 213). As with many other characters that populate NDiaye's fiction, self-awareness and self-delusion feed into and off one another, communicating through the conduit of a sensorial language akin to Nathalie Sarraute's "tropisms." Such is the case in the metamorphosis undergone by Nadia and her antiphrastically named husband Ange.

## Social Animals

Before manifesting itself in the characters' physical appearance, the change is initially perceptual and social. Others begin to question their humanity, displaying disgust at the sight of the couple and recognizing in them the radical negation of what Derrida calls "le rapport à soi d'une humanité d'abord jalouse et soucieuse de son propre" (Derrida 2006, 32). Under their gaze, the couple is reduced to the condition of animals. Since the first-person narrative precludes any certainty about what others truly think, Nadia's testimony fills the cognitive gap. Even as her interpretation alternates between hypothesis and assertion, it seizes upon the animality projected onto herself and her husband: "Des regards hargneux se posent sur nous, sans dissimulation, comme si nous étions des chiens fouineurs et si laids qu'on ne peut les regarder qu'avec rancune" (NDiaye 2007, 13). Their gradual transformation leads to a self-lacerating reflection about the reasons and the meaning of this inexplicable yet undeniable ostracism: "*Que voient-ils tous que je ne vois pas, que connaissent-ils donc que je ne connais pas ? Où étais-je, tout ce temps, quand il s'est agi de voir et de connaître ?*" (NDiaye 2007, 74, italics in the original).

At first, Nadia and Ange remain solidary, their domestic bond strengthened by their common decline into a sub-human state and the shame they experience as insults, at first vague and then more explicit, are hurled at them. A neighbor's remarks sum up the others' collective sense of disgust at their mere sight, a disgust all the more profound as it remains undefined, except through periphrasis, as an intolerable and repugnant "something": "Vous portez sur votre figure ce qu'on ne supporte pas d'y voir … sur aucune figure … et c'est quelque chose de proprement répugnant" (NDiaye 2007, 28). The spouses eventually come to resent each other and their solidarity turns to utter solitude when Ange sustains an injury that confines him to bed rest, leaving Nadia to care for him at the same time as she struggles with her ever-widening girth. Ange's festering wound will eventually be left in the care of strangers, like a synecdoche of the breach that engulfs the couple's quiet life built on middle- class certainties regarding work, social standing, family values and race. His martyrdom leads, through the attrition of his material body, to his eventual disappearance from the body of the narrative, later reversed by his matter-of-fact reappearance in the story's counterclimactic ending. Nadia's transformation therefore becomes the focus of the text, described in excruciating detail as it is experienced by the narrator herself. Powerless before her "chair excessivement abondante," her will surrenders to her stomach, which takes on a life of its own: "[il] remue, d'une vie propre, chaotique." A primal force is activated inside the former model citizen, who desperately clings to her image as a mother, wife and teacher of irreproachable repute while finding herself compelled to question the very foundations of that image: "*Et cette chose en moi, profite-t-elle de chaque bouchée?*" (NDiaye 2007, 256, italics in the original), "*Sous quel aspect exactement sortirait alors la chose, quels seraient sa nature et son degré de monstruosité ?*" (NDiaye 2007, 257, italics in the original), "*Des crimes que j'ai commis, quel est celui précisément que punit cette chose, cette abomination tapie ?*" (NDiaye 2007, 270, italics in the original). Such scenes summon traditional mind/body and instinct/reason dichotomies from the moralist and philosophical tradition, from Saint Augustine to Descartes, modern and post-modern images of human–animal hybridity and metamorphosis, running from Kafka and Pasolini to *Alien*-like movies, as well as cannibalistic imagery associated with early ethnographic writings and colonial literature.[1] Nadia describes her irrepressible need to eat with such medical lucidity that it, paradoxically, touches the reader on a visceral level, so to speak. This is the case when she points out the likeness between the meat she ingests and Ange's flesh: "*de petits bouts d'une viande ressemblant à du porc rosâtre et fibreux et la taille et l'aspect m'ont fait penser à de la viande humaine et par conséquent à des bouts de la chair d'Ange puisque j'ai vu ce matin*" (NDiaye 2007, 34, italics in the original). Nonetheless, the illuminating moments of self-awareness are submerged in an account possessing strong apologetic overtones, as if the character were tasked with defending a philosophical or religious position. Relying on lengthy explanations and self-serving justifications, Nadia appears to be the victim of an obscure force acting both from inside and outside herself, to which she refers as a thing, a monster and an abomination. The text reflects this psychological ambiguity through the typographic division between passages in Roman and Italic characters; the former convey the reasonable, "bien-pensant," and diurnal side of the protagonist's conscience; the latter indicate the disruption caused by her hidden anguish, her repressed memory, her remorse: that is, her nocturnal side. Forced to acknowledge her humble origins that she had forsaken in her efforts to climb the social ladder, Nadia returns to her parents' home, where she gives birth to her "bête noire": "[une] chose noire et luisante, fugitive, que j'ai vue glisser sur le plancher de ma chambre un soir [...] d'où aurait-elle pu jaillir, sinon de mon corps? Une chose noire, luisante, fugitive, qui laissa sur le plancher une légère trace de sang en direction de la porte" (NDiaye 2007, 295).

Nadia's "black thing" can take on several meanings, some of which are strongly supported by the diegesis, such as her social ambition and denial of her origins, the cold and calculating way in which she relates or, rather, avoids relating to others, and the daily violence of domestic interaction disguised under the pretense of manners that scarred her own son, leading to his estrangement. Other possible interpretations, such as the resurgence of a traumatic event, buried in the individual or collective psyche, are merely alluded to. Such is the case, for instance, in Nadia's descriptions of the city of Bordeaux, owing much of its fortune to the Atlantic slave trade yet resistant to own up to/admit its colonial legacy.[2] In *Ladivine* (2013), the story of Malinka/Clarisse, who spends her life covering up her métis identity, is defined by the rebellious gesture of running away from the city with her husband-to-be. The event of "cette fuite ensemble loin de Bordeaux" (NDiaye 2013, 69) appears as an accomplishment in itself, even acting as the foundation of her new identity. Yet the escape also brings about the slow unraveling of Clarisse Rivière, whose quiet middle-class life will be disturbed by a sense of duty that compels her to make furtive returns to the city where her mother lives: "se rendre secrètement à Bordeaux" (NDiaye 2013, 11). The heterodiegetic narrative of *Ladivine* mirrors the themes of *Mon cœur à l'étroit* while offering a multi-perspectival blueprint for mapping out the negative borders and implicit rules associated with French identity. If identity is anchored in an ideology of fantasmatic purity, suggested by the tropology of clarity, transparency, honesty and candor, NDiaye's narrative discourse undermines its monolithic message through the use of seriality, anamorphosis and animality.

### Inheriting the "Black Thing"

In contrast to *Mon cœur à l'étroit*, *Ladivine* does not conceal or defer the character's dual belonging, her conflicted sense of self or her struggle to erase one in favor of the other. Malinka is the daughter of a poor single mother who does not belong in the social and phenotypic setting of the city and the country she inhabits. The mother's portrayal is almost always indirect, as a reflection of the daughter's feelings toward her, combining love, duty and even respect with irrepressible shame and pity. Rather than being discussed at length, her blackness represents the vanishing spot of the narrative, often alluded to through a lexicon of circumlocution and rarely spelled out. The revelation of her mother's skin color marks the dreaded moment of social humiliation that Malinka sought to avoid by changing her name to Clarisse and hiding the truth about her family, even at the diegetic level. Like Nadia's "chose noire," Clarisse's mother appears one day in the restaurant where the young woman enjoys working as a waitress, prompting a triangular recognition mediated by her boss's watchful and disappointed gaze:

> Mais la patronne savait, elle savait tout et regardait Clarisse sans hostilité, avec une sorte de tristesse dure comme si Clarisse l'avait trompée mais qu'elle pût comprendre et admettre cela, puis ses yeux parcoururent encore les jambes longues de Clarisse, ses hanches étroites, sa figure mince, non sans doute, cette fois, pour évaluer la résistance de ce corps svelte mais pour établir à quel point il ressemblait à l'autre, celui de négresse assise bien droite près de la vitre. (NDiaye 2013, 50)

Even when the word "négresse" is finally uttered, its syntax detaches it from the person of the mother and associates it instead with the conflated images of the mother and daughter's bodies. This signals not only the alienation of the black body in a space where it does not belong but also, paradoxically, the failure of Malinka/Clarisse's attempt to alienate herself from her origins since, despite her fair beauty, her physical appearance can always be referred back to them. Furthermore, as A. Asibong notes in a comment situating *Ladivine* within a series of texts by NDiaye (*En famille, La Femme changée en bûche*) that display similar attempts to achieve *"blancness"*: "Perhaps the ultimate cruel irony is that these protagonists' anxious attachment to an always insecure *blancness* means that they can never properly enjoy the stupid, sleepy zombification that their 'unmarked' contemporaries take for granted" (Asibong 22).

As a young girl, Malinka uses this physical difference to reconstruct her personal history and spin a compensatory tale in which she herself is a princess, her mother a mere servant and her unknown father a well-to-do and kindly man who speaks without an accent, "à la voix mélodieuse dépouvue d'accent" (NDiaye 2013, 29). Instead of serving as a transitional fantasy to be overcome, according to the Freudian developmental scheme, by the acceptance of reality at a later age, Malinka's childhood fiction becomes the cornerstone of a life-long effort to refashion herself as a white, middle-class, "French" woman. On the one hand, her make-up routine presents a toned-down version of the more radical practices depicted in Paule Constant's *White Spirit*: "À quinze ans, Malinka accentuait la pâleur naturelle de son visage par un maquillage blême" (NDiaye 2013, 31). On the other hand, her emotional life, defined by the relationship with her husband, Richard Rivière, provides a constant validation of her supreme whiteness, represented by the imagery of a fair and bright body (white teeth and bright blue eyes) offered to her lover as a "sumptuous" lily flower, an object loaded with religious (Christian) and historical (the heraldic symbol of the Bourbon dynasty) connotations:

> Elle sentait tout son visage se tendre vers lui dans un miroitement de dents blanches et d'yeux clairs scintillants, elle sentait et voyait son visage se donner à lui comme une splendide fleur de lis qu'elle lui eût présentée fièrement et sans précaution, assurée de la valeur de son offrande, et la souple tige de son corps se penchait vers lui également, entraînée par le poids de la fleur somptueuse. (NDiaye 2013, 60)

However, far from being a postcolonial "aliénée," Clarisse does not privilege one allegiance over another but, instead, assumes them both. As Lydie Moudileno shows in her study of the "discombobulated subject" in NDiaye's fiction, the "and"-coordination of the following sentence suggests a juxtaposition that sustains the discourse "of/on banality and the quotidian" (Moudileno 2006, 84) throughout the novel. At the same time, the expression "l'envers et l'endroit" points to a meaning stronger than a simple reference to the two sides of a coin, perhaps to the Camusian "betwixt and between": "et, tranquillement, elle considérait son existence à venir et se la figurait vouée à deux commandements qui étaient l'envers et l'endroit d'une même mission, renier la mère de Malinka et adorer Richard Rivière tout en ne manquant jamais, pour l'un comme pour l'autre, au moindre de ses devoirs" (NDiaye 2013, 68).

Clarisse is therefore caught in a double spiral of seriality and anamorphosis; as one link in an infinite series of similar physical features, emotions and social gestures, she is never quite herself, always other than herself and other to herself. Moreover, the uncertainty principle that she embodies has repercussions for virtually all the characters caught in her identitarian maelstrom, from her mother and daughter, both called Ladivine, to Richard's second wife, whose first name is Clarisse as well.

As a young girl, while she works to erase all indications of her foreign origins, she also secretly searches for information on her mother's homeland, a nameless place only indexed as "la région où la mère de Malinka était née" (NDiaye 2013, 15). The malaise she experiences and her implicit promise never to visit the land of her ancestors do not prevent her from noticing the delicate features of the natives. It is precisely these features that trigger her anger, since they become the tangible proof of a hereditary bond that deprives her of the right to will herself different:

> Et que sa mère eût ainsi hérité les caractéristiques physiques de toute une postérité, puis les eût transmises à sa fille (les traits, les bras, la longueur de la silhouette et, grâce à Dieu, c'était tout) avait autrefois étourdi de colère Clarisse Rivière, car comment échapper durablement si l'on était ainsi marqué, comment prétendre n'être pas ce qu'on ne voulait pas être, ce qu'on avait pourtant le droit de ne point vouloir être? (NDiaye 2013, 16)

The indirect free speech registers the dramatic realization that she bears the mark of her ancestors all the more menacingly since it is invisible but known, therefore always present. The textual space of the black skin is carved out by that which it is not: of all the physical features the mother passed on to her daughter, the one that remains unseen is the most powerful and the most binding. Clarisse's choice of work before meeting her husband, who will help her flee Bordeaux, further tightens this connection, as she moves away from her mother's menial job as a "servante" (a domestic) to the position of "serveuse" (waitress) in a restaurant, trading the hidden shame she felt as a child about her mother's social status to the pride she feels for participating in the public spectacle of serving. However, as the lexical and semantic link between the two words first signals and the recognition scene analyzed above confirms with the force of a paracolonial *anagnorisis*, further strengthened by the conclusion of the narrative focalized on Richard Rivière, who admits, in Aristotelian terms, that "une sorte d'horreur et de crainte l'avaient chassé loin de chez lui, loin de Clarisse Rivière" (NDiaye 2013, 346), the difference is merely one of degree and not of essence. Malinka/Clarisse can no more transcend the condition she inherits than she can help passing it on to her own child: "Quand l'enfant fut née, elle la prénomma Ladivine. C'était le prénom de la servante" (NDiaye 2013, 76). Even as her story unfolds away from her mother and her native France, Ladivine Rivière, who lives in Germany with her husband and her children, "ces deux petits Allemands [qui] paraissaient être également deux parfaits petits êtres humains" (NDiaye 2013, 344), experiences a similar yearning for perfection in her children and her domestic life, for purity of appearance, blood and language. Her feelings of exile are muted, blending melancholy and contentment: "elle pouvait, même, jouir mélancoliquement du sentiment d'exil et de solitude quand elle tombait par hasard, à la télévision, sur une image de campagne française éternelle et radieuse" (NDiaye 2013, 183). However, Ladivine's dissatisfaction is evidenced by her self-portrayal, as she finds herself wanting in relation to the French, and particularly Parisian, standards of physical appearance, style and speech:

> Ah non, elle ne s'aimait guère physiquement, tout en considérant ces questions avec une distance moqueuse, un dédain réel même si récent et conquis de haute lutte contre de vieux rêves naïfs de beauté renversante ou, plus simplement, de charme piquant à la parisienne – elle aurait aimé être, ici, une petite chose aussi svelte que distinguée, raffinée et coquine, dont le glamoreux accent français aurait achevé le portrait à la perfection. (NDiaye 2013, 185–186)

Her discomfort is further increased by the foreboding story of her parents' separation and her mother's violent end at the hands of her live-in boyfriend. As the interrogative sentence unfolds, it lays out the atavistic pattern of anxiety at the heart of NDiaye's fiction, from the fear of repeating her parents' story through the questioning of the character's lack of "grace" in contrast with her perfect and unattainable partner, which in the process reveals the cracks in their relationship, to the fatidic mark of her mother's blood as it hyperbolically contaminates not only the scene of her death but also the daughter's dwelling place (home, city, natural environment) across time and national borders:

> Craignait-elle que, à l'exemple de Richard Rivière qui avait compris dans la force de l'âge que rien, ni loi ni morale, ne l'obligeait à rester vivre en la compagnie d'une femme pour laquelle il ressentirait toujours une infinie tendresse mais dont les singularités de caractère le fatiguaient et l'ennuyaient, un Marko soudain conscient de sa grâce ne pût que s'éloigner d'elle, Ladivine Rivière, que souillait définitivement le sang de sa mère répandu à profusion dans un pavillon de province, ruisselant jusque chez eux, à Berlin, maculant les trottoirs de leur quartier, altérant même le ciel de printemps? (NDiaye 2013, 223)

The female characters are not the only ones being swept into the cycle of seriality and anamorphosis, although they are protagonists of the story and thus its main passive agents, if this oxymoron can capture their ambiguous status. One cannot help but notice that the uncertainty principle is at work again in confusing their number: Does Ladivine refer to one or two characters, to grandmother and granddaughter or to the return of the former, Ladivine Sylla, under the guise of the latter, Ladivine

Berger *née* Rivière? Should Malinka/Clarisse be added to the count or even be considered the sole protagonist of a story that, fittingly, does not bear her name? And what of Richard's second wife, Clarisse, who occupies an important role in what would be metafictionally qualified as "l'histoire de Richard, le drame de Richard" (NDiaye 2013, 163) and serves to illuminate, if not Malinka/Clarisse's mystery, at least Richard's quest for it? Each of them appears to be "étrangère à elle-même," to paraphrase the term Julia Kristeva uses to describe the psychic experience of being an outsider; these different yet identical characters personify the idea that "we are our own foreigners" (Kristeva 1991, 183). Far from remaining "unmarked," as Asibong puts it, male characters, such as Richard Rivière and Marko, Ladivine's German husband, are swept into this maelstrom as well. In fact, their peripheral and belated involvement underscores the diegetic and ideological importance of the questions of belonging, identity and the authenticity of one's Frenchness through a stream of negations, circumvolutions, dysfunctions and maladies.

Richard's feelings after his divorce mirror Malinka/Clarisse's own ambivalence toward her mother whom she forsakes socially, only to find herself even more attached to her emotionally and morally: "Comme elle aimait cette femme pourtant, et plus encore maintenant qu'elle la voyait souffrir! Comme elle se sentait sinueuse et abjecte près de la servante légère, claire et vaillante dans son attachement!" (NDiaye 2013, 57). In a confounding chiasmus, the epithets used to define the daughter's ideal of humanity now apply to her mother, while the young woman projects onto herself the same adjectives that describe Nadia's monstrous offspring in *Mon cœur à l'étroit*. Similarly, after having ended his first marriage out of an inexplicable but relentless sense of falsity and unease, Richard ends up marrying another woman named Clarisse whose transparent face, "franc et simple, sans mystère," and unimpeachable demeanor recommend her as the "impersonnelle, irréprochable et candide" (NDiaye 2013, 363) reflection of his first wife, causing him to feel a violent but never actualized desire to see one face emerge while the other fades away: "Et Richard Rivière se sentait déchiré entre le respect qu'il devait à ce visage et son désir violent de la voir s'effacer pour laisser l'autre survenir" (NDiaye 2013, 365). The two women are nominally identical and thus interchangeable, while at the same time containing the reversed and distorted image of each other. The obvious imageries of the mask, and implicitly of black skin/white masks, in which one is the original and the other the copy, are brought to mind without being overtly stated. NDiaye's writing dwells in the in-between space where the reader is made to feel, as Richard Rivière does, "à la fois hors de lui-même et pleinement dedans" (NDiaye 2013, 356).

In the last section of the narrative, internal focalization grants Richard the questionable privilege of searching for an understanding akin to solving the mystery of Malika/Clarisse. Under his scrutiny, their life together appears as an unspeakable, perverted and counterfeit experience, a simulacrum or a dream to which his own weakness made him complicit and from which he suddenly awoke in a moment of recognition mixed with disgust:

> Toute rencontre avec sa fille, toute discussion avec elle au téléphone, toute rêverie autour de son enfant le ramenait à cet affreux sentiment qu'ils avaient vécu tous les trois ensemble une existence déformée par quelque chose d'indicible et de considérable, qui avait flotté au-dessus d'eux sans jamais se dévoiler ni disparaître et qui avait fait de leur vie une vie factice. [...]
>
> C'est ce qu'il pensait. Il pensait encore à présent que Clarisse Rivière n'avait été coupable de rien.
>
> Et lui, Richard Rivière, avait accepté de dériver dans cette vie contrefaite parce qu'il s'était senti faible et démuni, puis il s'était comme réveillé et l'écœurement, une sorte d'horreur et de crainte l'avaient chassé loin de chez lui, loin de Clarisse Rivière. (NDiaye 2013, 345–346)

If Richard longs for the face of his former wife to reveal itself beneath the appearance of his current spouse, his motivation is not so much affective as it is cognitive. Although the woman with whom he shared a sham life is "not guilty of anything" and his inability to represent her true being is "his own fault," her presence in his thoughts remains a scandal that disrupts the order of things and a mystery demanding to be illuminated: "Mais toujours il y revenait et scrutait ces traits en quête d'une illumination: il saurait, enfin, qui avait été Clarisse Rivière, espérait-il éperdument" (NDiaye 2013, 363). Moreover, understanding her is tantamount to fulfilling the unrealized promise of the unrepresentable and unimaginable being within her, to elucidating a truth she herself could not comprehend: "Car Clarisse Rivière ne lui manquait pas mais la femme qu'aurait dû ou pu être Clarisse Rivière et qu'il ne connaissait pas, qu'il ne pouvait même se représenter, par sa propre faute, lui semblait-il" (NDiaye 2013, 341).

The desire to grasp once and for all the nature of the obscure "thing" that disrupts one's train of life, acting as a burden not only on the conscience but also on the body (physical and political), is just as manifest in Nadia's insistence on providing a clinical description of the creature to which she gives birth: "une courte et grasse anguille, bien qu'il ne soit pas exclu que cette chose ait été velue, un poil collé et lissé par l'humidité, le sang, les glaires." However, far from indicating a wish to recognize or claim her monstrous offspring as her own, the reluctant mother's efforts to name and rename reveal her intention to sever all connection with it, ensuring that she is exempt from any future responsibility for her child in the event that someone might think to bring it back to her (NDiaye 2007, 296).

The oscillation between the search for meaning and its obfuscation, which, in Marie NDiaye's characterization techniques, occupies a fine line between conscience and instinct or between subject-driven intention and de-individualized, process-triggered intentionality, is analogous with the human/animal relation in her works. Michael Sheringham identifies six facets of animal representation in the works of Marie NDiaye. It is first associated with suffering, shifting the narrative focus from the Cartesian primacy of reason to Bentham and Derrida's emphasis on emotion. It can convey the anxiety of the concept of "being-on-the- watch" (l'être-aux-aguets), studied by Deleuze in Kafka's writing, while evoking the idea of the open gaze cast upon the world, as thematized by Rilke and Agamben. The presence of animals in fiction harkens back to their fabulous diversity and their proximity to the human species that, since ancient times, has never ceased to intrigue artists and thinkers. It thus follows that hybridity and metamorphosis haunt NDiaye's books not only as formal components of the fantastic genre to which her writing often veers but insofar as they gesture toward the "existential transformation of the human being" (Sheringham 51–56). However, I argue that, instead of signaling what Sheringham calls "the cognitive evolution of the hero" (Sheringham 57), interspecies relations and mutations reveal not only the plasticity and malleability of the corporeal substance constituting the beings that populate the world but also the indistinctness of their cognitive abilities and ontological status.

One finds a telling example in *Trois femmes puissantes*, a book that earned NDiaye the Prix Goncourt in 2009. The protagonist of the final section of the triptych, where personal identity and political belonging are foregrounded, is a young African widow named Khady Demba, who is forced by her husband's family to embark on a grueling and ultimately deadly journey to Europe. All throughout her infernal descent into the dehumanizing condition of an immigrant, culminating in a pathos-filled ending, Khady is constantly shunted between the human and the animal condition. While her ordeal turns her into a beast of labor whose connection to the world is fundamentally sensorial, either through pain or lack of it, it expands her awareness of herself – in other words, of her irreducible identity. Khady's demise on the electric fence that separates the immigrants from Europe marks the highest point of her *prise de conscience* at the very moment when her human body is obliterated:

> C'était moi, Khady Demba, songeait-elle encore à l'instant où son crâne heurta le sol et où, les yeux grands ouverts, elle voyait planer lentement par-dessus le grillage un oiseau aux longues ailes grises – c'est moi, Khady Demba, songea-t-elle dans l'éblouissement de cette révélation, sachant qu'elle était cet oiseau et que l'oiseau le savait. (NDiaye 2009, 333)[3]

Whether one chooses to interpret this scene as a Sisyphus-like apotheosis, in the existentialist tradition established by Camus, or an escapist aestheticization of a grave political issue, *via* Benjamin or Lyotard, its literal meaning points to a transition, be it only of perspective and not of substance, from human to animal, from the woman's head hitting the ground to her eyes looking unto a bird flying in the sky above her. NDiaye deploys a rhetorical constellation reminiscent of Hélène Cixous's reflection on the *vol*-atile relation between women, birds and thieves: "What is interesting is that birds, writings, and many women are considered abominable, threatening and are rejected, because others, the rejectors, feel something is taken away from them" (Cixous 2004, 170). A similar progression away from an anthropocentric and anthropomorphic imagination or, in Nancy's terms, to "les autres corps ouverts" pointing toward "un autre que l'homme" (Nancy 2010, 43), accompanies Malinka/Clarisse's narrative evolution in *Ladivine* through the seemingly random but recurrent appearance of a dog, reminiscent at first of Malinka's mother ("ce chien aux manières élégantes avait les yeux de la mère de Malinka," NDiaye 2013, 81), later associated with Clarisse's unhappiness and guilt after being abandoned by her husband ("son corps lui semblait être une vieux chien qu'on ne châtierait jamais assez pour avoir, par exemple, dévoré un petit enfant," NDiaye 2013, 99) and finally representing her posthumous presence in the eyes of her daugher, who finds herself followed by a mysterious dog during her outings in Berlin and even while away on vacation in an unnamed exotic country that could be Ladivine Sylla's native land. More importantly, the dog reappears on the very last page of the book in front of the "palais de justice," its presence not only noticed but understood to be that of Malinka by Richard Rivière and Ladivine Sylla, who meet for the first time, thereby bringing the two halves of the woman's life together in the same space. The justice-bearing dog is also carrying Malinka's heart, signaling the possibility of a new form of clarity. The scene itself relies on the uncanny interplay of stylistic clarity and symbolic obscurity:

> Ladivine Sylla ouvrit la porte, le grand chien brun entra avec délicatesse sur ses pattes fines, frissonnates.
> Elle carressa son poil rêche, entre les oreilles petites et droites, et le chien tourna vers elle ses yeux savants, ses yeux chastes.
> Elle en eut un éblouissement de bonheur.
> Elle fut certaine qu'il est venu leur apprendre tout ce qu'il savait, qu'il avait traversé pour cela bien des tourments et des fatigues.
> Il leur rapportait le cœur palpitant de Malinka et peut-être aussi, pensait-elle dans l'ardeur de sa joie, la promesse d'une clarté nouvelle posée sur chaque jour. (NDiaye 2013, 403)

If the ending of *Ladivine* can be read as a positive portrayal of a character who has shed her divided, anguish-ridden and counterfeit identity in order to acquire superior intellectual and moral qualities, indicated by the adjectives "savants" and "chastes," Malinka/Clarisse reaches an exemplary condition by forsaking her humanity or, rather, being forced to forsake it. Only at the end of her trials as a woman, which include the separation from her mother, a failed marriage and a violent death, does she transcend her duality and ascend to true feeling, denoted by "a beating heart" and a knowledge beyond reason, or "a new clarity." Whereas the presence of an animal can trouble the ideological assumptions of the characters and shake the ontological foundations of their fictional world, the transformation from human to animal further destabilizes the fragile boundaries of identity in Marie NDiaye's writing. Fragility, thematized as weakness, simplicity, delicacy (as in the quotation above) and, often, "grace," can foreshadow (in *Trois femmes puissantes*) or follow (in *Mon cœur à l'étroit* and *Ladivine*) the sacrifice of one's humanity, leading to a deeper understanding akin to spiritual wisdom. Lydie Moudileno's examination of the dialectics of "puissance/impuissance," particularly as it participates in the portrayal of African women in the writer's work, invites us to complicate this dichotomy and its moral and political implications (Moudileno 2013, 67). Moreover, in an interview from 2009 about *Trois femmes puissantes*, the writer explains the meaning of Khady Demba's death by using, very reluctantly, the word "glory":

> Je n'avais pas envie que chaque fin soit lugubre. Cela peut vous paraître curieux mais pour moi c'est un livre gai, joyeux. Si à la fin de la troisième

histoire il y a la mort, cela ne jette pas un voile de tristesse sur l'histoire. Elle meurt certes, mais elle meurt dans la "gloire": – même si je me méfie de ce mot, trop empreint de catholicisme, et je ne suis pas du tout mystique. L'histoire malheureuse de cette femme n'est pas désespérée car c'est quelqu'un qui ne s'oublie jamais, qui n'oublie jamais qui elle est même si c'est un être assez simple, et Je n'avais pas envie que chaque fin soit lugubre. Cela peut vous paraître curieux mais pour moi c'est un livre gai, joyeux. Si à la fin de la troisième histoire il y a la mort, cela ne jette pas un voile de tristesse sur l'histoire. Elle meurt certes, mais elle meurt dans la "gloire": – même si je me méfie de ce mot, trop empreint de catholicisme, et je ne suis pas du tout mystique. L'histoire malheureuse de cette femme n'est pas désespérée car c'est quelqu'un qui ne s'oublie jamais, qui n'oublie jamais qui elle est même si c'est un être assez simple, et même si cela ne tient qu'à un nom, son nom propre, Khady Demba, qu'elle se répète, mais un nom c'est beaucoup.[4]

Even though we may remain skeptical toward any self-exegesis intended to establish authorial control over the meaning of one's work, it is interesting to notice a tension between the spiritual, even salvific interpretation of fragility, on the one hand, and its didactic and moralistic value, on the other. Despite their apparent similarity, the former points to a post- human and anti-humanistic interpretation that obviates any connection between NDiaye's fiction and the social and political circumstances surrounding it, while the latter calls attention precisely to such connections in a humanist tradition of commitment, albeit reimagined as a post-Barthesian "morale de la forme" (Barthes 1953, 15). Consequently, scholars question the ethics of NDiaye's aesthetic choices by reading into the undecidability, or "blankness," of her style, as A. Asibong puts it, a compromise between her artistic ambitions and her desire to achieve recognition as a representative of the postcolonial canon. In his discussion of Khady Demba, whose "saintly" or "Christ-like" portrayal undermines the social and psychological verisimilitude of the narrative, Asibong contends that NDiaye's highly stylized, allusive and indeterminable writing – what I have called her uncertainty principle – reduces her character's portrayal to a tokenistic and "disingenous" representation of female Africanness. For the author of *Marie NDiaye: Blankness and Recognition*, the issues raised by her aesthetic choices in this case go beyond the mere question of verisimilitude or style, calling for a reassessment of the political and ideological implications of the writer's work: "There is something problematic, for me at least, about how much the figure of the dark-skinned Khady Demba is made to 'carry', in terms of physical destruction and accompanying ideological 'optimism':

it is as though she is nothing more than the result of a condescendingly Africanized – and strangely black – projection" (Asibong 103). Does the fact that NDiaye's characters lack social and psychological verisimilitude – for this remark could be extended to many, if not all, of her protagonists – weaken or even invalidate the philosophical, moral and political stance of her writing? One could attempt an answer by turning to other novels that seem to follow more closely implicit rules of a contemporary poetics of commitment.

## "We Others" – Global Citizens, Postcolonial Sons

Stéphane Audeguy's *Nous autres* (2009) illustrates, according to the volume's back cover, the genre of the "intime planétaire," a novel expression that could lend itself to a translation such as "intimate planetarity." The publicity blurb explains this surprizing oxymoron as follows: "L'action de ce roman se passe au Kenya, c'est-à-dire partout." Does the narrative, written by a white French metropolitan author and recounted in the present tense and in the first person plural through the voice of the region's manes, endow the East African country with a universal, exemplary or simply tokenistic value? Herein lies the question raised by this story featuring Pierre, a photojournalist who travels to Kenya upon receiving word of the death of his estranged father, Michel Figuier. After identifying the body being held at the central morgue in Nairobi, the 33-year-old man retraces his father's steps from the capital city to Mombassa and then back to the poor Nairobi neighborhood of Kibera while slowly immersing himself into the region's nature, culture and history.

Far from marking a new experience for the protagonist, this African journey of filiation brings a culmination to his long-standing passion for the continent, stirred up by the discovery, at the age of thirteen, of his father's identity or, rather, of his location. By synecdochal association, the previously unknown author of his life and the continent he inhabits combine in Pierre's mind. Audeguy's ironic style, characterized by a fast-moving narration and alternating focalization (reminiscent of a camera zooming in and out) brings out the Bovarystic nuance in the character's infatuation: "cette apparition d'un père romanesque coïncide chez lui avec une passion vive pour tout ce qui concerne l'Afrique, ses animaux d'abord, puis sa géographie, bientôt son histoire" (Audeguy 45). Like Le Clézio's African father, Michel Figuier serves as an inter-continental and intercultural "passeur," a guide for the son's own discovery of an unknown world hidden under the layers of stereotypical representations and cultural prejudice; unlike his son, Michel engenders a narrative that walks on the razor's edge of the postcolonial exotic. As Huggan defines it, the postcolonial exotic reflects "a pathology of cultural representation under late capitalism – a result of the spiraling commodification of cultural difference" (Huggan 45). In the case of Audeguy and other white metropolitan writers, such as the previously discussed Gaudé and Darrieussecq, this is undertaken not by postcolonial Francophone writers but by their metropolitan peers, who turn their attention outwards in both a geographic and a thematic sense. In *Nous autres*, the move to explore the margins of this continent of inspiration and incorporate it into the mainstream literary substance is mirrored by the novel's plot. Additionally, the novel's alternal tone, with its shifting voices, vacillates between testimonial pathos and undecidable irony, depending on whether it is focused on events preceding Pierre's arrival in Africa, on the span of time from precolonial times to the death of Michel Figuier, or on the life of the protagonist himself.

The alternating structure of the narrative reveals that the true legacy of Pierre's father lies not in his few material possessions but in the son's emotional and experiential journey. Nairobi is at first experienced as a collection of objects (streets, crowds, buildings) to be photographed in order to document its strange and excessive qualities. Pierre's retinal contact with the objects echoes his tangential insertion into the space:

> Il se répète qu'il est en Afrique, il sait bien qu'il n'existe rien qui soit vraiment l'Afrique, il sait bien que l'Afrique n'existe pas, qu'il ne se dirait pas en marchant à Milan qu'il est en Europe, mais tout de même il sourit dans la rue, il sourit à cette rue grise et luisante de pluie, à ses petits escrocs, aux mendiants, aux hommes d'affaires en costume rayé, aux femmes qui passent, aux vendeurs de journaux, aux Indiens qui téléphonent sous des porches. (Audeguy 56)

Pierre's experience is a more self-aware and thus less illusion-ridden repetition of his father's African journey. Although the son carries on its sentimental legacy, the decades that have passed since decolonization tempered the idealism so commonly found among the previous generation. Michel's own motivation, however, reveals his exotic prejudice cloaked under the veil of humanitarianism and the critique of late capitalism. While he came to Kibera to escape the failings and corruption of the Western world, he finds himself surrounded by its long-ranging deleterious effects: "il se trouve au cœur de ses effets les plus étranges et les plus pervers" (Audeguy 133). Faced with the reality of the inescapable neocolonial order, he is forced to trade his primitivist dream of helping to build a new society on an emerging continent populated by an ideal version of humanity for provisional and mostly inconsequential acts, such as helping the locals file requests with international organizations: "De plus en plus on leur fait rédiger des lettres à destination du monde entier: ils remplissent des demandes de bourses, ils sollicitent l'aide des fondations situées en Afrique du Sud, en Angleterre, aux États-Unis, en Union Soviétique" (Audeguy 133). Eventually, tired of witnessing the cycle of violence rooted in colonial prejudice, postcolonial greed and neocolonial indifference, he commits suicide by auto-asphyxiation after killing a rapist whose crime had gone unpunished. Additionally, Michel's relationships with the people of his adoptive country are alluded to without being fully developed. Several characters, such as Kahina, Elizabeth and Anyango, are sketched out merely to represent stock figures of Third-World suffering and post-colonial resistance as victims of violence, sectarian conflicts and exploitation by the global economic order. The father's story-within-the-story is replete with "these almost clichéd statements [that] rehash many tried-and-true imperialist stereotypes, along with their Orientalizing, homogenizing, and other racialized undercurrents" (Anker 38).

The tone of the narrative alternates between the jocular and the pathetic, sometimes even combining them as a way to introduce a distance between the gravity of the narrated events and the act of narration itself. In one laughter-provoking scene, Pierre watches a program on the international French station TV5-Monde, ironically described by the narrator as a "chaîne international de la France mère des arts et des lois" (Audeguy 113). It is a documentary on "nos ancêtres de la préhistoire." Badly dressed, "ils patronnent et ils cousent comme des manches, un peu comme des Nègres du temps jadis; d'ailleurs, l'action se passe dans un pays chaud qui a le sens du rythme" (Audeguy 114).

Through prosopopoeia, the author gives a voice to the spirits of the dead and, more importantly, opposes a local yet transhistoric counter-narrative to the mainstream discourse of African misery:

> Après le départ de Pierre nous sommes restés seuls dans la savane, pour autant que nous puissions être seuls, car les chiffres parlent d'eux-mêmes, depuis le commencement des temps 80 milliards de morts, les 7 milliards de ceux qu'on appelle les vivants ne font pas le poids. Nous avons marché dans ces herbes hautes et nous avons dormi dans ces arbres avant même

que les mots n'existent pour désigner les arbres, les herbes, la savane. Il faudrait pouvoir dire à quel point le monde sans mots pouvait être menaçant et sournois. Mais ça n'a plus d'importance maintenant, nous avons l'habitude, nous en avons vu d'autres, depuis le temps, et dans cette nuit du Kenya nous veillons sur les morts et sur nos descendants, sur les bantous qui jadis s'en allèrent vers la côte, il y a de ça bien deux mille deux cents ans, sur les colons arabes et sur les colons persans, sur les nomades nilotiques, sur les Portugais et même sur les Anglais. (Audeguy 29)

By telescoping past and present, the collective narrative discourse underscores the circular movement of history, from contemporary ethnic violence in Africa back to the Bruxelles conference of 1890. While the stated purpose of the meeting between the great colonial powers of late nineteenth-century Europe was to pacify and civilize the continent, its true purpose was to exploit it. Widening the breach between ideological pretense and political reality, the narrative riffs off the official phraseology before stripping it of its humanist pretense to lay bare the meaning hidden under the rich rhetorical folds of the civilizing mission. Furthermore, antithesis elucidates the true intentions of history-makers, all the more so when it is constructed by those on whose backs history was made: from "mettre un terme aux crimes et aux dévastations qu'engendre la traite des esclaves africains, afin de protéger efficacement les populations aborigènes de l'Afrique et d'assurer à ce vaste continent les bienfaits de la paix et de la civilisation," the discourse swiftly shifts into explanatory mode: "Il est question de développer l'Afrique. C'est-à-dire [...] de l'exploiter [...] La conférence de Bruxelles appelle de ses vœux, nous nous penchons par-dessus des épaules" (Audeguy 29–30). Hypotyposis, the technique of vivid description that echoes the protagonist's profession as a photographer, creates a triangular relation in which the collective voice of Africa serves as a conduit between the past colonialist's actions or the contemporary tourist's gaze and the conscience of the reader. As a group of tourists stop to gaze at a leopard in the Massai Mara National Park, the narration glides from the amazed contemplation of the wild animal to feelings of displacement and discomfort and finally to a meditation on death in post-World War II Europe:

Et plus les clients contemplent le fauve et plus la perfection de sa présence les atteint, et plus leur présence, dans ce véhicule puant qui refroidit lentement dans le soir descendant, dans ce métal craquant pour des raisons obscures, dans ces effluves mornes de plastique et d'essence, plus cette présence leur pèse, et c'est alors qu'ils voudraient mettre pied à terre, non pas pour se rapprocher de l'animal, mais pour se défaire de leur solidarité abjecte avec ce véhicule automobile désormais obscène, avec cette bête étrange, avec ce monstre d'ingéniosité où des systèmes électroniques qui n'ont pas vingt ans voisinent avec la roue qui en compte dix mille, avec ce Pajero qui depuis le matin salit le paysage, avec lequel ils creusent sur tous les chemins de la réserve des ornières toujours plus dangereuses, de sorte que bien vite ils doivent contourner les plus profondes d'entre elles, en traçant de nouvelles, déplaçant les chemins comme d'affreux et obstinés lombrics à labourer stérilement la terre oui, dans la honte d'être un homme, l'illusoire possibilité de mettre pied à terre, d'avancer vers le fauve en méprisant la mort, mais évidemment personne ne descend, personne en Europe ne méprise plus la mort depuis la Seconde Guerre mondiale. (Audeguy 13)

In the passage above the vocabulary expressing the tourists' admiration of nature stands in contrast with the technical terminology and establishes a series of parallels that oppose simplicity, tradition and beauty with complexity, modernity and ugliness. However, these parallel lines intersect another set of antinomies: wilderness and risk, on the one hand, and comfort and security, on the other. While the rhetorical progression of the sentence runs along the lines of an expected antithesis between Western and African values, the ending swerves in an unforeseen direction, by folding another – seemingly unconnected – event into the historical narrative of *Nous autres*. The trauma of mass murder and genocide that haunts European consciousness in the aftermath of Auschwitz and Hiroshima seems both incongruous, for it is left undeveloped, and entirely fitting in the context of a narrative about contemporary Africa, while at the same time fulfilling the implicit argument of Audeguy's narrative about Africa as a space of exploration, initiation and (self-)discovery. The last sections of the novel trade irony, reserved for the hordes of tourists that ebb and flow with the seasons, for tenderness, indicating the protagonist's acculturation to his adoptive homeland. The emphasis on grace, beauty and kindness casts a soft light on his intimate encounter with Anyango and his meeting with his half-brother Akwam, foreshadowing his decision to return to and perhaps settle in Kenya. Akwam, who works on a project to create a natural preserve for lacertilians, literally takes him by the hand to introduce him to the wonders of the natural world. In keeping with the theme of crustacean salvation, Pierre saves a crab lost in the desert by bringing it back to the water. This small encounter touches the young photographer in unexpected ways: the creature's aquatic movements become a metaphor for writing itself, and the life he saves rewards him in return with a sense of grace: "l'écriture vacillante de cette vie inconnue lui semble le signe le plus émouvant de la grâce du monde" (Audeguy 253). Epiphany and vitality meet on the African shore to open the traveler's – and the reader's – eyes to the pure beauty of life: "Sa joie est pure comme celle du crustacé ingrat maintenant absorbé par les joies délicates de la vie en lagon, et le vent le plus fou ne nous fera pas taire, et nos mots sur la terre un immense tombeau" (Audeguy 253). Yet the *non sequitur* in the novel's closing sentence signals a larger disconnect between two plotlines that seem to compete without converging or even communicating: the individual story of the European man whose journey leads to privileged, if evanescent, moments of pure joy and the collective endeavor of the African dead who strive, against all adversities, to verbalize and memorialize the obscured past.

Through their distinct mappings of identity, NDiaye's and Adeguy's texts raise a larger question. Is realism – and, if so, which kind: psychological, social, *roman à thèse* – the only aesthetic technique able to convey the complexity of our globalized world and the urgency of addressing its inequalities and injustices without falling into the pitfall of condescending *misérabilisme* or detached idealization? Or should the narrative genre itself, particularly in its "storytelling" instantiations, be reassessed along with the contemporary political and cultural system that favors it over other forms of expression? I use the term in the sense accorded to it by Christian Salmon in his 2007 book *Storytelling: la machine à fabriquer des histoires et à formater les esprits* and futher developed by him and Yves Citton, among others, to indicate a form of strategic, goal-oriented and usually non-literary narrative communication used in politics, business and media to convey a clear message and incite to action in cases such as a candidate's political campaign or the sale of a product. In an article written after the election of Barack Obama to the office of President of the United States in 2008, Salmon lays out the elements of the "magic square" used by the winning candidate's communication team:

> 1. Raconter une histoire capable de constituer l'identité narrative du candidat (*storyline*). 2. Inscrire l'histoire dans le temps de la campagne, gérer les rythmes, la tension narrative tout au long de la campagne (*timing*). 3. Cadrer le message idéologique du candidat (*framing*), c'est-à-dire encadrer le débat comme le préconise le linguiste Georges Lakoff, en imposant un "*registre de langage cohérent*" et en "*créant des métaphores*". 4. Créer le réseau sur Internet et sur le terrain, c'est-à-dire

un environnement hybride et contagieux susceptible de capter l'attention et de structurer l'audience du candidat (*networking*).[5]

By contrast, literature offers a space of resistance against this form of neoliberal storytelling by imagining counter-narratives (Salmon 213) or counter-fictions, according to Yves Citton.[6] From this perspective, NDiaye's writing undermines each corner of the communicative structure by blurring identities and storylines, amalgamating temporal lines, allowing the characters' fluid subjectivity to shape their story and maintaining an authorial distance to the narrative that invites reflection rather than empathy on the part of the reader. It resists the siren call of reparative, recuperative or salvific storytelling not because it does not believe in its ethical and didactic potential but because it cultivates the dimension that Walter Benjamin in his interpretation of storytelling calls "the continuation of a story which is in the process of unfolding" (Benjamin 146) rather than the authoritative lesson of a completed story. In so doing, her fiction dovetails with the genre of "the human rights bestseller" while refusing to participate in the exotization of suffering through its sublimation into what Anker calls "an alchemy of horror, wonder, and enthrallment" (Anker 39). Conversely, Stéphane Audeguy's novel features two narratives – of individual self-discovery and communal endurance – that fail to engage with one another, except tangentially and superficially, casting doubt on the very idea of the cultural and affective encounter upon which this and other human rights novels are predicated.

## Notes

1 Jean-Marie Seillan identifies four types of colonial novels: narratives of knowledge which focus on exploration and discovery, narratives of having emphasizing the economic endeavors of the colonizers, narratives of power which tend to its political implications and narratives of duty which stress the necessity to follow and implement the ideals of the colonial mission (Jean-Marie Seillan, "Le roman d'aventures coloniales africaines (1863–1914): ébauche de typologie" in Durand and Sévry 99–12).

2 For a historical overview of the city's colonial past, see Éric Saugera, *Bordeaux, port négrier, XVIIᵉ–XIXᵉ siècles*, Paris: Karthala, 2002. For the present forms of recognition but also occultation of that past, an article published in 2014 on the website www.rue89bordeaux.com offers a glimpse into the current state of the debate. http://rue89bordeaux.com/2014/05/bordeaux-difficile-memoire-lesclavage/ (accessed February 20, 2017).

3 For an analysis of this topic, see Hall Bjørnstad and Oana Panaïté,

"'Roiseau Pensant': Marie NDiaye and Blaise Pascal", in Panaïté 2016, 154–167.

4 http://www.lesinrocks.com/2009/08/30/actualite/lecrivain-marie-ndiaye-aux-prises-avec-le-monde-1137985/ (accessed February 20, 2017).

5 Christian Salmon, "Le carré magique d'Obama", *Le Monde.fr*, 17/10/2008. http://www.lemonde.fr/idees/article/2008/10/17/le-carre-magique-d-obama-par-christian-salmon_1108146_3232.html (accessed February 20, 2017).

6 Yves Citton, "Contre-fictions en médiocratie", *Revue Critique de Fixxion Française Contemporaine*, n°6, 2013. http://www.revue-critique-de-fixxion-francaise-contemporaine.org/rcffc/article/view/fx06.14/726 (accessed February 20, 2017); "Contre-fictions politiques", *Multitudes*, No. 481, March 2012, 70–148.

# PART THREE

# Colonial Remanence

Contemporary writers create narratives that delve into the residual effects of Western colonization while integrating them into a larger ethical discussion about the complicity and responsibility of the colonizers as well as the formerly colonized. In so doing, late twentieth- and early twenty-first-century authors such as the French–Algerian Leïla Sebbar and the Algerian-born Jewish–French Hélène Cixous, whose works are situated in the larger framework of memorial writing about colonial Algeria, engage with the melancholic behaviors rooted in the traumas of the past, as both individual and collective phenomena. The concept of "postcolonial melancholia" theorized by Paul Gilroy proves especially productive for illuminating the cultural and ideological context in which these narratives emerge. In the chapter entitled "The Negative Dialectics of Conviviality," Gilroy paints a vivid picture of the ideological contradictions characteristic of contemporary Britain's race relations and immigration policies. His critique is sometimes couched in sympathetic storytelling:

> They [immigrants] have been among us, but they were never actually of us. [...] The real source of their treacherous choices is likely to remain a private, spiritual matter disconnected from the patterns of everyday life inside Britain. Their fundamentalism is no more or less alien than was their misguided introduction into this country in the first place. They are traitors because immigrants are doomed in perpetuity to be outsiders. Becoming an enemy terrorist only makes explicit what was already implicit in their tragic and marginal position. Irrespective of where they

are born, even their children and grandchildren will never really belong. (Gilroy 122)

To be sure, the author of *Postcolonial Melancholia* elucidates such oblique accounts of the justifications (failure to integrate, unemployment, religious differences and terrorism) for unavowed segregation and discriminatory practices with careful explanations that are, in fact, the focus of his discussion: "Ethnic absolutism comprehends their evil and their affiliation to fundamentalist Islam as neither a choice nor an act of will. It sees this outcome as the result of their instinctive responses to the combined pressures of ethnohistory, divergent tradition, and biocultural or even genomic division" (Gilroy 123). However, the theorist reveals a larger issue that he describes as a vicious circle intrinsic to defining the very notion of the alien: "the rioters rioted because they were alien. The proof of their alienness was the fact that they rioted" (Gilroy 123). Thus, the politics of assimilation and integration is by its own nature – that is, by the nature of its founding concept – circular. Furthermore, its critique also displays a discursive circularity whereby in order to deconstruct it one needs to espouse, be it for heuristic purposes only, its arguments and internal logic.

# CHAPTER FIVE

# Algeria's Mortified Memory

In 1991 the French historian Benjamin Stora observed in a study entitled *La Gangrène et l'oubli*: "In France, in the seventies and eighties, Pieds-noirs, Harkis and soldiers represent groups that each carry separate memories of Algeria" (Stora 1991, 256). These dissimilarities notwithstanding, fourteen years later the French National Assembly passed the controversial "loi française n° 2005–158 du 23 février 2005 portant reconnaissance de la Nation et contribution nationale en faveur des Français rapatriés," a law meant as an official gesture of acknowledgement for the work and sacrifice of the former French inhabitants of Algeria. After a heated public debate, article 4 of the law, which affirmed the beneficial – in other words, fortunate – influence of colonialism over the territories formerly under French control, was repealed, but the contentious fight over what constitutes the most appropriate symbolic and material forms of national recognition for a formerly marginalized social group is still ongoing, reminiscent of Gilroy's remark that "the problematic of assimilation lost its grip on the postcolonial world long, long ago" (Gilroy 131). The heterogeneous nature of the group itself has long been at the heart of the debate.

In the French imagination, starting from the early nineteenth century, when the memory of Napoleon's campaign in Egypt was coeval with the successful attempts by the Restoration to conquer Algiers, "Algeria lingers there with the ontological strangeness of something missing but still felt: a phantom limb, as it were, and a big one" (Bell 35). Dorian Bell shows that in several novels by Balzac, such as *La Cousine Bette*, *Le Programme d'une jeune veuve*, *La Duchesse de Langeais*, *Le Député d'Arcis* and *Une passion dans le désert*, North Africa is often depicted as a deadly yet destiny-fulfilling place for military heroes, gallant adventurers and social-climbing bourgeois or small nobility. Balzac, Bell argues, displays his nationalistic support for the French control of

Algeria ("cette seconde France") in his journalistic writing while at the same time using his novels to delve deeply into the political, economic and moral corruption of the colonial administration. However, Bell further asserts that Balzac's "desert odyssey" presents him with a particular challenge, as the expanding colonial space contests the social stratification and spatial symbolism of realist representation. The closing sentence of *Une passion dans le désert* –

> "Dans le désert, voyez-vous, il y a tout, et il n'y a rien" (1232) – reads as Balzac's own revealing conclusion about a canvas so simultaneously enticing and forbidding to him as the empire. If Napoleonic Egypt, in its historical finitude, had perhaps at first seemed an easier imperial frontier to render than the still-ongoing Algerian adventure, it had not proven so. (Bell 50)

Over a century later the French colony, home to a million Pieds-noirs and object of a fierce struggle for independence, remains as mysterious and disquieting as ever, a strangely "measureless" or "illimited" realm inhabited by "miserable lords" reminiscent of Pascal's disposed king who embodies the human condition itself, yet holding the promise of meaning and liberation:

> Depuis toujours, sur la terre sèche, raclée jusqu'à l'os, de ce pays démesuré, quelques hommes cheminaient sans trêve, qui ne possédaient rien mais ne servaient personne, seigneurs misérables et libres d'un étrange royaume. Janine ne savait pas pourquoi cette idée l'emplissait d'une tristesse si douce et si vaste qu'elle lui fermait les yeux. Elle savait seulement que ce royaume, de tout temps, lui avait été promis et que jamais, pourtant, il ne serait le sien, plus jamais, sinon à ce fugitif instant, peut-être, où elle rouvrit les yeux sur le ciel soudain immobile, et sur ses flots de lumière figée, pendant que les voix qui montaient de la ville arabe se taisaient brusquement. (Camus 1957, 23)

Stora's own work attributes the roots of the war and the continued dissent that marked its aftermath to the inferior political status of Muslim Algerians, who, despite being the demographic majority, were considered "false citizens" required to forsake their "personal status" as Muslims in order to be granted French nationality. The 1944 decrees and the 1947 law brought an extension of the right to vote to all French citizens of Algeria, albeit in a two-tier college, signaling a greater commitment to integration. Therefore, the perceived discrepancy between these signs of political and administrative progress post-World War II, on the one hand, and the extreme violence of the war, on the other, has generated an image of Algeria's transition to independence as a violent divorce following a relatively happy marriage. In this dramatic conflation of the familial and the political, the Pieds-noirs – that is, French settlers in Algeria from 1830 to 1962 – as well as the Harkis Algerian auxiliary forces in the French army during the 1954–1962 war and the Chibanis – Algerians working and living in France in the 1960s and 1970s – are cast in the role of abandoned children, innocent victims of an unnecessary divorce. In reaction to the imagery of marriage and domesticity used (as we have seen above, in Camus's writing) to reinscribe a historical power dynamic in a natural paradigm, Frantz Fanon is among those who counteract with scientific explanations the colonial attempts to obfuscate the elements of a contingent situation. In an open letter addressed to the Governor General of Algeria, published in July 1956 in the journal *Action*, the future author of *L'An V de la révolution algérienne* states: "Si la Phychiâtrie [sic] est la technique médicale qui se propose de permettre à l'homme de ne plus être étranger à son environnement, je me dois d'affirmer que l'Arabe, aliéné permanent dans son pays, vit dans un état de dépersonnalisation absolue" (Brun and Penot-Lacassagne 84).

The narrative of victimization had previously shaped the anticolonial discourse and paved the way for militant claims to independence. Writers such as Kateb Yacine and Mohammed Dib and intellectuals such as Mostefa Lacheraf and Frantz Fanon rely, rhetorically and ideologically, on the evocation of past crimes, spectacular acts of violence and a long history of pain, injuries and humiliations. The French government, at first, and radical colonial groups and organizations, later, rejected these claims, emphasizing France's civilizing contribution (a journal article from 1957 reminds readers that French colonization modernized Algeria, taking it "from tent to building" – "de la tente au building"[1]). Moreover, they refuted the idea of colonial guilt at the same time that the country's military engagement in the North African colony led to the use of more extreme tactics, thereby compromising the army's integrity and widening the rift caused by the Algerian debate in metropolitan France (comparable to the one caused by the Dreyfus affair half a century before). The most striking and jarring example is the official, yet not public, sanction of torture as a means of "pacification" during the battle of Algiers of 1957, used by the DOP ("détachements opérationnels de protection") and special intelligence units, but also by the military ("unités du contingent"), a practice which, in Stora's assessment, is a sub-product of a war predicated on the secrecy of its tactics and goals (Stora 1991, 30). When the information ultimately transpired in the

French papers, the Pieds-noirs would level accusations against "defeatist" journalists and intellectuals for defaming the army and betraying their co-nationals in Algeria.

Another topic of contention for all sides was the unrecognized or under-recognized massacres, such as the one that occurred in October 1961 in Paris. After forty-two policemen were killed in attacks spearheaded by the Algerian insurrectional political party, the FLN (Front de Libération Nationale), the "préfet de police," Maurice Papon, issued an official order of curfew for "certain French citizens," meaning "Algerian workers" and "French Muslims." At a protest against this order 11,000 people were arrested and, in the absence of official police reports, several dozen dead bodies found in the Seine further aroused suspicion among the public and fed speculation in the press. Similar events occured in Algeria, arguably the most disputed being the shooting of rue d'Isly in Algiers on March 26, 1962 during the Evian negotiations that would eventually end the hostilities and lead to independence. As the war drew to an end, the French pro-colonial militia known as OAS (Organisation Armée Secrète) intensified its activities. Considering the French forces a foreign occupation army, its members set up acts of armed resistance and called Europeans to participate in a general strike and a march in Algiers. As a result of violent confrontations between protesters and soldiers, forty-six were left dead and 200 wounded (twenty of whom died later) in an atmosphere of confusion and mutual accusations: some suspected an OAS provocation, others accused the French army of shooting upon orders from Paris, while yet others placed the blame on Muslim soldiers in French uniforms. Reprisals by the Pieds-noirs would later cause the deaths of ten Algerians.

In the years following the war, France witnessed the phenomenon called "nostalgérie," the most salient aspect of which was a surge in publications about the former colony. Aside from the works of French writers and intellectuals who had supported Algerian independence, such as François Mauriac and Raymond Aron, the majority of these books are favorable to the continued French presence in North Africa. Despite this profusion of scriptural memorialization and mythologization, the 1960s and 1970s also marked a period of silent reconciliation, as the country tried to adjust to the reality of life after the empire while avoiding a public debate about its failed colonial project. Government policies were implemented to oversee the repatriation of the almost one million Pieds-noirs, as well as that of the Harkis. Each of these groups was fraught with internal divisions between, for instance,

"Pieds-rouges" (French communists, some of whom requested Algerian citizenship after the country's independence) and former members of the paramilitary group OAS (fiercely opposed to the decolonization of Algeria), or, according to the racialist categories introduced into the French legal system by the "Code noir" of 1685, between Pieds-noirs and "Pieds-gris" (the latter referring to the offspring of French colonists from Algeria), or Pieds-noirs and metropolitan French. Moreover, each of these groups elicited public anger and were subjected to various forms of incivility, from indifference to open resentment and discrimination. To illustrate the consequences of war fatigue in the early 1960s, Stora offers the following example: a survey conducted in April 1962 showed that 75 percent of French people were "preoccupied" by the Algerian question; yet, at the end of the summer break, in September 1962, only 13 percent of French society thought that Algeria and the repatriation of the Pieds-noirs were major issues of public concern (Stora 1991, 117). The former French colonists became the object of social contempt, as their return to the motherland was perceived as an undue economic burden by some at the same time as they were being held accountable by others for the loss of the most important colony of the French empire. Despite strong initial objections from politicians, including President De Gaulle, the former Algerian auxiliaries were relocated into special areas – rural camps or suburban neighborhoods build on the outskirts of French cities. Their successful integration into the "French melting pot" has been hampered by acts of discrimination justified by the perceived "incivility" introduced in French society by North African immigrants and their descendants, deemed impervious and even hostile to French republican values.

In this context, Paul Gilory's conclusion regarding Great Britain can apply to postcolonial France: "There is no governmental interest in the forms of conviviality and intermixture that appear to have evolved spontaneously and organically from the intervention of anti-racists and the ordinary multiculture of the postcolonial metropolis" (Gilroy 124). As state policies and public discourse often manifest the fragile and contradictory relation between socialistic principles and welfare-state inclusivity, on the one hand, and the increasing move toward privatization and market liberalism, on the other, they also betray a considerable level of confusion regarding past and present immigration and the treatment of their own citizens born of immigrant parents:

> the beleaguered regimes have produced strangers and aliens as the populist limit against which increasingly evasive national particularity

can be seen, felt, measured, and then, if need be, negatively discharged. The raw material for that perilous exercise is not supplied by aging representatives of the incoming caste of settler-citizens but by the two succeeding generations of their locally born descendants. That group gets trapped in the vulnerable role of perpetual outsider, but their local sense of entitlement leaves them reluctant to make common cause against racism and xenophobia with more recently arrived refugees and asylum seekers. To do so would be to accede to the secondariness and marginality with which racism associates them. (Gilroy 123)

In recent years, veterans' organizations and immigrants' associations in France have become increasingly vocal about the recognition of their rights, legal and symbolic, which led to the highly controversial 2005 law about "the benefits of colonialism" and, as a direct consequence of that legislative action, to what Stora dubbed "the war of memories" (*la guerre des mémoires*).[2] One could see in this a structural reverberation of the "war without name." Similarly, the written expression coined in 1963, "la guerre de l'écrit" (the war of writing), provides another homology between past and present (Brun and Penot-Lacassagne 13). During the last years of the war the number of publications devoted to the conflict ranged in the hundreds: "Les dernières années du conflit voient se multiplier les textes et les études consacrées à la guerre: récits de vie, plaidoyers, témoignages, enquêtes" (Brun and Penot-Lacassagne 19).

Commemorative acts that were in the past associated with the singular initiative of notable writers and intellectuals, such as Albert Camus, Marie Cardinal, Leïla Sebbar, Jacques Derrida and Hélène Cixous, have metamorphosed into a collective cultural phenomenon. Events such as the 2011 National Congress of Harkis and Pieds-noirs, organized to prepare for the fiftieth anniversary of the end of the French–Algerian war in 2012, have been furthermore disseminated by a host of books written either by the participants of the war or by their children. One could legitimately ask in this case, as Antonious Robben does in regard to similar manifestations elicited by Argentina's Dirty War: "Why this incessant return to a painful past? Are these individuals, groups, and organizations concerned about how the past will be remembered or how they will be judged by history? Are their public confrontations a manifestation of a politics of memory aimed at imposing a master narrative [...]?" (Robben 121).

I contend that in this recent convergence between writings by Harkis and Pieds-noirs we are faced with two distinct yet interconnected types of memorial writing that recollect or re-enact the colonial past by setting it in contrast with the post-colonial present. Through the interconnected narratives of personal remembrance and historical discourse, these personal stories hark back to lost examples of civility. I will examine how, in books published by Pieds-noirs and Harkis and their children, French Algeria is depicted as a genteel polity, conjured up through childhood memories, parents' testimonies and collages from old newspaper and journal articles and supported by documentary fiction. The following remarks by Robben about the fractures of social memory in Argentina carry a particular resonance for the former French colony:

> Memory, violence, and trauma coexist here in contradictory ways. Past acts of human degradation have evoked their indomitable intrusion on individuals and society alike. The forgetting of violence is inextricably linked to the remembrance of violence because traumatic experiences are characterized by the inability to be either completely recalled or completely forgotten. It is precisely this obstruction to either total recall or total erasure, and the unending search for comprehensive understanding, that makes trauma so indigestible and memory so obsessive. (Robben 122)

## From Memory Wars to Anger Consensus

Anger and incivility are integral parts of the post-colonial *ethos* that oriented France's response to the violent dismantling of its colonial empire in the wake of World War II. From the Franco-Vietnamese War (1945–1954) to the Franco-Algerian war (1954–1962), decolonization was marred by confrontations not only in the colonies but also in the metropolis. In addition to the conflict between French colonists and the indigenous colonized, there were clashes between different groups and factions of French society and internecine collisions among Vietnamese and Algerian peoples.

Among the publications reflecting the point of view of the Pieds-noirs, I will focus on two volumes that illustrate these characteristics. The first is a nostalgic, personal collection of memories containing written and visual materials about "French Algeria" by Maurice Calmein and Christiane Lacoste-Adrover, evocatively titled *Dis, c'était comment, l'Algérie française?* (2002). The second, a memoir by Marie-Jeanne Rey, *Mémoires d'une écorchée vive. Alger 1954–1962* (2004), recounts the life story of a young woman torn ("skinned alive") between the deep sense of belonging to her adoptive "native land" of Algeria and the feeling of alienation after her family's relocation to France, her unknown and unwelcoming "motherland." Rey's memoir presents some of the ideological and discursive traits associated with "settler self-mystification" (Dine 149–150) and epitomized by *Le Premier Homme*, without exhibiting any of the artistic or self-reflective qualities present in Camus's posthumous text.

The perspective of the Harkis transpires in the work of a daughter who writes her father's biography as an Algerian refugee whose presence in France is both concealed by the government and resented by the public: Fatima Besnaci-Lancou, *Fille de Harki* (2003). Besnaci-Lancou's publications, which include two collections of testimonies by former Harkis (*Treize chibanis harkis*, 2006) and Harkis' wives (*Nos mères, paroles blessées. Une autre histoire de harkis*, 2006), have been instrumental in drawing attention to the plight of her community. Moreover, the synergy created by a host of similar books written mainly by daughters of Harkis, such as Dalila Kerchouche (*Mon père, ce harki*, 2003), Zahia Rahmani (*Moze*, 2003) and Hadjila Kemoum (*Mohand le harki*, 2003), even though male authors such as Boussad Azni (*Harkis, crimes d'État. Généalogie d'un abandon*, 2002) also participated in this phenomenon, has led to a generational effect with cultural, political and literary implications. As it is apparent from their dates of publication, all these titles accompanied or closely followed the 40th anniversary of the end of the war in Algeria.

I will conclude by turning my attention to two books by Algerian–French writer Leïla Sebbar. One is an edited volume of short testimonies, recollections and reflections by twenty-five French-language writers, journalists, historians and intellectuals; the other is Sebbar's own autobiographical work entitled *Je ne parle pas la langue de mon père*. The texts perused in this chapter display an obvious formal and aesthetic heterogeneity, ranging from history books, memoirs and biographies to literary pieces. In order to grasp the memorial modulations of the colonial fortune as they relate (and relate to) an event that, though past, still marks a gaping wound in the collective consciousness of two countries, I have decided to read "against the current," in the words of Christopher L. Miller, "by bracketing questions of literary and stylistic quality" (Miller 1998, 60) while focusing on the texts' rhetorical devices and their aesthetic and ideological effects.

These texts develop, albeit with various degrees of pathos and intensity, several common themes, such as the desire to unveil the truth for a French audience unfamiliar with the realities of colonial life and to highlight the intercultural nature of a society created by the synthesis of Arab, Berber, Jewish, Hispanic and more generally European cultures in the Mediterranean cradle. Dennis Walder defines this medley as an "uncanny mix of individual and social desires that prompts the search for remembered times and places that constitute it" (Walder 1). Produced by contemporary migration and displacement, postcolonial nostalgia comes in forms that are plural, manifold and hybrid: "Not only is nostalgia deeply implicated in the political life of people, it is a part of their historical sense of themselves" (Walder 3). Yet Walder's hypothesis that postcolonial nostalgia "begins in desire and may end in truth" warrants closer scrutiny as the types of writing I will examine below (propaganda pamphlets, memoirs and short testimonials) seem to embody that which Paul Ricœur defines as "the pitfall of the imaginary, inasmuch as putting-into-images, bordering on the hallucinatory function of imagination, constitutes a sort of weakness, a discredit, a loss of reliability for memory" (Ricœur 2004, 55).

Is postcolonial nostalgia a writing practice that aims to heal the open wound of melancholy? Is the positivity of storytelling, the sense of narrative closure, the escape into a reimagined past an answer to the repetitive, circular and inescapable prison of melancholia?

Unlike mourning, defined by Freud as the process of grieving over the loss of a loved object, melancholia perpetuates the grief for an object that continues to exist and is therefore experienced as "a loss of a more ideal kind. The object has not perhaps actually died, but has been lost as an object of love" (Freud 245). The melancholic thought pattern, according to Julia Kristeva, revolves around a contradictory statement:

> "I love that object", is what that person seems to say about the lost object, "but even more so I hate it because I love it, and in order not to lose it, I imbued it in myself; but because I hate it that other within myself is a bad self, I am bad, I am non-existent, I shall kill myself." (Kristeva 1989, 11)

While nostalgia results from a longing for a "mythical return," melancholy is a depressive mood brought about by the loss of an object as a loved object.

Through a contrastive analysis of the ethical and the cognitive tasks of memory and history, in which one finds the baseline formula: "the duty of memory consists essentially in a duty not to forget" (Ricœur 2004, 30), Ricœur offers a critique of the cultural paradigm of memorialization that has become dominant since the 1980s, spurred, in France, by official policies and government initiatives of commemoration and magnified by the lasting impact of Pierre Nora's monumental project *Les Lieux de mémoire*. The memorial stance places the experience of the past, with the deictic "j'y étais" of the subject and the effort to recreate and reinhabit the site of memory, at its center; in so doing, it unsettles and even supplants the archival approach, predicated on veracity and unveiling the traces of the past. This engenders a paradigm harking back to Jules Michelet's "résurrection de la vie intégrale" (Michelet iv), which invited deeply subjective, highly imaginative and even hallucinatory narrative forms.

I inscribe my own reading of contemporary memorial writing about French Algeria within the conceptual framework offered by Walder and Ricœur by pursuing the following questions: What rhetorical and indexical strategies are utilized by these authors in order to inscribe the ideas of moral responsibility and historic retribution specific to each group's political agenda? In what manner does each text contend for a more "authentic" and more "ethical" memorial model? While all these works rely on narratives that contrast past and present, how do individual authors thematize the political and cultural tropes of "loss," "forgetting" and "decline"? How can we understand the seemingly paradoxical consensus among these authors about the lack of social and political recognition of both Pieds-noirs and Harkis in contemporary France as well as their shared denunciation of the French government and the French public for the collective act of forgetting? In 1958 the Algerian francophone writer Jean Amrouche made a remark that could describe today's state of affairs: "Entre Algériens francophones et Français, la langue est commune, non le langage."[3] Does expressing anger through personal memories and favoring the experiential level of history truly allow these two groups to overcome and move away from "memory wars" toward a place of civility and dialogue?

Interesting examples of corrective writing are found in propaganda books that seek to fill a perceived gap in current school programs or to correct supposed errors in the younger generation's historical education. *Dis, c'était comment, l'Algérie française?*, published in a symbolically titled series "SOS Outre-mer," bears the subtitle "20 questions and answers addressed to the Pieds-noir youth." It begins with a personal introduction, as do all writings in this category,[4] which grounds the educational intentions of the authors' undertaking in the necessity to preserve and pass on a legacy that is both familial and communal. The book also purports to go against the grain of mainstream discourse and rectify the stereotypical, even caricatural popular representations of the French from Algeria. As such, it borrows the paternalistic tone of a grandfatherly story and the sapiential stance of a classroom handbook, combining emotion and fact for the greatest persuasive effect. The twenty chapters hastily cover a wide variety of topics, ranging from a brief history of Algeria to lists of Pieds-noir artists, intellectuals and successful professionals, while an addendum provides a list of alternative sources of information (print materials, websites and databases) for further reading.

The treatment of these topics professes several colonial and postcolonial themes, first among which is the emphasis on France's right to occupy and develop a virgin land full of potential as well as the benefits brought to Algeria through the implementation of a modern system of infrastructure, agriculture and industry. Strengthening this claim to technological progress, the duty to civilize the natives and improve their living conditions through education, a health-care system and steady employment adds a humanitarian argument in favor of colonization.

The second theme lies in the description of a harmonious, well-ordered and peaceful coexistence within the French–Algerian melting pot. An interesting difference with the other memorial writings by Pieds-noirs, which favor the euphemism "events," is the use by Calmein and Lacoste-Adrover of the expression "guerre d'Algérie," in quotation marks for the first occurrence, and without any marks of punctuation afterwards. This indicates that in their 2002 pamphlet the long-held collective fear that naming the war might split the body of the "one and indivisible Republic," as Stora remarks, and the belief that without its North African colony France itself would cease to exist – "Plus d'Algérie française, plus de France!" proclaimed the posters of Jacques Soustelle's organization "Union pour le salut et le renouveau de l'Algérie française" in 1957 (Brun and Penot-Lacassagne 81) – have been overcome and/or replaced by the urgency emanating from the authors' political project of revealing a forgotten truth to the younger generations.

A third theme explains the demise of French Algeria as the result of an international conspiracy catalyzed by the mounting influence of the Communist bloc with the consent of the United States and its allies. Their impact allowed the fledgling movement for independence to soar and become a major threat to the existing order: "une main invisible cherch[e] à ruiner les solidarités invisibles France-Afrique du Nord."[5] A corollary of a military and moral victory thus turned into political defeat by the indifferent and even hostile attitude of the metropolitan French population and the mismanagement of the situation by the French administration (De Gaulle and his cabinet).

The downward spiral of the Algerian state after 1962 caused by the abdication of moral and political values along with the loss of economic know-how (resource management, infrastructure maintenance) that accompanied the forced departure of the French administrators and the Pied-noir population offers the authors a fourth line of attack:

> La France avait construit là-bas un pays riche, créé des villes à partir de rien, mis la terre en valeur, fourni de l'emploi et élevé le niveau de vie et d'instruction de la population. Aujourd'hui, l'agriculture a dépéri, la vigne a été en grande partie arrachée pour des raisons religieuses, les usines, les ateliers et bien des commerces ont fermé leurs portes, l'économie est en panne et le pays s'enfonce dans le chômage, la misère et la violence. Seuls restent le pétrole et le gaz, mais pour combien de temps? (Calmein and Lacoste-Adrover 27)

It is also worth noting the constant efforts to reframe the conflict by highlighting the enduring aspects of the struggle between civilization and barbarism through the connection between the French military operations in Algeria from 1954 to 1962 and the US-led wars in the Middle East in the aftermath of September 11, 2001. The attempt to perpetuate the relevance of the past in the present or even to conflate the symbolism of past and present events is complemented by self-ethnographic passages meant to immerse young readers into the daily lives of the Pieds-noirs via their dialect (*pataouète*) and their cuisine and customs (the ritual of summer holidays, family celebrations etc.). These forms of "narrative recovery" (Henke xxii) emerge from a real need in contemporary societies "for a more sophisticated and political understanding of cultural change, influence, and adaptation that can defend and explain the spontaneous tolerance and openness evident in the underworld of [the country's] convivial culture" (Gilroy 131). However, revisionist writing about French Algeria cannot break free from the psychological mechanisms and ideological overdetermination of postcolonial melancholia as described by Gilroy:

> Pending the belated arrival of that long-delayed intervention, postcolonial melancholia invites us to pass the time not by laughing at ourselves and our national plight, but by laughing at immigrants and strangers and, in particular, finding distraction and respite in the uneven results of the country's incomplete transition to cultural diversity and plurality. (Gilroy 131–132)

*Dis, c'était comment, l'Algérie française?* calls upon some accurate information: for instance, reminding readers that Algeria's annexation to France precedes that of some metropolitan regions, such as Savoie, thereby explaining the attachment to the North African colony, or explaining that the vast majority of Pieds-noirs were not rich colonists, as their income was inferior to that of their compatriots in the Hexagon, or pointing out that they did not form a homogeneous ideological bloc. It nonetheless offers biased interpretations of the facts, which have become discursive tropes of the French–Algerian memorialization.

Marie-Jeanne Rey's *Mémoires d'une écorchée-vive* invites, from its pathos-filled title to its ecstatic conclusion, a restorative or energetic reading, in the rhetorical sense developed by Quintilian in the wake of Aristotle and Cicero: "*Insequitur* enargeia, *quae a Cicerone* illustratio *et* evidentia *nominatur, quae non tam dicere videtur quam ostendere* [...] *et adfectus non aliter, quam si rebus ipsis intersimus, sequentur*" (Quintilian 60). Feeling isolated in France and unable to share her painful memories with her coworkers, friends and even family members, a woman "skinned alive" reactualizes her past (*energeia*) as a young Pied-noir woman caught in the whirlwind of the war by undertaking a monumental autobiographical project (*enargeia*). The closing scene strikingly displays these two reappropriations of the past as its four paragraphs conjure up, one by one, faith, truth, nostalgia and the imaginary return to the homeland:

> Je fis ce geste qui m'a toujours aidée chaque fois que je me suis sentie à bout. Je pris les Evangiles, posai l'ongle au hasard sur la tranche, ouvris le volume, et je lus: "Que la lumière ne demeure pas sous le boisseau".
>
> Je ne crois pas pour autant posséder "La Lumière", ni même la vérité entière. Cependant, s'il se pouvait qu'un jour j'éprouve le sentiment d'avoir, par ce récit, permis qu'on lance un regard un peu différent sur quelques-uns des miens, ces parias qu'on n'a pas intégrés, alors oui, je serai libérée.
>
> Ce jour-là, je fermerai les yeux. Je descendrai en courant l'escalier de la maison, je serai légère, j'aurai douze ans, je sauterai les sept dernières marches, j'ouvrirai la porte en bois un peu rugueux, elle m'écorchera les doigts. Enfin, je sortirai dans la lumière, je tendrai la main vers ce ciel lisse, ce ciel de satin lourd, je le caresserai. Je prendrai par le boulevard Laferrière. Je marcherai dans les jardins vers la mer. Et la terre de mon pays sera vraie et chaude sous mes pieds. (Rey 467)

With its complex layering of intimate moments and political events, tender family scenes and tense social interactions, this narrative of self-memorialization weaves the thread of an individual's coming-of-age with those of a collective awakening and upheaval. It is an exercise in "scriptotherapy" that promises "both the recovery of past experience through narrative articulation and the psychological reintegration of a traumatically shattered subject" (Henke xxii).

Even though, or perhaps precisely because, the narrative goes to great lengths to provide a reassuring picture of everyday life in Algiers, tears in the social fabric are strikingly apparent. One such example depicts a group of schoolboys, whom the narrator calls the "horribles garçons kabyles" and "mes bourreaux," who mock and taunt the young girl because of the homophony between her name and that of Maréchal Pétain:

> Les affreux garçons kabyles, qui allaient à l'école, eux, y avaient appris une chanson, la même que tous les autres écoliers français de l'époque. Cela commençait … "Marichane, nous voilà!" … Du moins était-ce ce qu'ils chantaient. Et comme ils prononçaient mon prénom de la même manière, ils avaient pris l'habitude de venir m'en donner la sérénade. J'avais beau verser des torrents de larmes, ces cœurs endurcis continuaient, impitoyables, en se tordant de rire. (Rey 19)

These insidious displays of common incivility escalate to verbal intimidation and other threatening acts, shouts and insults, angry faces and shaken fists, eventually leading to direct physical attacks that first foreshadow and then echo the violent attacks perpetrated by both sides during the war. The mounting climate of violence that precipitates the young woman's political radicalization is a direct consequence of her community's feeling of abandonment by the Motherland ("mère-patrie"):

> Cette guerre qui nous broyait depuis six ans et demi, ce n'était pas nous qui l'avions voulue. Nous n'avions pas non plus demandé à notre Patrie de nous trahir, ni encore moins à l'armée française de nous combattre comme des criminels. On nous attaquait de toutes parts et la défense de notre terre apparaissait comme un devoir sacré. Cette lutte ne pouvait se passer de meurtres. Pour la plupart, nous étions incapables de nous livrer à cette terrifiante forme de combat, mais tous l'approuvaient, moi la première. (Rey 268)

The French officials' behavior is denounced as "ridiculous," a unilateral desertion by the forces of reason in the face of primitive savagery, a collective humiliation and an inexplicable abdication of a great country's rights afforded by its history and prestige: "Jamais, dans toute l'Histoire, jamais, on n'avait vu cela. Un chef d'État prestigieux ordonnait à ses troupes de ne plus se battre, de laisser commettre tous les crimes, sans intervenir" (Rey 268).

In this context, not only does the memoirist refuse to conceal her former support for the Organisation Armée Secrète, she further reaffirms it in the present of her writing by endorsing the organization's message and actions as "the flicker of hope" for those ready to sacrifice themselves for the famous slogan: "Algérie française ou mourir." The patriotism of the Pieds-noirs is all the more manifest as both officials and the metropolitan population are perceived to be indifferent, defeatist or oblivious of the national values promoted theretofore in the colonial enterprise. Maintaining the French presence in Algeria is motivated not by a selfish desire but by patriotic altruism: "Nous garderions l'Algérie à la France! Pour la France, bien plus que pour nous-mêmes! [...] Que deviendrait-elle sans l'Algérie? Une médiocre, une très médiocre chose." The embattled community takes it upon itself to protect the essence of its nation and to restore it to its past greatness: "Mériterait-elle alors le nom de Patrie? Et comment, comment, vivre sans patrie?" (Rey 268).

Yet the most effective strategy, because it operates on a common-sensical, emotional level to which any reader can relate, is the use of anecdotes that cast the OAS members in the role of guardians of civility. The organization and its sympathizers collect funds, extend their protection to people in danger from either militant Algerians or French law forces and provide financial support for victims' families. Rey conveys their message when she ends an argument with the proclamation: "Tout le monde a le droit de parler, à condition d'être poli" (Rey 272). These moments are the most effective because they represent a very subtle affirmation of the French norms of civilized behavior (being polite in disagreement or using reason instead of brute force). Moreover, Rey's memoir sets up an antithesis between the surrounding incivility and violence, on the one hand, and the narrator's contained reactions despite her inner turmoil, on the other. In one instance, the memoirist recalls her unuttered insults brought on by a feeling of "ferocious hatred" for a screaming Algerian women pursued by OAS armed assailants: "Sale fellaghate! Va te faire tuer ailleurs!" Her thoughts are nonetheless transcribed in order to stand in contrast with the threatening words shouted by French policemen in a scene where the "boys" of the OAS shoot and kill an Algerian man in the street while Marie-Jeanne and her husband are allowed to pass unharmed. Afterwards, when the police arrive to investigate, their brutal words – "Rentre salope! Rentre ou je te descends!" – shock the woman, who, after a moment's hesitation, decides to disobey the order and to display her resistance in the name of self-respect and civility: "Si je rentre maintenant, je perds ma propre estime" (Rey 293). This leads to what could have been a tragic event as one of the policemen points his machine gun at her, ready to shoot. She is saved, *in extremis*, by the dramatic intervention of her younger sister, who pulls her back into the house, only to be rewarded with a slap. This episode demonstrates that public incivility is the gateway to violence and fear, which in turn generate more incivility in the private sphere.

The scene exemplifies another dimension of self-memorialization highlighted in Walder's essay: whereas nostalgia is defined as a sentimental longing or wistful affection for the past, usually a period or place associated with happiness and security, in the colonial context of "re-membered, or recreated identities" shaped by "the many migrations – voluntary or enforced – of empire and its aftermath," self-affection is often accompanied by blindness toward others' past suffering (Walder 49). While Rey strives to reaffirm and illustrate the French presence in North Africa as a vector of civilization and social progress, especially in children's education and women's rights, indigenous characters are often cast in ambiguous roles, particularly in the moments when ideology takes a back seat to emotion. In an early scene of her coming-of-age tale, the narrator describes her grandfather's blind friend, Hamou, whose daily visits fill the young girl with a mixed sense of fascination and revulsion: "une immense silhouette [...] une gandourah douteuse recouverte d'un large bournous, montagne crasseuse surmontée d'une face imposante [...] Des traits du visage, je n'ai gardé aucun souvenir, sans doute à cause de la fascination mêlée de répulsion que provoquait le regard blanc et vide. C'était Hamou l'aveugle, ami de Grand-père" (Rey 17). Afterwards, Marie-Jeanne tries to fulfill her secular apostolate as a teacher in an Algerian school in the "haute Casbah, quartier misérable" (Rey 101), with classes overpopulated by flea-ridden, violent and ignorant children of refugees. As the war rages on, she is openly confronted by a student, Saïd, whose somewhat unsettling physical portrait – "[il] avait une grande bouche, toujours largement fendue en un sourire gouailleur et des yeux rusés" – portends a dark moral makeup. One day, after his teacher gives him "sa fessée quotidienne," he avenges his humiliation with a veiled threat, telling her that the French soldiers in the Zoauves regiment befriended him:

> Le lendemain Saïd posa sa "preuve" sur mon bureau d'un air vainqueur. C'était un petit journal militaire édité par les Zouaves. En plein milieu de la première page, la photographie de mon Saïd, avec son sourire coquin.
>      Le gamin me fixait, bombant le torse. Je lus alors la légende: "Sous le sourire des enfants perce déjà le rictus du voyou." (Rey 105)

To counteract these conflictual encounters, the memoirist depicts scenes of peaceful coexistence with Algerian neighbors, acquaintances and even strangers. Such is the case of Marie-Jeanne's spontaneous gesture of fraternization during a political meeting when she, transported by their shared passion for the French–Algerian cause, takes the hand of the man sitting next to her, a "Mozabite vêtu du traditionnel costume à large pantalon plissé" (Rey 159). However, the narrative stages these instances of social harmony in a counterpuntal structure as if to underscore their fragile and precarious nature. Under the growing threat of the Algerian FLN (Front de Libération Nationale), whose combatants are a faceless yet ubiquitous presence "brandissant des couteaux, des barres de fer, des haches, et de nombreux pistolets" (Rey 222), the last pieces of the social fabric holding together colonial society are torn up by bloodshed among natives. In Rey's narrative, the killing of the Harkis offers the ultimate proof of the senselessness characterizing the Algerian claims to independence: "On profita de l'opportunité pour se débarrasser des Musulmans trop francophiles, une trentaine d'égorgés et d'autres tués par armes à feu" (Rey 223).

Despite a number of publications whose authors sought, as the war drew to its inevitable conclusion, to bring attention to the tenuous status of the Algerians enlisted in the French auxiliary forces and to highlight the government's responsibility toward them, such as the journal *Les Cahiers libres*'s special issue "Les Harkis à Paris," edited by Paulette Péju in 1961, and Pierre Vidal-Naquet's article "La guerre révolutionnaire et la tragédie des harkis," which came out in *Le Monde* the following year (Brun and Penot-Lacassagne 221–222), the Harkis have never enjoyed a great deal of public or academic attention. Thus, in the Pieds-noirs' pedagogical and memorial literature they are cast as the forsaken and forgotten children of France, the innocent victims of a senseless conflict whose silent suffering mirrors that of the Pieds-noirs themselves, while also offering the latter group an opportunity for endorsing an altruistic cause. Even though in post-war France the Algerian refugees will be relegated to a politically and socially marginalized place, this situation can be perceived either as an improvement on their former colonial status, which the majority of them shared with all Algerians, as imperial subjects or potential citizens with limited rights, or even as a life-saving solution in contrast with their untenable political situation in Algeria, where they were branded as traitors and often condemnded to random reprisals or state prosecution following France's defeat.

In Fatima Besnaci-Lancou's autobiography *Fille de harki*, one finds a project akin to Marie-Jeanne Rey's, although, considering its more limited length and scope, I would term it a personal testimonial rather than a memoir. Her autobiographical project was prompted by the controversial statement of the Algerian president, Abdelaziz Bouteflika, during his visit to Paris in June 2000: "the conditions are not yet favorable for the Harkis to visit Algeria" (Besnaci-Lancou 11). The foreword by the editors, whose intent to instrumentalize the text is made clear in the pathos-filled subtitle: "Le bouleversant témoignage d'une enfant de la guerre d'Algérie," speaks of "martyrdom," while the author herself prefaces her life story with reflections on the "burden of guilt" carried by those who tragically came out of the confrontation as traitors to both sides. Although as a child she was unable to fathom the complex ramifications of her community's compromised situation, she did internalize the "sentiment douloureux" of their abandonment by the French. Since their fathers and brothers were treated as a band of thieves, "des bandits," by the French authorities in full retreat from the lost colony, their families experienced the hurt, shame and stigma in indirect but pervasive and insidious ways. Adding to the lasting feeling of unfairness, the daily lives of women and children were defined by the men's often random, even "absurd" affiliation to the French military auxiliaries. In a striking similarity to Rey's memoir, Besnaci-Lancou emphasizes the arbitrariness of most Algerians' political positioning during the war: whether they were on the side of the FLN revolutionary "maquis" or the French army was not so much a matter of deliberate choice or political conviction as an inevitable association with the least dangerous camp. They are the puppets of history whose true agency lies elsewhere, with political and military leaders, either anonymous and ominous entities acting in the shadows (as is the case of the FLN "fellaghas") or great public icons who embody the promise of safety but also the threat of rejection (President De Gaulle). Consequently, in both the monumental memoir and the personal testimonial, dates are highly symbolic, as they bring about a rupture in historical time with lasting consequences for lived time: for instance, October 17, 1961 for the Chibanis; March 19, 1962 for the Harkis; March 26, 1962 for the Pieds-noirs.[6] Yet, they are ultimately meaningless, indicating a mere exchange of political labels, revealing opportunism on the part of some and sheer haplessness for others. For the "Harki's daughter," war leads to the definitive demise of pre-colonial customs and social rules, of all the traditional "civilizing" restraints (where the term is used in the sense given by Norbert Elias in his study of the civilizing process[7]) left relatively unchanged by the French "civilizing" policies (where the same word is contaminated by the colonial ideology famously illustrated by Jules Ferry's political speeches). Among these one finds references to the preeminence of elders, forms of ethnic and religious authority, particularly at the local level, the precedence of family ties over political allegiances and women's rights in the private and communal sphere.

Written on behalf of the Harki community, the book engages with the inequalities of French rule in Algeria predicated on political separation between republican citizens and imperial subjects as well as social segregation reflected by the two-tier employment scheme. Furthermore, Besnaci-Lancou's narrative is punctuated with references to daily acts of humiliation, practiced even in institutions charged with carrying out the ideology of assimilation. One such example is an unsettling memory that depicts Algerian schoolgirls being required to show their underwear to the teacher daily before class so that she can ascertain their level of hygiene. Relegation to a medicalized category as such separates the individual from the social body and causes her to experience what Gilroy calls "the compression of time," which "makes the immigrants always seem to be stuck in the present. Devoid of historicity, their immediate circumstances are invested with an incontrovertible priority" (Gilroy 123). As the constant focus of a whole host of issues, such as hygiene, education, language proficiency, crime, unemployment, affordable housing and religion, immigrants and their offspring manifest an ever-present symptom of the lack of national homogeneity and social solidarity, which, in turn, prompts more debates on national identity and the failures of assimilation.

These painful memories notwithstanding, the narrator portrays the French presence in Algeria as the guarantor of safety and order, an external authority that allows life to continue even in the most distressing circumstances. Fatima's family endures endless upheavals due to fraternal rifts, as brothers and cousins are enlisted in different fighting camps, separation, as men of fighting age leave the household while women, children and the elderly are left to cope with the consequences of their political associations, and home displacement, as varied yet continuous threats force those left behind to flee the town and hide in the countryside. With the exception of French education, which governs the narrator's life story as a generational staple, French influence manifests itself rather distantly in her family's life, taking the form of a superimposed set of constraints and values that hem in everyday life without truly permeating it. Throughout the trying times of the war, the fabric of their life is weaved by house and land work, religious rites and immemorial customs, chief among which are the respect for traditional social hierarchy and storytelling.

Despite the haunting presence of the past in Harki literature, which has been the subject of several studies in recent years (Ireland 2013; Moser 2014), Besnaci-Lancou's narrative seeks to provide an example of successful integration in French society. Seemingly insurmountable obstacles hinder her progress: the anxious wait in the Béni-Messous military camp, to which her family is whisked away after the fateful day of March 19, 1962; trying times in the Rivesaltes relocation camp, formerly used by the Vichy regime as a Jewish detention center in France; the complete lack of professional opportunities afforded to her parents, whose immigrant status places them on the outer fringes of the workforce; and restrictive state policies along with discriminatory social behaviors. These limitations notwithstanding, some of Besnaci-Lancou's personal achievements are highlighted in order to bolster her argument, including her ability to overcome cultural differences and political prejudice in the Hexagon, her marriage to a French man and her professional accomplishments as she completes her MA degree and becomes the CEO of a medical publishing house. Hers is, in fact, a two-edged story, much as Marie-Jeanne Rey's was: it represents an indictment of those held responsible for wartime violence and the postwar distortions of a mortified memory, paralyzed in its own primal scene and unable to acknowledge other forms of rememoration, but also an exculpation of those who were wrongly accused and ultimately revealed to be victims. Time's passing and France's willingness to forget enable the progressive erasure of political differences – in other words, the "blurring of [the] boundaries between perpetratos and victims" (Eldrige 123) – while also hampering the individuals' successful social integration. Working against the modern strategies of "a history that is constituted by the way it disappears from consciousness, that eludes or erases memory in the very act of creating new events" (Caruth xii) and "emerges as the performance of its own disappearance" (Caruth xii), these memorial projects resist erasure and forgetting on behalf of communities that reject the mainstream strategies employed to deny injustices, ignore suffering and renounce accountability. Yet Rey's lengthy memoir and Besnaci-Lancou's short testimonial narrative engage in a form of "conflictive memory work" that "does not facilitate working through, but slows it down, and turns reenactment into a compulsive practice" (Robben 127).

## Notes

1 Article by Robert Lacoste, *Le Bled*, no. 66, June 8, 1957, in Calmein and Lacoste-Adrover 11.

2 The Harkis seem to have scored a symbolic victory in François Hollande's public statement delivered on the national day of Harki commemoration, September 25, 2016. On behalf of the French government, the President recognized, in highly problematic terms, the group's "abandonment" after the Évian agreements and "the French Muslims's sacrifice" for "our freedom and our flag." http://www.lemonde.fr/politique/article/2016/09/25/francois-hollande-reconnait-la-responsabilite-des-gouvernements-francais-dans-l-abandon-des-harkis_5003061_823448.html (accessed February 20, 2017).

3 Jean Amrouche, "Pour un dialogue entre Algériens et Français", *France-Observateur*, 16 janvier 1958 (Brun and Penot-Lacassagne 14).

4 *Le Livre interdit. Livre blanc, Alger, le 26 mars 1962*, Freidberg/Bayern: Atlantis, 2000 [1962, 1991]; Francine Dessaigne and Marie-Jeanne Rey, *Un crime sans assassins: Alger, 26 mars 1962*.

5 Pierre Albin Martel, *Le Monde*, 2 novembre 1954, in Stora 1991, 14.

6 On October 17, 1961 Algerians working in France conducted a protest in Paris against a curfew ordinance clash with police, which resulted in a large yet indeterminate number of casualties, as the press and the public were left to speculate without an official and reliable police report. The subsequent retrieval of several bodies from the Seine escalated the climate of suspicion and anger around this tragic event. On March 19, 1962 the ceasefire signaled the beginning of the negotiations leading to the Evian treaty, which left Harkis in a tenuous and increasingly dangerous position. March 26, 1962 marks the date of the shooting of the rue d'Isly, in Algiers, that occured in the context of a Pieds-noirs protest against the Évian treaty.

7 See chapters 2 and 3 of Norbert Elias's *The History of Manners*, vols I–II, tr. Edmun Jephcott, New York: Pantheon Books, 1978 for his study of shame, repugnance and pacification.

# CHAPTER SIX

# A Place of Dialogue

Buffeted between "inside" and "outside," between the desire to return to the origin and the acute consciousness of foreignness, diasporic imagination is often cast as a yearning for one's "native land" based on a "[m]utual imbrication rather than clear opposition between a desire for roots and an embrace of diasporic existence" (Hirsch and Miller 2). However, Hirsch and Miller dispute the mythifying inscription of the diasporic self, committing instead to "contingent, ambiguous definitions of self" (Hirsch and Miller 4). To emphasize the specificity of their new paradigm of memorialization and self-writing, Hirsch puts forward the concept of "post-memory," while Miller develops the idea of "transpersonal" experience, which circumscribes "a zone of relation that is social, affective, material, and inevitably public" (Hirsch and Miller 5). The motivation behind this memorial model is to "shift the focus from *diaspora* to *return*," where the term "return" is redefined as a state between "*routes*" and "*roots*" (Hirsch and Miller 6), between errantry and rootedness (what Glissant calls "enracinement"), loss and recovery.

Insofar as it describes the current memorialization of French Algeria, the model proffered by Hirsch and Miller invites a closer examination of the dynamics of knowledge and ignorance, certainty and doubt, as they are shaped by the desire to know and the fear of the unknown with regard to the individual and collective past.

## I Do Not Speak – the Limits of Knowledge and the Possibility of Dialogue

The ambiguous relationship between knowledge and ignorance is central to the works of Leïla Sebbar, an established French writer born in the Oran region of French and Algerian parents. Her mixed lineage, reflected in her own fiction and autobiographical writing, indicates a level of personal investment in the memorialization of French Algeria akin to that of Rey or Besnaci-Lancou. Sebbar's style claims its dual French and Algerian kinship, displaying both the Orientalist opulence of the sentence and the crude lyricism of the "beur" slang, confronting clashing cultures and discordant memories. Moreover, in her personal testimonies she underscores the latent but ever-present and potentially deadly struggle that characterized her own upbringing as a child of French and Algerian parents growing up in the colony: "Je recherche, je crois, ce que j'ai aperçu dans l'enfance algérienne, coloniale et qui m'a troublée, jusqu'à toujours l'écrire, le croisement fécond ou meurtrier de l'étranger avec l'étranger."[1] On the one hand, the author of *La Seine était rouge. Paris, Octobre 1961* relentlessly questions the issues of identity, memory, exile, the return to her origins and colonial as well as postcolonial violence. On the other hand, Sebbar refuses to be enrolled in an ideological camp or associated with a political agenda, even as she engages with the linguistic and cultural breach separating the first generation of Algerians living in France and their "Beur" children in *Parle, mon fils, parle à ta mère* or takes on, as in *Les Femmes au bain*, the place of Muslim women in Algerian society. Instead of transcribing history or mining the archives in search of a truth both factual and emotional, Sebbar favors a poetics of evocation in which the past is revisited in fantasmatic and, sometimes, hallucinatory forms. In the autobiographical narrative *Je ne parle pas la langue de mon père*, the combination of historical details and hypothesis born of ignorance, personal recollection and historical testimony generates a sense of the past not as it was but as it *could* or *should* have been:

> Je ne comprenais pas la langue de mon père, je l'entendais, dépourvue de sens, et je savais, à la voix, que mon père n'avait rien à craindre, au moment même où, peut-être, ces hommes des maisons pauvres lui apprenaient que l'OAS sillonnait les quartiers arabes pour accomplir les missions de l'honneur dont ses membres étaient chargés, les plus enragés, ceux qui ne se trompaient pas de cible, les Arabes de la liste, et si possible les autres, en plus, pour la cause. Mon père riait, en arabe, avec des hommes inconnus. Ce qu'ils se racontaient les faisait rire, je ne savais pas, je ne saurai pas ce qu'ils se disaient alors [...]. Les femmes se parlaient dans le soir, fort, toujours. Je les entendais. (Sebbar 2003, 19)

Sebbar's memorial writing contains within it its own ghost without trying to dismiss it through an epic gesture, such as the deliverance of a great narrative or the definition of its meaning through verifiable facts or an ultimate cathartic revelation. In this respect, Sebbar's *Je ne parle pas la langue de mon père* bears a number of similarities with *Si près* by Hélène Cixous (2007). Cixous's book is a travelogue, a "non-return narrative" (Hubbell 2012, 73) undertaken by the Jewish–French author whose childhood, like that of her friend Jacques Derrida, who appears as a spectral interlocutor in Cixous's work and protagonist of his own visual non-return to Algeria in the short film *D'ailleurs, Derrida* (co-authored with Saafa Fathy in 1999), was forever marked by life in Algeria under the Vichy Régime. The impossible task of recovering a past that irrupted into her writing after years of absence (which also provides the topic of her 2000 book, *La Rêveries de la femme sauvage. Scènes primitives*) is spelled out from the very beginning of the travelogue, as the writer admits defeat "à faire obstacle à l'entrée de la Chose Algérie dans ses livres" (Cixous 2007, 19). However, even though Cixous sets out on her trip back to Oran, "la ville de mémoire," where she is to visit her father's grave, the closeness announced in the title is, and can only be, hypothetical and ultimately ghostly, as the traveler emphasizes her non-belonging in a country where she never felt at home and yet the memory of which she wishes to preserve untainted by the experience of the return: "J'ai voulu arriver en Algérie, [...] mais c'était impossible. Si bien que j'ai atteint l'impossibilité, et cela sans l'avoir calculé. Aujourd'hui comment ne pas m'en réjouir ? *Atteindre l'impossibilité* n'est ni un but, ni une possibilité, c'est une impossibilité délivrée en notre absence" (Cixous 2007, 18). If the original intention of the narrator as she undertakes the trip is to recover her "algériance" (Cixous 2007, 21), the book itself bears testimony to the impossibility of turning Algeria – a resisting subject, with its own agency – into a narrative object: "je ne suis pas en train d'écrire le Livre-que-je-n'écris-pas et que je n'écrirai jamais [...] je crains d'être repoussée de ce volume par un force secrète venue du Sujet" (Cixous 2007, 40). Instead, the narrative recapitulates the various instances of writerly loss into which the other loss, of the "Chose-Algérie," is absorbed:

> Le signe, je le reconnais: chaque fois que j'ai voulu écrire sur l'Algérie, il y a eu compulsion-disparition de mes premières pages de notes. Je le constate. Ce sont de petits événements mais affreux et doués de pouvoirs obsessionnels extraordinaires. 1) Je dispose des notes sur quelques pages. Elles sont d'une portée si profonde que, voyant déjà tout le livre, en germination, satisfaite, je me repose. 2) Le mardi les pages sont introuvables. 3) Dans une troisième partie je passe plusieurs jours à chercher des pages dont je sais par expérience qu'elles sont introuvables. 4) Au

lieu d'utiliser ces jours si précieux à écrire. 5) Je me rends folle et je suis traversée par la pensée que je suis en train de me suicider. 6) Ma fille me demande doucement au téléphone: tu les as retrouvées ? 7) Non, dis-je. Je n'y pense plus. (Cixous 2007, 40)

In *Specters of Marx* Jacques Derrida asks: "Qu'est-ce que suivre un fantôme? Et si cela revenait à être suivi par lui, toujours, persécutés par la chasse même que nous lui faisons?" (Derrida 1993, 31). In this much-discussed "hauntology," the present construed as an end-point in a teleological and elucidating version of history can never be reconciled with an unresolved and insolvent past in an open-ended interpretation of history. While Leïla Sebbar's works remind the present of its own disjointedness, they do not fall in with the literature of postcolonial haunting and self-victimization described by Michael O'Riley. They instead present the reader, in narrative or essayistic ways, with the same questions that O'Riley raises about Assia Djebar's later novels: "What if the active agent of the haunting becomes consumed with the memory of colonialism and abjection he or she transmits? What if he or she, or a significant number of formerly oppressed subjects, turn the repetition of the history of abjection into a politics of memory based upon the victim's position?" (O'Riley 8).

Sebbar's writing is neutral not in the sense of unfeeling or indifferent, but rather sensitive, without displays of emotion or affectation. Yet it is also attentive to the myriad manifestations of the world and it attends, in an almost phenomenological way, to its signifying potential. These traits are salient in *Je ne parle pas la langue de mon père*, where the duty to recreate the past compels the writer to retrace important moments of her family's life in Algeria while scrutinizing her own recollections in order to uncover the hidden truths and the shared secrets that held the family together but left a negative imprint on her memory. It is precisely the negativity, the absence, the lack of knowledge that anchors the memorial narrative. Further accentuating the dissonance between the subject and her object is the fact that a historical event, the war in Algeria, lies at the core of this personal journey. The rememorating subject's identity is defined by that which she does not know about her father's life as an Algerian schoolteacher, married to a French woman, living in colonial Algeria, and about his mother tongue, Arabic, which he never taught his daughter. Not-knowing becomes a leitmotiv that provides, in subtly varied ways, the *incipit* of each section of the narrative: "Mon père ne m'a jamais appris la langue de sa mère" (Sebbar 2003, 33), "Je n'ai pas parlé la langue d'Aïsha et de Fatima" (Sebbar 2003, 49), "Mon père ne m'a jamais appris la langue des femmes de son peuple" (Sebbar 2003, 59) and "Je n'ai pas appris la langue de mon père" (Sebbar 2003, 79). Each iteration widens the familial and communal circle while at the same time accentuating the distance between the subject and her kith and kin. While her autobiographical return to her childhood in wartime Algeria cannot mend the ties that were never formed, it revisits the world that gravitated around not-knowing with its complex relationships, its unspoken rules, its deadly secrets and its sobering lessons. Thus not-knowing does not denote mere ignorance, as it is pregnant with the awareness of what the subject has not been taught or has not learned. Sebbar's rememorating subject becomes an interpreter of a language not only of familiar yet foreign sounds but also of emotions, gestures and customs.

The unknowing interpreter becomes, in *Je ne parle pas la langue de mon père*, a defining figure for the postcolonial present's attempt to understand the colonial past. The subject's presence at a time when the war in Algeria was unfolding and in places touched by the traumatic effects of the war allows her to claim the privileged position of the witness, *testis*, yet her limited understanding precludes her from being an *istor* (Bouju 51–60), an eye-witness who can assume the function of the historian. Perhaps her resistance to becoming an eyewitness is the reason for the adult subject's decision not to learn her father's language, which would signify an attempt to recover the missing pieces of her memory or even to repent for her past ignorance. Instead, the book closes on a brief and poignant chapter that could be read as a prayer to not-knowing: "Je n'apprendrai pas la langue de mon père. // Je veux l'entendre, au hasard de mes pérégrinations. Entendre la voix de l'étranger bien aimé, la voix de la terre et du corps de mon père que j'écris dans la langue de ma mère" (Sebbar 2003, 125). The refusal is not a rejection of the country Sebbar left behind when her family moved to France or a sign of resentment for her father's land, but a catalyst of her work as a writer whose self-imposed duty is to fill "la citadelle de la langue de la mère" with the foreign sounds of the father's language.

Sebbar's and Cixous's texts present a hybrid case of memorial–testimonial writing, one that could be read alongside the production of their North African male counterparts such as Albert Memmi, Dris Chraïbi or Mouloud Feraoun as they support the move away from the restrictive and ethnographic deployment of postcolonial autobiography as "an interpretative lens or reading strategy" (Brozgal xiii) and toward a better understanding of the genre as a place of theoretical production.

Their writings carve out a generic and thematic median place between the monumental scope and pathos-filled tone of the former, whose goal is to transcend the individual, who is nonetheless at the center of an exemplary story, and the more intimate tone of the latter, where the individual testifies humbly on behalf of her community. Faced with the duty of "tuterappelles" (Cixous 2000, 16), the two writers recognize the phantasmagorical power of the process of remembering and, rather than suppressing it in order to foreground a narrative of elucidation, they amplify and deepen it:

> Je reconnais qu'une allégorie a depuis trente-cinq ans pris la place de l'Algérie dans ma tête. Et dès avant que l'allégorie se produise, je n'ai de mémoire que si profondément plantée dans les replis de ma chair, si gravée dans ma grotte personnelle, qu'il me semble, dès que je dis cette phrase, être dans l'Antiquité d'une fiction que j'invente et dont je suis l'invention. (Cixous 2007, 121)

The narratives previously discussed in this chapter were predicated on three objectives: first, the retrieval of forgotten or concealed information (names, events); second, the emphasis on the discrepancy between individual or communal experiences of history, on the one hand, and the collective or official inscription of the same events, with the ethical implication that the latter seeks to erase, conceal and forget traumatic events and forego responsibility, on the other; and, third, the call to restorative or corrective action (individual remembering or learning and collective acts such as the passing of laws or the establishment of memorial sites). Sebbar is the editor of *C'était leur France. En Algérie, avant l'independance*, which also features a text by Cixous entitled "L'Affrance," an occurrence far from singular given the long-standing relationship between the two writers (Sebbar included a text by Cixous in *Enfance algérienne*, another collected volume issued by Gallimard in 1999). Unlike the many pamphlets and memoirs self-published or printed by niche presses, this volume was issued by Gallimard in its "Témoins" series. The three similarities outlined previously notwithstanding, this volume is not predicated on sharing a communal experience through the transmission of individual stories. It contains short texts by twenty-five French-language writers, academics and journalists, journalists who are Pieds-noirs, Harkis and Algerian exiles of Jewish, Berber or *métis* descent, invited to share not their memories of "French Algeria," a political construct, but of "France in Algeria," a composite idea made up of psychological, social and cultural strands. Whereas the theme fits into the general memorial paradigm, the book's content indicates the intent to treat this topic as "remanence": that is, by acknowledging its continuation or permanence in present-day consciousness while presenting it as a multiplicity of dissimilar residues. Through discontinuity, fragmentation, polyvocality and juxtaposition, the collection allows for individual acts of recollection, where one's "search for truth" is not subsumed into a totalizing, narrative and ideological project.

One could speculate about whether these non-consensual forms of writing constitute an abdication of the duty of memory or, on the contrary, a return to civility through artistic creation envisioned as a space of dialogue. Sebbar's and Cixous's works are moved by the belief in the elucidative quality of writing, even as the object and the manner of their elucidation remain intensely singular.

### Note

1   "3 questions à Leïla Sebbar", *Harfang*, May 2004: 56–59, 56.

# An Unpayable Debt:
# For a Paracolonial Aesthetics

The issues of political responsibility, moral recognition and material reparation have come to the forefront of public attention several times in recent decades, spurred by a series of controversies surrounding legal intiatives and commemorative acts. Among these, one can list the 2001 "Taubira" law, recognizing the Atlantic slave trade and slavery as laws against humanity, the demands for colonial reparations made in 2003 by Haitian president Jean-Betrand Aristide, the 2004 and 2010 measures prohibiting, respectively, the ostentatious display of religious symbols and the concealment of the face in public places (interpreted as laws against the Islamic scarf), the 2005 law requiring high-school teachers to highlight the "positive role of the French presence abroad," the increased attention given to the lack of recognition and the adminis-trative mistreatment of indigenous soldiers who fought in the French army during the First and Second World Wars (such as the Senegalese sharpshooters), and the fiftieth anniversary of the end of the war in Algeria celebrated in 2012.

The topic of reparation has often been brought up in these debates, but, rather than serving to clarify matters, it has served as a catalyst for exposing their political and ideological ambivalence. Thus, the term has been used not only in a symbolic but also in a material sense to refer both to the gratitude that formerly colonized countries should display toward their colonizers and the latter's responsibility for the damage caused by their subjugation and exploitation of the former. Moral and pecuniary worth, market and symbolic value, sacrificial and civilizing ethics are thus inextricably entangled.The idea of colonial debt, innervated by the symbolism of recognition and reparation, exhibits a considerable degree of plasticity being associated with symbolic notions (moral and political) incompatible and incommensurable with a given monetary value, yet it persistently translates into the claim for material reparations that alone can express the historical and ethical enormity to which it refers. Moreover, the reversible nature of the concept proves a fertile ground for the literary imagination.

The political and literary genealogy of the colonial debt can hardly be overestimated. Originating in the messianic pathos that, in the nineteenth century, binds together the ideologies of nationalism, progress, vitalism and the civilizing mission, the relationship between France and its colonies is shaped, both implicitly and explicitly, by the rhetoric of public figures, especially writers and politicians such as Victor Hugo and Victor Schœlcher. A speech delivered by the Romantic poet at the opening of the 1849 Congrès de la Paix paints in hyperbolic terms the transformational effects of France's influence in the world:

> la face du monde serait changée. Les isthmes seraient coupés, les fleuves creusés, la marine marchande du globe aurait centuplé, [...] on creuserait des villes là où il n'y a encore que solitudes; on creuserait des ports là où il n'y a encore que des écueils; l'Asie serait rendue à la civilisation, l'Afrique serait rendue à l'homme. [...] Au lieu de faire des révolutions, on ferait des colonies ! Au lieu d'apporter la barbarie à la civilisation, on apporterait la civilisation à la barbarie. (Hugo I, 289)

The colonial entreprise involves nothing less than changing the face of the world: cutting new paths through land and sea, erecting cities in the desert, "returning" Asia to civilization and "Africa" to mankind. Conquest and construction appear as gestures of gift-giving, of bestowing material objects and lost values upon a world waiting to be both restored to an edenic state and led forward toward a promised future. This sets up a rhetorical duality relying simultaneously on instrumentalization and magnanimity. However, a hierarchy is subtly established that predicates the success of the latter upon the former. In the famous passage that rehearses the Hegelian argument about Africa's historical condition, Hugo's use of causative verbs highlights the passivity of the dark continent in the interaction with its munificent white counterpart: "L'Afrique n'a pas d'histoire; une sorte de légende vaste et obscure l'enveloppe. [...] Au XIX$^e$ siècle, le Blanc a fait du Noir un homme, au XX$^e$ siècle, l'Europe fera de l'Afrique un monde" (Hugo IV, 425).

One finds a similar emphasis on the emancipatory agency of the colonizer in the oratory work of Victor Schœlcher, the governor of Martinique tasked with delivering the good news of the abolition of slavery by the 1848 Republic. France appears not only as a liberating force, but also as a generous creditor who has agreed to buy out the Caribbean slaves from the plantation owners to whom they belong. Moreover, his speech draws a powerful parallel between the policies of the July Monarchy that stipulated the slaves' right to buy their freedom as individuals and the new regime's sweeping decision to buy them all out, one might say, "in bulk": "Louis-Philippe n'est plus roi! C'est lui qui enrayait votre libération, pace qu'il voulait que chacun de vous se rachetât, et la République au contraire va vous racheter tous à la fois" (Glissant 1997, 78).

In his analysis of Schœlcher's rhetoric, Édouard Glissant observes that its pecuniary overtones "légitime[nt] le principe de l'indemnisation." By recognizing the institution of slave ownership as an economic reality rather than dismissing it as a moral and political aberration, the messenger of the Republic thus announces to the future free citizens of French Antilles: "Vous étiez donc la propriété *légitime* de vos maîtres" (Glissant 1997, 74). Glissant's parenthetical comment – "(L'histoire se répète.)" – may point to the circularity of the Atlantic slave trade and the Republican liberation insofar as they belong to the same logic of capitalism, but it also applies to the colonial discourse of stewardship and obligation. In 1885, several decades after the abolition of slavery, as France is about to engage in an intense competition over new markets and new resources in Africa and Asia, Jules Ferry urges his peers in the Chamber to pursue this enterprise for economic as well as moral reasons: "Il faut dire ouvertement que les races supérieures ont un droit vis-à-vis des races inférieures. Je répète qu'il y a pour les races supérieures un droit, parce qu'il y a un devoir pour elles. Elles ont le devoir de civiliser les races inférieures."[1] The same subtle equation of natural rights and ethical duty underlies Léon Blum's account of the universalist and humanitarian dimensions of the colonial endeavor: "Nous admettons le droit et même le devoir des races supérieures d'attirer à elles celles qui ne sont pas parvenues au même degré de culture, et de les appeler aux progrès réalisés grâce aux efforts de la science et de l'industrie."[2] Achille Mbembe calls attention to the fundamental contradiction between care for a humanity in need of rescuing from its own abject condition and disdain for the very condition that justifies the caring intervention. These ideas are often invoked together by the champions of "l'art de coloniser" (Mbembe 2000, 55), such as Maurice Delafosse and Albert Sarraute, in support of their policies: "Le potentat colonial s'offre [...] comme une donation libre qui se propose de soulager son objet de ses misères et de l'affranchir de sa condition d'avilissement en le relevant au rang d'un être humain" (Mbembe 2000, 57).

In *Morning Yet on Creation Day*, the Nigerian writer Chinua Achebe quotes *Prester John* by Johns Buchanan, a classic of British colonial literature that captured the imagination of generations in the first half of the twentieth century, which rehearses Kipling's "white man's burden": "That is the difference between white and black, the gift or responsibility, the power of being in a little way a king, and so long as we know and practice it we will rule not in Africa alone but wherever there are dark men who live only for their bellies" (Achebe 114). Such is the white man's burden: giving the colonial gift means contracting an unpayable and reversible debt. Unpayable because, as a gesture ruled by the principles of *potlach*, it can never be fully acknowledged and repaid by its recipient; reversible because, as its circular and open rhetoric prefigures, the donation requires some form of recognition, through recompense – that "inferior races" show their gratitude for the gift of civilization – or equivalence – that they follow the path opened by the civilizing mission to raise themselves above their pre-colonial condition. These notions inform, to various degrees, the discourse of colonialism; their plasticity allows them to be used in conservative and religious as well as progressive and secular ideologies. Furthermore, they permeate postcolonial discourses of emancipation (the reciprocity underscored by headings such as the empire writes back, thinks back, eats back...) that maintain the relationship with the colonizer in order to reject, contest or subvert it. In his work, the Congolese scholar Désiré Kazadi Wa Kabwe shows the ideological and symbolic function of the discourse of colonial debt in the construction of postcolonial African identity. He examines, for instance, the novel *La Dette coloniale*, by Zaïre-born writer Maguy Kabamba,[3] in which the experience of postcolonial immigration between Africa, France and Canada mirrors the triangular Atlantic slave trade of the colonial era. Nonetheless, the difficulty of formulating in precise terms the claims for reparation (should they be legal, moral or monetary, and who should participate in this process?) is further complicated in the doubly troubled context determined by "des relations inégales entre les ex-métropoles et les nouveaux pouvoirs postcoloniaux," on the one hand, and "des indépendances africaines, caractérisées par le durcissement des régimes militaires qui confisquent les libertés fondamentales," on the other (Kazadi Wa Kabwe 141). The consequences of this ambiguity play out in the social and political arena, where they generate behaviors that may appear "irrational" or "bipolar" to the external observer. Immigrants find themselves isolated in their new countries by their posture of unassimilable exiles suffering from depression or madness, while, in the former colonies, the phrase "payer la dette du peuple" is brandished by representatives of new regimes as a means of legitimizing their populist agendas and predatory actions.

However, Susan Buck-Morss's work illustrates how the reversibility of the colonial debt can become a productive conceptual instrument. In her examination of the historical and intellectual roots of Hegel's Master–Slave dialectics she contends that this was not only coeval with the events of the Haitian revolution but also, and more importantly, influenced by them. In turning anticolonial struggle into the *explanans* of Hegelian thought instead of its *explanandum*, as has so often been the case, Buck-Morss's approach goes beyond the postcolonial *doxa* of resistance or subversion to the very heart of colonial genealogy. To paraphrase David Scott's formula, it is important to acknowledge that the vector of history runs both ways.[4]

In their writings, Lyonel Trouillot, Régis Jauffret and Léonora Miano ponder, probe and reimagine the contradictory connotations of colonial debt. I contend that the texts in which issues of political, moral and cultural debt are most effectively addressed turn away from the dominant models of storytelling (such as the third-person *Bildungsroman* or autobiographical fiction), espousing instead hybrid or parasitic forms such as the lyrical and dramatic narrative, the short story or the essay. These texts reveal that at the heart of the discourse of the colonial debt lies a phenomenon described by Éric Méchoulan as "le *désir de la médiation* – et [...] *l'oubli de l'immédiateté*" (Méchoulan 102).

## Postcolonial Failure between Neoliberal Economics and Moral Bankruptcy

In Lyonel Trouillot's *La Parabole du failli* Pedro, a young Haitian actor, commits suicide by jumping off the twelfth floor of a modern building in a European metropolis. His life is recounted by one of his best friends in a second-person narrative striated by multi-perspectival stories and poetry quotations, intense dialogue and philosophical reflection. The discourse of History is disrupted, as is the story-oriented novelistic structure. Instead of engaging in what Yves Citton calls scenario-writing ("activité de scénarisation") (Citton 2010a, 65–90), Trouillot shapes the emotional, ideological and political substance of his text in a series of intermittent yet interwoven fragments that diffract rather than connect the different facets of the absent hero's life. By intercalating monologues and dialogues with verse and stream-of-consciousness discourse, *La Parabole du failli* resists what C. Salmon calls the New Narrative Order (in French, NON) "qui preside au formatage des désirs et à la propagation des émotions" (Citton 2010a, 66) in the neoliberal age. These discursive suspensions and narrative disruptions transform the story of Pedro's victimization as a despondent and eventually suicidal young Haitian artist into a meditation on value, debt and poverty:

> Oui, le jour où tu t'es jeté du douzième étage de cet immeuble d'une grande ville l'Estropié et moi nous étions occupés à faire nos calculs de parias: le riz, le rhum, la décharge, des cigarettes au détail et quelques pièces en plus, de la petite monnaie pour la folle et les enfants abandonnés qui ne manqueraient pas de nous solliciter. (Trouillot 28)

The text carves out a triangular space for its departed protagonist between the rememoration of the facts that formed his life, the memory of the artworks that informed his own creation and, at its apex, money as it relates to the value of both life and art. The tenuous plotline revolves around the lack of money, an economic state affecting Pedro and his friends – poor Haitian artists – to a degree so fundamental that it acquires the status of an ontological condition. Translated into the vocabulary of capital and possession, human life becomes both a highly valued resource and disposable waste in the terms theorized by Zygmunt Bauman. Pedro's struggle to run his theater company despite the lack of funds underscores the connection between economic and political discrimination during his theater troop's French tour. The second-person description of the Haitian actor's experience in France performs a critique of everyday neocolonial racism and bureaucratic anti-immigration policies in which money is but one in a series of stereotypes (accented language, sexual prowess) used simultaneously as signs of distinction and exclusion:

> Et tu as joué les impresarios et les producteurs, le public rare dans la petite salle municipale, la vieille dame raciste et débonnaire qui appréciait cet accent venu d'ailleurs: *"le parfum d'exotisme qui embellit la langue"*, la jeune femme qui avait frappé à la porte d'un comédien pour vérifier si les Noirs l'ont vraiment plus grosse que les Blancs, et la première personne qui t'avait adressé la parole à ta descente de l'avion, la femme en uniforme de la police des frontières qui t'a posé les questions de routine: "Montrez-moi votre réservation d'hôtel ou votre

lettre d'hébergement. Vous disposez de combien d'argent pour votre séjour? [...]." (Trouillot 138)

M^me Armand, the generous money-lender, an oxymoronic character who is both greedy and prodigal, cold and maternal, embodies both capitalist greed and postcolonial solidarity with the disenfranchised while reflecting the disparity between the excessive accumulation of wealth and the scarcity of feeling. By refusing to engage with her clients' justificatory storytelling, she rejects the postcolonial humanitarian *ethos* and exhibits instead the blunt logic of exchange:

> ce que disent les gens qui viennent chez elle lui emprunter de l'argent, mis à part le montant, les gages et les traites, elle n'y accorde nulle importance: "Dis-moi juste combien il te faut. Le reste, les causes et motifs, les pourquoi, les parce que, inductions, déductions, garde-le pour les imbéciles. Épargne-moi les exposés. Indique-moi juste le montant ... ." (Trouillot 48)

Her disenchantment, captured in her signature phrase "je n'aime rien," is an interiorization of the cacophony of human experiences gathered in the capharnaum upon which she reigns. Moreover, from the perspective of her unfortunate clients and protégés, her wealth is to be both coveted as the mirror of a forbidden world and feared as a *memento* of the human vanities: "Les objets accumulés dans son rez-de-chaussée, ce n'est pas seulement une immense fortune, plus d'argent qu'une femme n'en peut dépenser durant toute une vie. C'est aussi une bibliothèque, un musée des horreurs, toutes les preuves de leurs défauts et appétits laissées par ses clients" (Trouillot 47). Yet, it is the money-lender's indifference to the narrative undertow of her trade that leads her to become the group's unlikely benefactress. Despite her protestations, in encountering Pedro and his friends she comes face-to-face with her reversed mirror image, which triggers in her the need to give without a guarantee or an expectation of receiving anything in return. Their indigence transcends any and all material need and is matched only by their disinterest or "lack of project" for the source of their livelihood:

> Nous avions bu le café puis elle nous a donné de l'argent en disant: "Ne revenez jamais." Le lendemain, nous y sommes retournés et elle nous a encore donné de l'argent en disant: "Ne revenez jamais. Moi, les garçons, je n'aime rien. Et comme je vous vois là si je vous prête de l'argent avec quoi vous allez me le rendre?" Nous n'avions nul désir de lui emprunter de l'argent. Nous n'avions rien à lui laisser comme garantie. Et nous ne nourrissions aucun projet. C'était son choix de nous donner de l'argent,

dont nous avions besoin et pas besoin. Nous en avions besoin pour les choses courantes, et nous n'en avions pas besoin, nous contentant de faire avec les mêmes choses courantes, juste un peu plus. C'était un jeu. [...] Voilà comment Madame Armand est devenue notre mécène. (Trouillot 48–49)

Refusing to surrender to the capitalist imperative of work for consumption as the central value of individual worth and social life, Pedro and his friends are forced to live on the economic fringes of society. Yet they do more than merely inhabit the margins where countless people try to survive and make ends meet. L'Estropié, who is identified only by his surname, "the cripple," remembers Pedro's efforts to create a book collection destined to be open as a free library to all children in his neighborhood:

Sa collection, il l'a payée avec ses économies et la garde dans l'idée de créer un jour une bibliothèque qui fonctionnerait un peu comme une cantine populaire dans ce quartier pourri de Saint-Antoine. [...] Sa collection, c'est son trésor, son cadeau aux enfants de ce quartier où personne ne donne rien à personne. (Trouillot 92)

The generosity of the artist marks a singular and desperate attempt to counterbalance the dismal state of the schools in which teachers, students and parents are all prisoners of a system ruled by poverty and corruption:

La direction de l'établissement paie les maîtres avec des semaines de retard, le temps de forcer les élèves à convaincre leurs parents de verser une partie de la somme due pour les frais de scolarité. Une partie, en espérant que le restant sera versé à la fin de l'année scolaire, sans quoi l'élève n'aura pas le droit au dernier bulletin, le plus important, qui atteste sa réussite. (Trouillot 158)

Disheartened by the lack of prospects in a dysfunctional society plagued at every level by a circular logic that turns institutions against individuals and individuals against one another, Pedro also reveals his desire to forsake his native land for a better life elsewhere:

"Tu comprends? Quand on a la chance de sortir, il ne faut pas revenir. Pourquoi revenir? Pour voir que la poussière a augmenté, que le chômage a augmenté, que les prix des choses qu'on ne pouvait déjà pas s'acheter a augmenté [...] Elle [ma mère] apprécie le directeur de la troupe qui nous donne de l'argent de sa poche quand les choses vont vraiment très mal à la maison." (Trouillot 140–141)

This is indeed his ultimate choice, but one that proves fatal for the young artist, as leaving Haiti can only mean carrying the burden of its suffering without being able to alleviate it.

Between solidarity and despair, *La Parabole du failli* depicts humanity at odds with the terms of the narrative into which it is cast by the incongruous discourse of global aid and national responsibility, of postcolonial remorse and neoliberal development. Trouillot's book offers not a solution but an alternative to this nexus of contradictions, a way out – a walking away or a flying away from existing relations (Goh 166). Moreover, this emerges not from the narrative thread but from the writing itself, from its layered composition teeming with intertextual references in which Villon meets René Philoctète and Baudelaire dialogues with Pablo Neruda. Not only are Pedro's story and his art built on borrowed words, but they are others' words. Their foreignness or "étrangèreté" (Panaïté 2014, 797) and the text's debt to them is acknowledged both in italics in the text and in an index of works cited at the end of it. The Cripple warns him early on not to waste them: "Arrête de gaspiller les mots des autres" (Trouillot 96). Yet the one who quotes Anthony Phelps to express the incommensurable acts of creation and communication through a metaphor joining commerce and the cosmos – *"J'ai mis la voie lactée en vente pour un peu d'amour mais n'ai point trouvé d'acquéreur nul ne veut s'embarrasser de trente milliards d'étoiles"* (Trouillot 23) – also divests himself of any claims to authorship. The memorial chorus voices out an alternative to the circular logic of the market in proclaiming their friend's sacrifice, evanescent as it may be: "Dans l'amour, tu aimais le don. Tu as payé ce vœu de fausse chevalerie d'une chute de douze étages [...] L'Estropié à calculé que ton taux de présence dans la mémoire du monde suivra le tracé d'une courbe descendante' (Trouillot 158). The language of love and generosity is contiguous with the jargon of accounting and calculating, without nullifying each other. While Pedro's story fails to provide a redeeming lesson for physical survival or posthumous permanence, his anachronistic persona as suggested by the "vœu de fausse chevalerie" expression exudes "une odeur d'offrande sans sacrifice," to borrow a line from Lyonel Trouillot's collection of poems *Le Doux Parfum des temps à venir.*[5] Faced with the untenable situation of the colonial debt – that is, with the other's refusal to acknowledge its burden – Trouillot's character removes himself from the tyranny of the other's narrative. Already a social and historical reject, he disengages from the space of clashing subjectivities and becomes an active reject, claiming "the right to disappear" as a form of radical resistance against an unfair global system. While his radical act of self-annihilation can be read as a metaphor for Haiti's tragic condition and, more generally, for the condition to which former colonial countries have been condemned by the contemporary balance of power, it nevertheless constitutes a violent reminder that politics "must maintain every being's liberty to free itself from any present relation and to form new ones beyond the determination of politics" (Goh 166).

## The Paracolonial Fade-out

The very impossibility of turning away from the colonial debt without really facing it, but rather allowing it to subtend the writing, to irrigate the capillaries of fiction, is at work in *Microfictions*, by Régis Jauffret. The self-proclaimed novel represents a literary *tour de force* not only because of its thousand-page length but also because of its fragmented and fractal structure. The large edifice is composed of short and sometimes minuscule stories or anecdotes, most of which are bizarre, fantastical and even absurd, yet retain a strangely realistic quality. Through the lines of these would-be novels that refuse to deploy their epic folds one can catch glimpses of a present past, creating a technique that I propose to call the paracolonial fade-out. The first "microfiction," bearing the name of Albert Londres, the early twentieth-century pioneer of investigative journalism and acerbic critic of colonization, begins with the following passage:

> Nous avons filmé ces scènes de torture et de meurtre afin d'en dénoncer le caractère intolérable et la barbarie. Vous ne pouvez pas reprocher à une chaîne d'information de montrer la réalité. S'il est bien évident que nous blâmons leur conduite, nous devons aussi rendre hommage à ces tortionnaires de nous avoir permis d'apprécier à sa juste valeur le prix du bien-être et de la vie. Il est vrai que nous nous sommes rapprochés d'eux peu à peu. (Jauffret 11)

Thus the opening segment sets the tone for the entire book in two distinct ways: first, by transposing the sharp, critical tone of Londres's famous collection of articles, *Terre d'ébène*, into the context of today's audio-visual journalism; and, second, by subverting the very stance of "reportage" through the disparity between subject matter and its treatment. Following in the footsteps of their celebrated predecessor, today's journalists, identified only as an amalgamated "nous," approach a topic of the same magnitude as forced labor in colonial Senegal and the French Congo – that is, torture. Yet their humanitarian agenda is thwarted by the very means of representation, as they appear more concerned with delivering a spectacular version of reality according to the codes and expectations of the 24-hour news media and reality TV than with objectivity and truth. Moreover, so fascinated are the reporters with the subject of their investigation that they cross moral boundaries, humanizing and even lionizing the "tortionnaires" themselves. Translated into the language of the twenty-first century, the banality of evil truly becomes the ordinariness of evil, described in excruciating detail by a camera indifferent to the event it documents but interested in prolonging its unfolding as a valuable source of newsfeed. Rather than questioning in order to understand how the impossible becomes possible, how crimes against humanity can be perpetrated by seemingly ordinary human beings, the journalistic discourse uses its deontological rules to justify its lack of ethics. Thus, the collective voice does away with any concerns about the sensationalistic portrayal of female torture and the secrecy regarding the location of the site in brief and matter-of-fact terms. By invoking the politically correct fact that most of the crew is composed of women, which would exclude the possibility of any bias, and the journalists' rights to protect their sources under any circumstances, the heirs of Albert Londres prompt the reader and their fictional viewer to imagine what has remained of his legacy and, therefore, what the function and value of today's journalistic storytelling is in today's world.

Another example of paracolonial fade-out appears in the microfiction "Gagne-pain." Recounted by a man whose wife attempts to buy a child during a trip to Africa, the story refers to the incident in which the woman offers to purchase the child from his parents (thus equating it with the source of income in the section's title) casually, as a minor, if bothersome, detail of his domestic life: "À vingt-trois ans, j'ai épousé par intérêt une femme sans enfants, ménopausée depuis des lustres. [...] Lors d'un voyage en Afrique, elle s'est entichée d'un bébé dont la famille vivait dans une case que visitaient les touristes. Elle a voulu le négocier, mais le père s'est opposé à la vente" (Jauffret 285). Jauffret's style is rife with the traits of impassibility, ironic distance and autorial self-deprecation, which render the random allusions to neocolonialism both seamless within a larger aesthetic of sarcasm and striking because of the stark contrast between the book's general tone and the references to the mediatic spectacle of third-world poverty, the pervasiveness of "exotic" prostitution and the occasional racist and xenophobic remarks **k** proferred by characters and narrators.

## An Indivisible Legacy

If disappearing in Trouillot and fading out in Jauffret offer indirect and oblique forms of engaging with the colonial debt, Léonora Miano's insistence on "Afropean" amalgamation indicates the desire to move away from a hyphenated identitarian model. The Cameroonian writer lays claim to both African and European legacies and to their harrowing encounter. In her lectures and essays she deploys a set of arguments aimed at recovering the colonial, non-metropolitan and especially non-African dimensions of French history while refuting the nativist ideals espoused by the Négritude movement and the ideology of a return to the pre-colonial roots. Miano's fiction addresses in equal measure postcolonial alienation, peri-colonial contamination of African cultures by the early European presence and African responsibility for and participation in the slave trade. If, as Jean-Marc Moura contends, exoticism is the totality of the debt Europe has contracted with the other cultures (Moura 38), Miano's writing shows the inseparability of the contributions in creating contemporary Afropean culture. Miano focuses on music and food to buttress her argument on mutual acculturation and the irreversible effects of colonization. It also speaks to the paracolonial scope of creolization as it is powerfully redefined by Valérie Loichot through the lens of the culinary imagination: a "process: never a fixed product, never a stabilized recipe, but not a lawless chaos either" (Loichot 2013a, xxxii).

In *Soulfood équatoriale*, the writer focuses on social and commercial practices and traditions surrounding food, which allow her to retrace a tri-continental pattern of influence and circulation. As Sylvie Durmelat notes: "Food and foodways are a crucial addition to this list of elements of material culture in which imperial histories have 'crystallised'" (Durmelat 118). Moreover, while ingredients and dishes can be perceived as "lieux de mémoire," they remain sites of constant creation and reinvention. Miano approaches food as a unique cultural site where the past meets the present in living, evolving and multiple ways. This calls into question the national narrative and blurs the seemingly clear lines that define a country's or a continent's identity: "Les populations d'ascendance africaine ont donc métissé le contenu de leurs assiettes depuis des siècles, au point même, pour les Africains en particulier, de s'imaginer qu'ils se nourrissent comme le faisaient leurs ancêtres" (Miano 29). Similarly, the United States are the birthplace of *soul food*, not as the result of a political will for racial or cultural mixing but rather as a counter-effect of the slavery system: "La *soul food* prend donc ses racines dans la période de l'esclavage étasunien, en devenant un des tous premiers éléments de métissage entre des peuples appelés à vivre ensemble. De fait" (Miano 28). The last sentence, "in fact," is an ellipsis that could be interpreted as an emphasis on the actuality of the "métissage" while indicating by opposition to the phrase "de droit" ("by law"). Food confirms the reality of races living together that is not acknowledged by law. The Africans forcibly brought to the Southern plantations of the New World to serve the descendants of the English settlers use their native ingredients and culinary techniques to create dishes far superior to anything their new masters may have known. The telescopic summary of slavery, colonization and cuisine serves as both a necessary reminder of historical facts and a form of comic relief that dedramatizes their burden while underscoring their importance for the present: "On sait que les esclaves servant dans les maisons des planteurs du Sud apportèrent leur savoir-faire et leur plantes africaines sur la table. La descendance des colons anglais installés dans le Nouveau Monde ne s'en plaignit pas, tant elle était dépourvue de capacités culinaires, comme chacun le sait" (Miano 28). The argument reaches its ironic conclusion that turns the logic of the civilizing mission on its head: "Puisque cette civilisation est, d'après nous, surtout dans l'assiette, il n'est pas exagéré d'affirmer que les États-Unis doivent une partie de ce qu'ils ont de civilisation à cette cuisine imprégnée de l'Afrique" (Miano 28).

Still, the writer uses food to go against the grain of nativist or purist thinking that equates collective identity with certain ingredients, dishes and culinary practices. She calls into question the fact that, although "[e]ating, indeed, brings about commensality and exchanges," "it also contributes to the intimate construction of social and racial stratifications, ethnic delineations, gender differences, religious identities and national distinctions" (Durmelat 119). Manioc, for instance, has become an integral part and a symbol of African cuisine and culture: "Cet aliment s'est si bien intégré aux cultures afro-caribéennes, qui ont épuisé les manières de l'utiliser, que le simple fait de prétendre ne pas en manger devient synonyme de complexe de couleur" (Miano 30). However, its presence on the African continent is a product of colonial globalization subtended by layers of history that saw it arrive from South America aboard Portuguese slave ships during the sixteenth century. Miano stresses the random nature of the encounter to argue against any essentialist interpretation of food habits: "Pourtant, il n'y a pas de raison objective qu'un Africain aime le manioc, tubercule implanté en Afrique par les Portugais qui le firent venir d'Amazonie, par les navires destinés au commerce des esclaves" (Miano 30). The transformation of a foreign plant into a natural symbol for African taste occurred in spite of its somber history, serving as a reminder that forms of cultural mixing transcend racial divisions and national conflicts: "Il est très vite apparu à ceux qui le [*le manioc*] goutèrent les premiers qu'ils perdraient quelque chose à ne pas l'adopter. La tradition orale de nos peuples rapporte bien des histoires du temps jadis, mais aucune, cependant, où il soit question de tourner le dos aux aliments venus d'ailleurs" (Miano 31). The writer's interpretation suggests that food establishes an intimate relationship between the local and the global, the familiar and the foreign, governed by principles of openness and addition rather than closure and subtraction. Welcoming the strange and unknown in the kitchen and on the plate transforms border thinking into a truly creative activity.

### The Colonial Fortune from Colonial Debt to Paracolonial Aesthetics

Literary analysis or theoretical discussions may seem quite removed from the tragic urgency of the Black Lives Matter movement that originated in the US and has inspired similar actions elsewhere, from the UK to South Africa and Kenya, or from the divisive arguments around immigration in Europe and the US, or, yet again, from the revival in France of the debate over the *jus sanguinis* vs. *jus soli* meant to protect society against the "half-blood," the citizen who, never fully integrated, is destined to become the enemy within. Furthermore, given the current context of a "global civil war" in which "the state of exception tends increasingly to appear as the dominant paradigm of government" (Agamben 2), the individual who stands out because of the color of his skin, her garb, his way of praying or her accent can quickly devolve, as did the "public enemy" in ancient Rome, from a human who, even though he or she is not or no longer a citizen, still enjoys the protection of *ius gentium* (the law of the people or, in the current terminology, human rights) into a *hostis iudicatus* – that is, a suspect "radically deprived of any legal status [who] could therefore be stripped of his belongings and put to death at any moment" (Agamben 80). Literature and theory can shed light on the burdensome, incommensurable and indivisible colonial heritage that continues to shape our era's violent struggles, ideological incomprehensions and myopic or even catastrophic public policies. They can show that reckoning with irreconcilable visions of the past may lead to imagining a common future and they can call to a particular kind of action in which powerful emotions foster careful reflection.

Throughout the readings offered here, *The Colonial Fortune* has highlighted the features of a paracolonial aesthetics that emanates from a significant – yet by no means complete – body of contemporary texts, both Hexagonal and non-metropolitan, signed by writers directly involved in the debate about the colonial past and its remanence and by those who do not overtly manifest such a concern.

I have shown how these questions are modeled through stylistic dissemination (Michon, Constant), vocational fiction (Glissant), empathy (Le Clézio, Gaudé), alternal narratives (Monénembo, Darrieussecq, Audeguy), indirection (NDiaye) and mediation (Sebbar, Cixous). The focus on "colonial fortune" narratives draws attention not to a set of colonial themes, conceived as static phenomena, but to a number of thematic concerns, ideological stances and discursive features crystallized around the idea of the colonial. Moreover, this approach underscores continuities as well as discontinuities between literary and testimonial texts (fiction, autobiography and essay).

At the outset I asked whether a non-antagonistic reading of the subtle yet persistent colonial scenes, events and tropes in contemporary French-language fiction can offer a better, more nuanced understanding of today's political and cultural imaginary. Dialogical readings that have placed texts and writers in critical relation to one another while allowing them to echo each other have called attention to the pitfalls of subaltern cosmopolitanism, self-exoticization and memorial mortification manifest in these works.

Rather than setting the emphasis on colonialism as a theme, *The Colonial Fortune* has sought to delineate a shared imaginary space expressed through paracolonial aesthetic practices which incorporate symbolic, rhetorical and conceptual aspects of the colonial and postcolonial eras. First, the term's etymology signals the heterogeneous continuity of colonialism. While remaining vigilant to the effects of history, it refuses to subscribe to a strictly chronological view of modern colonialism that severs time into *pre-* and *post-* colonial eras, and resists its attempts to impose a divisive logic on our relation to the world. Second, the paracolonial refers to the revival, resurgence and remanence; in other words, a residue indicating a form of discrete permanence of the colonial in the contemporary imagination. And, third, it addresses the reimagining, revisiting and recasting of the colonial in current works of literature.

The idea of colonial fortune emerges as an interface between our era's concern with issues of fate, economics, legacy and debt, stemming from the understudied persistence of the colonial in today's political and cultural conversation, and literature's ways of making sense of them both sensorially and sensibly.

## Notes

1  Jules Ferry, "Les fondements de la politique coloniale" (28 July 1885), http://www2.assemblee-nationale.fr/decouvrir-l-assemblee/histoire/grands-moments-d-eloquence/jules-ferry-1885-les-fondements-de-la-politique-coloniale-28-juillet-1885 (accessed February 20, 2017).

2  Léon Blum, "Débat sur le budget des Colonies à la Chambre des députés", 9 July 1925.

3  Montréal: Humanitas, 1995.

4  "There is a familiar conceit that the colonial relation was not a mutually or reciprocally constitutive one, that the vector of influence ran rather one way than the other, that is, from Europe to its colonies, not vice versa" (David Scott, "Antinomies of Slavery, Enlightenment, and Universal History", *Small Axe*, No. 33 (Vol. 14, No. 3), November 2010: 152–162, 154.)

5  Arles: Actes Sud 2013, 58.

# Bibliography

**Primary texts**

AUDEGUY, Stéphane. *Nous autres*, Paris: Gallimard, 2009.

BESNACI-LANCOU, Fatima. *Fille de harki*, Ivry-sur-Seine: Éditions de l'Atelier, 2003.

CONSTANT, Paule. *White Spirit*, Paris: Gallimard, 1989.

DARRIEUSSECQ, Marie. *Il faut beaucoup aimer les hommes*, Paris: P.O.L, 2013.

GAUDÉ, Laurent. *La Mort du roi Tsongor*, Arles: Actes Sud, 2002.

——. *Cris*, Arles: Actes Sud, 2001.

——. *Eldorado*, Arles: Actes Sud, 2006.

GLISSANT, Édouard. *Ormerod*, Paris: Gallimard, 2003.

JAUFFRET, Régis. *Microfictions*, Paris: Gallimard, 2007.

LE CLÉZIO, Jean-Marie Gustave. *Désert*, Paris: Gallimard, 1980 [*Desert*, tr. C. Dickson, Boston: David R. Godine, 2009].

——. *Révolutions*, Paris: Gallimard, 2003.

——. *L'Africain*, Paris: Mercure de France, 2004.

MIANO, Léonora. *Souldfood équatoriale*, Paris: NIL, 2009.

MICHON, Pierre. *Vies minuscules*, Paris: Gallimard, 1984.

MONENEMBO, Tierno. *Le Roi de Kahel*, Paris: Seuil, 2008.

NDIAYE, Marie. *Mon cœur à l'étroit*, Paris: Gallimard, 2007.

——. *Trois femmes puissantes*, Paris: Gallimard, 2009.

——. *Ladivine*, Paris: Gallimard, 2013.

REY, Marie-Jeanne. *Mémoires d'une écorchée-vive*, Versailles: Éditions de l'Athlantrope, 1987.

SEBBAR, Leïla. *Je ne parle pas la langue de mon père*, Paris: Julliard, 2003.

——. *Les Femmes au bain*, Saint-Pourçain-sur-Sioule: Bleu autour, 2006.

—— (ed.). *C'était leur France. En Algérie, avant l'Indépendance*, Paris: Gallimard, 2007.

SIMON, Claude. *Histoire*, Paris: Minuit, 1967.

——. *L'Acacia*, Paris: Minuit, 1989.

TROUILLOT, Lyonel. *La Parabole du failli*, Arles: Actes Sud, 2013.

## Critical sources

*Le Livre interdit. Livre blanc, Alger, le 26 mars 1962*, Freidberg/Bayern: Atlantis, 2000.

*New Literary History*, Vol. 43, No. 1, Winter 2012.

——. Vol. 43, No. 2, Spring 2012.

ACHEBE, Chinua. *The Education of a British-Protected Child*, New York: Knopf, 2009.

ACHERAÏOU, Amar. *Rethinking Postcolonialism: Colonialist Discourse in Modern Literatures and the Legacy of Classical Writers*, New York: Palgrave Macmillan, 2008.

ACHING, Gerard. *Freedom from Liberation. Slavery, Sentiment and Literature in Cuba*, Bloomington: Indiana University Press, 2015.

AGAMBEN, Giorgio. *State of Exception*, tr. Kevin Attell, Chicago: The University of Chicago Press, 2005.

AMSELLE, Jean-Loup. *Branchements. Anthropologie de l'universalité des cultures*, Paris: Flammarion, 2001.

• ANDERSON, Warwick, JENSON, Deborah and KELLER, Richard C., *Unconscious Dominions: Psychoanalysis, Colonial Trauma, and Global Sovereignties*, Durham, NC: Duke University Press, 2011.

• ANKER, Elizabeth S. *Fictions of Dignity: Embodying Human Rights in World Literature*, Ithaca: Cornell University Press, 2012.

ANZALDÚA, Gloria. *Borderlands/La Frontera: The New Mestiza*, San Francisco: Aunt Lute Books, 1987.

APPIAH, Kwame Anthony. *In My Father's House: Africa in the Philosophy of Culture*. Oxford: Oxford University Press, 1993.

——. *The Ethics of Identity*, Princeton: Princeton University Press, 2005.

APTER, Emily. *The Translation Zone: A New Comparative Literature*, Princeton: Princeton University Press, 2005.

——. *Against World Literature: On the Politics of Untranslatability*, New York: Verso, 2013.

ARCHER, John Michael. *Old Worlds. Egypt, Southwest Asia, India, and Russia in Early Modern English Writing*, Standford: Stanford University Press, 2001.

ARENDT, Hannah. *The Origins of Totalitarianism*, new edition, New York: Harcourt Brace Inc., 1968 [1947].

ARISTOTLE. *The Complete Works of Aristotle*, ed. John Barnes, vol. 2, *Rhetoric*, tr. W. Rhys Roberts, Princeton: Princeton University Press, 1984.

ASIBONG, A. *Marie NDiaye. Blankness and Recognition*, Liverpool: Liverpool University Press, 2013.

ASSOCIATION DES LECTEURS DE JMG LE CLÉZIO. "Bibliographie critique." http://www.associationleclezio.com/ressources/bibliographie-critique/

ATTRIDGE, Derek. *The Singularity of Literature*, London and New York: Routledge, 2004.

AUGÉ, Marc. *Pour une anthropologie des mondes contemporains*, Paris: Aubier, 1994.

BARTHES, Roland. *Le Degré zéro de l'écriture*, Paris: Seuil, 1953.

——. *Mythologies*, Paris: Seuil, 1957

——. *Critique et vérité*, Paris: Seuil, 1966.

——. *L'Empire des signes*, Genève: Albert Skira, 1970.

——. *Nouveaux essais critiques*, Paris: Seuil, 1972.

——. *Œuvres complètes*, tome III, Paris: Seuil, 2002.

BAUDRILLARD, Jean. *Illusion, désillusion esthétiques*, Paris: Sens et Tonka, 1997.

——. *L'Esprit du terrorisme*, Paris: Galilée, 2002.

BAUMAN, Zygmunt. *Wasted Lives: Modernity and Its Outcasts*, Oxford: Polity, 2004.

BAZIÉ, Isaac and LUSEBRINK, Hans-Jürgen (eds.). *Violences postcoloniales. Représentations littéraires et perceptions médiatiques*, Berlin: LIT Verlag, 2011.

BECK, Ulrick. *World at Risk*, London: Polity, 2007.

——. "Critical Theory of World Risk Society: A Cosmopolitan Vision", *Constellations*, Vol. 16, No. 1, 2009: 3–22.

BELL, Dorian. "Balzac's Algeria: Realism and the Colonial", *Nineteenth-Century French Studies*, Vol. 40, No. 1–2, Fall–Winter 2011–2012: 35–56.

BENGSCH, Daniel and RUHE, Cornelia (eds.). *Une femme puissante. L'œuvre de Marie NDiaye*, Amsterdam, New York, Rodopi, 2013.

BENJAMIN, Walter. "The Storyteller: Observations on the Works of Nikolai Leskov", *Selected Writings, vol. 3: 1935–1938*, Howard Eiland and Michael W. Jennings (eds.), tr. Harry Zohn, Cambridge, MA: Belknap Press of Harvard University, 2002, 143–166.

BENSA, Alban. *La Fin de l'exotisme. Essais d'anthropologie critique*, Paris: Anacharsis, 2006.

BERNABÉ, Jean, CHAMOISEAU, Patrick and CONFIANT, Raphaël. *Éloge de la créolité/In Praise of Creolness*, Paris: Gallimard, 1989.

BESSIÈRE, Jean. *Énigmaticité de la littérature*, Paris: Presses Universitaires de France, 1993.

——. *Le Roman contemporain ou la problématicité du monde*, Paris: Presses Universitaires de France, 2010.

BEST, Stephen and MARCUS, Sharon (eds.). "Surface Reading: An Introduction", *Representations*, Vol. 108, No. 1, Fall 2009: 1–21.

BISANSWA, Justin K. and KAVWAHIREHI, Kasereka. "Liminaire", *Tangence*, No. 82, "Savoirs et poétique du roman francophone", 2006: 5–14.

BLANCHARD, Pascal, LEMAIRE, Sabrine and BANCEL, Nicolas. *La Fracture coloniale. La société française au prisme de l'héritage colonial*, Paris: Cahiers Libres, 2005.

——, LEMAIRE, Sabrine, BANCEL, Nicolas and THOMAS, Dominique (eds.). *Colonial Culture in France since the Revolution*, tr. Alexis Pernsteiner, Bloomington: Indiana University Press, 2014.

BLANCKMAN, Bruno, MURA-BRUNEL, Aline and DAMBRE Marc (eds.). *Le Roman français au tournant du XXIᵉ siècle*, Paris: Presses Sorbonne Nouvelle, 2004.

BON, François. *Exercice de la littérature. Formes neuves de récit pour une réalité transformée*, Berlin: Weidler Buchverlag, 2001.

BONGIE, Chris. "What's Literature Got To Do With It?" *Comparative Literature*, Vol. 54, No. 3, 2002: 256–267.

——. *Friends and Enemies: The Scribal Politics of Post/colonial Literature*, Liverpool: Liverpool University Press, 2008.

BOUJU, Emmanuel. "Force diagonale et compression du présent. Six propositions sur le roman *istorique* contemporain", *Écrire l'histoire*, No. 11, dossier "Présent (1)", Sylvie Aprile and Dominique Dupart (eds.), Marseille: Gaussen, 2013, 51–60.

BRATHWAITE, Kamau. *Words Need Love Too*, introduction by Stewart Brown, Cambridge: Salt, 2004.

BRINKER-GABLER, Gisella and SMITH, Sidonie. *Writing New Identities: Gender, Nation and Immigration in Contemporary Europe*, Minneapolis, University of Minnesota Press, 1997.

BRITTON, Celia. *Édouard Glissant and Postcolonial Theory. Strategies of Language and Resistance*, Charlottesville: University Press of Virginia, 1999.

BROZGAL, Lia Nicole. *Against Autobiography. Albert Memmi and the Production of Theory*, Lincoln and London: University of Nebraska Press, 2013.

BRUCKNER, Pascal. *The Tyranny of Guilt: An Essay on Western Masochism*, tr. Steven Rendall, Princeton: Princeton University Press, 2010.

BRUN, Catherine and PENOT-LACASSAGNE, Olivier. *Engagements et déchirements. Les intellectuels et la guerre d'Algérie*, Paris: Gallimard/IMEC, 2012.

BUCK-MORSS, Susan. "Radical Cosmopolitanism", *Third Text*, Vol. 23, No. 5, 2009: 547–549.

CALMEIN, Maurice and LACOSTE-ADROVER, Christiane. *Dis, c'était comment, l'Algérie française? 20 questions et réponses à l'intention des jeunes Pieds-Noirs*, Freidberg/Bayern: Atlantis, 2002.

CAMUS, Albert. *L'Exil et le Royaume*, Paris: Gallimard, 1957.

——. *Actuelles III. Chroniques algériennes 1939–1958*, Paris: Gallimard, 1958.

——. *Cahiers Albert Camus, Le Premier Homme*, Paris: Gallimard, 1994.

CARUTH, Cathy. *Literature in the Ashes of History*, Baltimore: Johns Hopkins •
University Press, 2013.

CASANOVA, Pascale. *La République mondiale des lettres*, Paris: Seuil, 1999.

CASTIGLIONE, Agnès. "Pierre Michon, l'autobiographie oblique", *Écriture de soi: secrets et réticences*, Bertrand Degott and Marie Miguet-Ollagnier (eds.), Paris: L'Harmattan, 2001, 321–337.

CAVELL, Stanley. *The World Viewed. Reflections on the Ontology of Film*, Cambridge, MA: Harvard University Press, 1979.

CAZENAVE, Odile. *Afrique sur Seine: une nouvelle génération de romanciers africains à Paris*, Paris: L'Harmattan, 2003.

—— and CELERIER, Patricia. *Contemporary Francophone African Writers and the Burden of Commitment*, Charlottesville: University of Virginia Press, 2011.

CÉSAIRE, Aimé. *Cahier d'un retour au pays natal*, Paris: Présence africaine, 1983 [1939].

CHAKRABARTY, Dipesh. "Postcolonial Studies and the Challenge of the •
Climate Change", *New Literary History*, Vol. 43, No. 1, 2012: 1–18.

CHAMBERS, Ross. *Story and Situation. Narrative Seduction and the Power of Fiction*, Minneapolis: University of Minnesota Press, 1984.

CHAMOISEAU, Patrick and CONFIANT, Raphaël. *Lettres créoles. Tracées antillaises et continentales de la littérature 1635–1975*, Paris: Gallimard, 1999.

CHEAH, Pheng. *What is a World? On Postcolonial Literature as World Literature*, Durham, NC: Duke University Press, 2016.

CITTON, Yves. *Mythocratie. Storytelling et imaginaire de gauche*, Paris: Éditions Amsterdam, 2010a.

——. *L'Avenir des humanités*, Paris: Éditions de la Découverte, 2010b.

——. "Contre-fictions politiques", *Multitudes*, No. 481, March 2012: 70–148.

——. "Contre-fictions en médiocratie", *Revue Critique de Fixxion Française Contemporaine*, No. 6, 2013. http://www.revue-critique-defixxion-francaise-contemporaine.org/rcffc/article/view/fx06.14/726 (accessed February 20, 2017).

CIXOUS, Hélène. *Les Rêveries de la femme sauvage. Scènes primitives*, Paris: Galilée, 2000.

——. "Birds, Women and Writing", *Animal Philosophy*, Matthew Calarco and Peter Atterton (eds.), London: Continuum, 2004, 167–173.

——. *Si près*, Paris: Galilée, 2007.

——. *Ayaï! Le cri de la littérature. Accompagné d'Adel Abdessemed*, Paris: Galilée, 2013.

CLIFF, Michelle. *The Land of Look Behind and Claiming*, Ann Arbor: Firebrand, 1985.

COETZEE, J. M. *White Writing. On the Culture of Letters in South Africa*, New Haven and London: Yale University Press, 1988.

COLLOT, Michel. *Pour une géographie littéraire*, Paris: Corti, 2014.

CONKLIN, Alice L. *A Mission to Civilize: The Republican Idea of Empire in France and West Africa, 1895–1930*, Stanford, CA: Stanford University Press, 1998.

CONRAD, Joseph. *Heart of Darkness*, London: Penguin, 1995 [1899].

COQUIO, Catherine (ed.). *Retours du colonial? Disculpation et réhabilitation de l'histoire coloniale française*, Nantes: L'Atalante, 2008.

COYAULT-DUBLANCHET, Sylviane. *La Province en héritage. Pierre Michon, Pierre Bergounioux, Richard Millet*, Genève: Droz, 2002.

CROWLEY, Patrick. "Empire and Intertext in Pierre Michon's 'Vie d'André Dufourneau'". Presented at Remembering Empire/Mémoires d'Empire, the Annual ASCALF Conference (Association for the Study of Caribbean and African Literatures in French and now the Society for Francophone Postcolonial Studies), London, The French Institute, November 29, 2001. Unpublished manuscript.

DABLA, Séwanou. *Nouvelles écritures africaines. Romanciers de la seconde génération*, Paris: L'Harmattan, 2000.

DASH, J. Michael. *Édouard Glissant*, Cambridge: Cambridge University Press, 1995.

DAVIS, Gregson. "'Homecoming without Home': Representations of (Post)colonial nostos (Homecoming) in the Lyric of Aimé Césaire and Derek Walcott", *Homer in the Twentieth Century: Between World Literature and the Western Canon*, Barbara Graziosi and Emily Greenwood (eds.), Oxford: Oxford University Press, 2011, 191–210.

• DAVIS, Oliver. *Rancière Now. Current Perspectives on Jacques Rancière*, Cambridge: Polity Press, 2013.

DEBAENE, Vincent, JEANNELLE, Jean-Louis, MACÉ, Marielle and MURAT, Michel (eds.). *L'Histoire littéraire des écrivains*, Paris: Presses de l'université Paris-Sorbonne, 2013.

DE CERTEAU, Michel. *L'Écriture de l'histoire*, Paris: Gallimard, 1975.

DELEUZE, Gilles. *Francis Bacon. La logique de la sensation*, Paris: La Découverte, 1981.

DERRIDA, Jacques. *Spectres de Marx*, Paris: Galilée, 1993.

——. 'Khora', *On the Name*, tr. Thomas Dutoit, Stanford, CA: Stanford University Press, 1995 [1993].

——. *Le Monolinguisme de l'autre ou la prothèse d'origine*, Paris: Galilée, 1996.

——. *L'Animal que donc je suis*, Paris: Galilée, 2006.

DESSAIGNE, Francine and REY Marie-Jeanne. *Un crime sans assassins: Alger, 26 mars 1962*, Alfortville: Confrérie-Castille, 1994.

DIDI-HUBERMAN, Georges. *L'Image survivante. Histoire de l'art et temps des fantômes selon Aby Warburg*, Paris: Minuit, 2002.

DINE, Philip. *Images of the Algerian War: French Fiction and Film, 1954–1992*, Oxford: Clarendon, 1994.

DUBOIS, Laurent. "La République métissée: Citizenship, Colonialism, and the Borders of French History", *Cultural Studies*, Vol. 14, No. 1, 2000: 15–34.

DUBREUIL, Laurent. *L'Empire du langage*, Paris: Hermann, 2008.

DUCROT, Oswald and SCHAEFFER, Jean-Marie (eds.). *Nouveau dictionnaire encyclopédique des sciences du langage*, Paris: Seuil, 1995.

DURAND, Jean-François and SÉVRY, Jean (eds.). *Littérature et Colonies*, Paris: Kailash Éditions, 2003.

DURAS, Marguerite. *Un barrage contre le Pacifique*, Paris: Gallimard, 1950.

———. *La Vie matérielle*, Paris: POL, 1987.

—— and PORTE, Michelle. *Les Lieux de Marguerite Duras*, entretiens et photos, Paris: Minuit, 1977.

DURMELAT, Sylvie. "Introduction: Colonial Culinary Encounters and Imperial Leftovers", *French Cultural Studies*, Vol. 26, No. 2, 2015: 115–129.

ELDRIGE, Claire. "Blurring the Boundaries between Perpetrators and Victims. Pied-Noir Memories and the Harki Community", *Memory Studies*, Vol. 3, No. 2, 2010: 123–136.

ELIAS, Norbert. *The History of Manners*, vols I–II, tr. Edmun Jephcott, New York: Pantheon Books, 1978.

FANON, Frantz. *Black Skin, White Masks*, tr. C. L. Markmann, New York: Grove Press, 1967 [*Peau noire, masques blancs*, Paris: Seuil, 1952].

———. *The Wretched of the Earth*, tr. Richard Philcox, New York: Grove Press, 2007 [*Les Damnés de la terre*, Paris: Maspéro, 1961].

FASSIN, Didier. *When Bodies Remember: Politics and Experiences of AIDS in South Africa*, Berkeley: University of California Press, 2007.

FELSKI, Rita. *The Limits of Critique*, Chicago: University of Chicago Press, 2015.

FLAUBERT, Gustave. *Madame Bovary*, Paris: Gallimard, 2001.

FORSDICK, Charles. "À quoi bon marcher: Uses of the peripatetic in contemporary travel literature in French", *Sites*, Vol. 5, No. 1, 2001: 47–62.

———. "Between 'French' and 'Francophone': French Studies and the Postcolonial Turn", *French Studies*, Vol. LIX, No. 4, 2005: 523–530.

—— and MURPHY, David (eds.). *Postcolonial Thought in the French-Speaking World*, Liverpool: Liverpool University Press, 2009.

FOUCAULT, Michel. *Security, Territory, Population. Lectures at the Collège de France, 1977–1978*, ed. Michel Senellart, tr. Graham Burchell, New York: Palgrave Macmillan, 2007.

FREUD, Sigmund. "Mourning and Melancholia", *The Standard Edition of the Complete Psychological Works*, tr. James Strachey, Vol. XIV, London: The Hogarth Press: 243–258.

FUENTES, Carlos. *Geografía de la novela*, Madrid: Alfaguara, 1993.

GALLO, Rubén. *Proust's Latin Americans*, Baltimore: Johns Hopkins University Press, 2014.

GEFEN, Alexandre. "Le Genre des noms: la biofiction dans la littérature française contemporaine", *Le Roman français au tournant du XXIᵉ siècle*, Bruno Blanckeman, Aline Mura-Brunel and Marc Dambre (eds.), Paris: Presses Sorbonne Nouvelle, 2004, 305–320.

GIKANDI, Simon. "Theory, Literature, and Moral Considerations", Research in African Literatures, Winter 2001, Vol. 32, Issue 4: 1–18.

——. "This Thing Called Literature … What Work Does It Do?", *PMLA*, Vol. 127, No. 1, January 2012: 9–21.

• GILROY, Paul. *Postcolonial Melancholia*, New York: Columbia University Press, 2006.

GLISSANT, Édouard. *Le Discours antillais*, Paris: Gallimard, 1997 [1981]. [*Caribbean Discourse*, tr. J. Michael Dash, Charlottesville: University Press of Virginia, 1989.]

——. *Introduction à une poétique du divers*, Montréal: Presses de l'Université de Montréal, 1995.

——. *Poetics of Relation*, tr. Betsy Wing, Ann Arbor: University of Michigan Press, 1997. [Poétique de la Relation (Poétique III), Paris: Gallimard, 1990.]

—— and CHAMOISEAU, Patrick. *Quand les murs tombent: l'identité nationale hors-la-loi?* Paris: Galaade, 2007.

——. *Philosophie de la Relation. Poésie en étendue*, Paris: Gallimard, 2009.

GOBINEAU, Joseph-Arthur (comte de). *The Inequality of Human Races*, tr. Adrian Collins, New York: H. Fertig, 1967 [Essai sur l'inégalité des races humaines, Paris: Éditions Pierre Belfond, 1967 (1853–1855)].

GOH, Irving. *The Reject. Community, Politics and Religion after the Subject*, New York: Fordham University Press, 2015.

GORDIMER, Nadine. *Writing and Being*, Cambridge: Harvard University Press, 1995.

GREEN, Mary Jay (ed.). *Beyond the Hexagon: Francophone Women Writers*, Minneapolis: University of Minnesota Press, 1996.

HA, Marie-Paule. "Reading the Colonial in Malraux's Asian Novels", *Revue André Malraux Review*, Vol. 26, no. 1–2, 1997: 27–40.

HAMEL, Jean-François. *Revenances de l'histoire. Répétition, narrativité, modernité*, Paris: Minuit, 2006.

HARGREAVES, Alec G. and MURPHY, David (eds.). *Journal of Postcolonial Writing*, "New Directions in Postcolonial Studies", Vol. 44, No. 3, September 2008.

——, FORSDICK, Charles and MURPHY, David (eds.). *Transnational French Studies: Postcolonialism and Littérature-Monde*, Liverpool: Liverpool University Press, 2013.

HARRISON, Nicholas. *Postcolonial Criticism: History, Theory and the Work of Fiction*, Hoboken: Wiley, 2003.

——. "Who Needs an Idea of the Literary?", *Paragraph*, "The Idea of the Literary", Vol. 28, Issue 2, 2005: 1–17.

——. "Metaphorical Memories: Freud, Conrad, and the Dark Continent", in *Postcolonial Poetics: Genre and Form*, Patrick Crowley and Jane Hiddleston (eds.), Liverpool: Liverpool University Press, 2011: 49–70.

HARTOG, François. *Régimes d'historicité: présentisme et expérience du temps*, Paris: Seuil, 2003.

HAVARD, Gilles and VIDAL, Cécile. *Histoire de l'Amérique française*, Paris: Flammarion, 2003.

HEFERNAN, Julián Jiménez. "'Empty About Me': Gordimer between the Singular and the Specific", *Research in African Literatures*, Vol. 41, No. 4, Winter 2010: 87–108.

HEISE, Ursula K. "Globality, Difference, and the International Turn in Ecocriticism", *PMLA*, Vol. 128, No. 3, 2013: 636–643.

HENKE, Suzette A. *Shattered Subjects: Trauma and Testimony in Women's Life-Writing*. New York: St. Martin's Press, 1998.

HIDDLESTON, Jane. *Understanding Postcolonialism*, London and New York: Routledge, 2009.

HIRSCH, Marianne and MILLER, Nancy K. (eds.). *Rites of Return. Diaspora Poetics and Politics of Memory*, New York: Columbia University Press, 2011.

HUBBELL, Amy L. "The Past Is Present: Pied-Noir Returns to Algeria", *Nottingham French Studies*, Vol. 51, No. 1, 2012: 66–77.

HUGGAN, Graham. *The Postcolonial Exotic. Marketing the Margins*, London and New York: Routledge, 2001.

—— and TIFFIN, Helen. *Postcolonial Ecocriticism: Literature, Animals, Environment*, London and New York: Routledge, 2010.

HUGO, Victor. *Actes et paroles*. Vols I–IV. Paris: Michel Lévy Frères, 1875.

HUSTON, Nancy. *L'espèce fabulatrice*, Arles: Acte Sud, 2008.

IMOROU, Abdoulaye. "Humaines et épanouies. Trois femmes puissantes et les figures littéraires des Africaines", *French Studies in Southern Africa*, Vol. 43, September 2013, 40–62.

IRELAND, Susan. "Trauma and Imprisonment in Works Representing the Harkis", *The Unspeakable. Representations of Trauma in Francophone Literature and Art*, Névine el Nossery and Amy L. Hubbell (eds.), Newcastle upon Tyne, Cambridge Scholars Publishing, 2013, 347–366

IRELE, Abiola F. *The African Imagination: Literature in Africa and the Black Diaspora*, Oxford: Oxford University Press, 2001.

JAMES, Alison. "Thinking the Everyday: Genre, Form, Fiction", *L'Esprit créateur*, Vol. 54, No. 3, 2014: 78–91.

JONES, Donna V. *The Racial Discourses of Life Philosophy: Négritude, Vitalism, and Modernity*, New York: Columbia University Press, 2010.

KABAMBA, Maguy. *La Dette coloniale*, Montréal: Humanitas, 1995.

KAZADI WA KABWE, Désiré. "Réparation, récupération et dette coloniale dans les romans congolais récents", *Cahiers d'études africaines*, 1/2004, No. 173–174: 141–150.

KEEN, Susan. *Empathy and the Novel*, Oxford: Oxford University Press, 2010.

KOM, Ambroise. "La littérature africaine et les paramètres du canon", *Études françaises*, Vol. 37, No. 2, 2001: 33–44.

KRISTEVA, Julia. *Black Sun: Depression and Melancholia*. tr. Leon S. Roudiez. New York: Columbia University Press, 1989.

——. *Strangers to Ourselves*, New York: Columbia University Press, 1991.

KUNDERA, Milan. *Les Testaments trahis*, Paris: Gallimard, 2000 [1993].

LAURETTE, Pierre and RUPRECHT Hans-George (eds.). *Poétiques et imaginaires. Francopolyphonie littéraire des Amériques*, Paris: L'Harmattan, 1995.

LE BRIS, Michel and ROUAUD, Jean (ed.). *Pour une littérature-monde*, Paris: Gallimard, 2007.

LE CLÉZIO, Jean-Marie Gustave. "The World Has no Center", *New Perspectives Quarterly*, Vol. 26, No. 3, Summer 2009, http://www.digitalnpq.org/archive/2009_summer/21_leclezio.html.

LÉGER, Thierry, ROUSSEL-GILLET, Isabel and SALLES, Marina (eds.). *Le Clézio, passeur des arts et des cultures*, Rennes: Presses Universitaires de Rennes, 2010.

LIONNET, Françoise. *The Unknown and the Uncertain: Creole Cosmopolitis of the Indian Ocean*, Mauritius: L'Atelier d'écriture, 2012.

——. "World Literature, Postcolonial Studies, and Collie Odysseys: J.-M.G. Le Clézio's and Amitav Gosh's Indian Ocean Novels", *Comparative Literature*, Vol. 67, No. 3, 2015: 287–311.

LOICHOT, Valérie. *Orphan Narratives: The Postplantation Literature of Faulkner, Glissant, Morrison, and Saint-John Perse*, Charlottesville: University of Virginia Press, 2007.

——. *The Tropics Bite Back. Culinary Coups in Caribbean Literature*, Minneapolis: University of Minnesota Press, 2013a.

——. "Édouard Glissant's Graves", *Callaloo*, Vol. 36, No. 4, Fall 2013b: 1014–1032.

LOKHA, Eileen. "Les femmes évanescentes du cycle mauricien: entretien avec Françoise Lionnet", *Les Cahiers Le Clézio*, Vol. 6, 2013: 113–123.

LORCIN, Patricia M. E. (ed.). *Algeria and France, 1800–2000: Identity, Memory, Nostalgia*, Syracuse: Syracuse UP, 2006.

MCDONALD, Christie and SULEIMAN, Susan R. (eds.). *French Global*, New York: Columbia UP, 2010.

MACÉ, Marielle. *Façons de lire, manières d'être*, Paris: Gallimard, 2011.

• MACKENZIE, Louisa and POSTHUMUS, Stephanie. *French Thinking about Animals*, East Lansing: Michigan State UP, 2015.

MADEIRA, Ana Isabel. "Portuguese, French and British Discourses on Colonial Education: Church–State Relations, School Expansion and Missionary Competition in Africa, 1890–1930", *Paedagogica Historica*, Vol. 41, Nos 1 & 2, February 2005: 31–60.

MAINGUENEAU, Dominique. *Les Livres d'école de la République (1870–1914). Discours et idéologie*, Paris: Le Sycomore, 1979.

——. *Le Discours littéraire. Paratopie et scène d'énonciation*, Paris: Armand Colin, 2004.

• MARSH, Kate. *Narratives of the French Empire: Fiction, Nostalgia, and Imperial Rivalries*, Lanham: Lexington Books, 2013.

—— and FRITH, Nicola (eds.). *France's Lost Empires: Fragmentation, Nostagia and 'La Fracture coloniale'*, Lanham: Lexington Books, 2010.

MARSHALL, Bill. *The French Atlantic. Travels in Culture and History*, Liverpool: Liverpool University Press, 2009.

MARTIN, Bronwen. *The Fiction of J. M. G. Le Clézio: A Postcolonial Reading*, Oxford: Peter Lang, 2012.

MBEMBE, Achille. *De la postcolonie. Essai sur l'imagination politique dans l'Afrique contemporaine*, Paris: Karthala, 2000.

——. *Critique de la conscience nègre*, Paris: La Découverte, 2013.

MÉCHOULAN, Éric. *Pour une histoire esthétique de la littérature*, Paris: Presses Universitaires de France, 2004.

MELZER, Sara E. *Colonizer or Colonized. The Hidden Stories of Early Modern French Culture*, Philadephia: University of Pennsylvania Press, 2012.

MERLIN-KAJMAN, Hélène. *La Langue est-elle fasciste? Langue, pouvoir, enseignement*, Paris: Seuil, 2003.

——. *L'Animal ensorcelé. Traumatismes, littérature, transitionnalité*, Paris: Ithaque, 2016.

MICHELET, Jules. *Œuvres complètes*, tome I, Paris: Flammarion, 1893.

MICHON, Pierre. *Le Roi vient quand il veut. Propos sur la littérature*, Paris: Albin Michel, 2007.

• MIGNOLO, Walter D. *Local Histories/Global Designs. Colonialities, Subaltern Knowledge and Border Thinking*, Princeton: Princeton University Press, 2000.

MILLER, Christopher L. *Theories of Africans: Francophone Literature and Anthropology in Africa*, Chicago: University of Chicago Press, 1990.

• ——. *Nationalists and Nomads. Essays on Francophone African Literature and Culture*, Chicago: University of Chicago Press, 1998.

——. *French Atlantic Triangle: Literature and Culture of the Slave Trade*, Durham, NC: Duke University Press, 2008.

—— and BENSMAIA, Réda (eds.). "French and Francophone. The Challenge of Expanding Horizons", *Yale French Studies*, Vol. 103, 2003: 1–6.

MOSER, Keith. *J.M.G. Le Clézio. A Concerned Citizen of the Global Village*, Langham: Lexington Books, 2013.

—— (ed.). *A Practical Guide to French Harki Literature*, Langham: Lexington Books, 2014.

MOTTE, Warren and MOUDILENO, Lydie (eds.). "Marie NDiaye's Worlds/ Mondes de Marie NDiaye", *L'Esprit créateur*, Vol. 53, No. 2, 2013: 1–3.

MOUDILENO, Lydie. "Marie Ndiaye's Discombobulated Subject", *SubStance*, Issue 111, Vol. 35, No. 3, 2006: 83–94.

——. "Trajectoires et apories du colonisateur de bonne volonté: d'*Onitsha* à *L'Africain*", *Les Cahiers J. M. G. Le Clézio*, Nos 3–4 "Migrations et métissages", Paris: Éditions Complicités, 2011: 63–82.

——. "Le manifeste comme écho. Échos du manifeste", *Trajectoires et dérives de la littérature-monde. Poétiques de la relation et du divers dans les espaces francophones*, Cécilia W. Francis and Robert Viau (eds.), Amsterdam, New York: Rodopi, 2013, 15–28.

MOUFFE, Chantal. *Agonistics. Thinking the World Politically*, London, New York: Verso, 2013.

MOURA, Jean-Marc. *La Littérature des lointains. Histoire de l'exotisme européen au XX$^e$ siècle*, Paris: Honoré Champion, 1998.

MOURALIS, Bernard. *Littérature et développement. Essai sur le statut, la fonction et la représentation de la littérature négro-africaine d'expression française*, Paris: Silex, 1984.

——. *Littératures africaines et Antiquité. Redire le face-à-face de l'Afrique et de l'Occident*, Paris: Honoré Champion, 2011.

MUDIMBE, V. Y., *The Invention of Africa: Gnosis, Philosophy, and the Order of Knowledge*, Bloomington: Indiana University Press, 1988.

NANCY, Jean-Luc. *La Déclosion: Déconstruction du christianisme*, tome 1, Paris: Galilée, 2005.

——. *L'Adoration: Déconstruction du christianisme*, tome 2, Paris: Galilée, 2010.

NDIAYE, Marie. "Je ne veux plus que la magie soit une ficelle », propos recueillis par Nathalie Crom", *Télérama*, 28 August 2009. http://www. telerama.fr/livre/marie-ndiaye-je-ne-veuxplus-que-la-magie-soit-une-ficelle-litteraire,46107.php (accessed 20 February 2017).

——. "L'écrivain Marie NDiaye aux prises avec le monde", entretien avec Nelly Kaprèlian, *Les Introckuptibles*, 30 August 2009. http://www. lesinrocks.com/2009/08/30/actualite/lecrivain-marie-ndiaye-aux-prises-avec-le-monde-1137985/ (accessed 20 February 2017).

NDIAYE, Pap. *La Condition noire. Essai sur une minorité française*, Paris: Gallimard, 2009.

NIXON, Rob. *Slow Violence and the Environmentalism of the Poor*, Cambridge, MA: Harvard University Press, 2011.

NORA, Pierre (ed.). *Les Lieux de mémoire*, Vol. 3, *Les France*, Paris: Gallimard, 1997.

O'RILEY, Michael. *Postcolonial Haunting: Anxiety, Affect, and the Situated*, Columbus: Ohio State University Press, 2007.

PANAÏTÉ, Oana. *Des littératures-mondes en français. Écritures singulières, poétiques transfrontalières dans la prose contemporaine*, Amsterdam/New York: Rodopi Press, 2012.

———. "Étrangèreté, non-savoir et écritures transfrontalières: Hélène Cixous, Nina Bouraoui et Leïla Sebbar". *Modern Language Notes*, Vol. 129, Issue 4, September 2014: 796–811.

——— (ed.). *Reading Communities. A Dialogical Approach to French and Francophone Literature/Communautés de lecture: pour une approche dialogique des œuvres classiques et contemporaines*, Newcastle upon Tyne: Cambridge Scholars, 2016.

PERROT-CORPET, Danielle and GAUVIN, Lise (eds.). *La Nation nommée Roman*, Paris: Garnier, 2011.

PERSE, Saint-John. *Œuvres complètes*, Paris: Bibliothèque de la Pléiade, 1972.

PHILIPPE, Gilles. *Le Discours en soi. La représentation du discours intérieur dans les romans de Sartre*, Paris: Honoré Champion, 1997.

——— (ed.). *Récits de la pensée*, Paris: SEDES, 2002.

PRATT, Mary Louise. *Imperial Eyes: Travel Writing and Transculturation*, London and New York: Routledge, 2007 [1992].

PRENDERGAST, Christopher and ANDERSON, Benedict (eds.). *Debating World Literature*, London, New York: Verso, 2004.

PRICE, Richard and PRICE, Sally. "Shadowboxing in the Mangrove: The Politics of Identity in Postcolonial Martinique", *Caribbean Romances. The Politics of Regional Representation*, Belinda J. Edmonson (ed.), Charlottesville: University of Virginia Press, 1999, 123–162.

PROUST, Marcel. *À la recherche du temps perdu*, Vols I–II, ed. Jean-Yves Tadié, Paris: Gallimard, 1987–1988.

QUINTILIAN. *The Orator's Education*, tr. Donald A. Russell, Book 6–8, Vol. III, Loeb Classical Library, Cambridge, MA: Harvard University Press, 2002.

RANCIÈRE, Jacques. *La chair des mots. Politiques de l'écriture*, Paris: Galilée, 1998a.

———. *La Parole muette. Essai sur les contradictions de la littérature*, Paris: Hachette, 1998b.

———. *Le Partage du sensible. Esthétique et politique*, Paris: La Fabrique éditions, 2000.

———. *Aisthesis: scènes du régime esthétique de l'art*, Paris: Galilée, 2011.

RICE, Alison. *Polygraphies. Francophone Women Writing Algeria*, Charlottesville: University of Virginia Press, 2012.

RICŒUR, Paul. *Temps et récit*, Vols I–III, Paris: Seuil, 1985.

——. *Oneself as Another*, tr. Kathleen Blamey, Chicago: The University of Chicago Press, 1992 [1990].

• ——. *Memory, History, Forgetting*, tr. Kathleen Blamey and David Pellauer, Chicago: University of Chicago Press, 2004. [2003].

RIGOLOT, Carol. *Forged Genealogies. Saint John Perse's Conversations with Culture*, Chapel Hill: North Carolina Studies in the Romance Languages and Literatures, 2001.

• ROBBEN, Antonious G. C. M. "How Traumatized Societies Remember: The Aftermath of Argentina's Dirty War", *Cultural Critique*, 59, Winter 2005, 120–164.

ROCHLITZ, Rainer. *Logiques et résistances de la modernité*, Paris: Seuil, 1998a.

——. *L'Art au banc d'essai: esthétique et critique*, Paris: Gallimard, 1998b.

ROSE, Nikolas. *The Politics of Life Itself: Biomedicine, Power and Subjectivity in the Twenty-First Century*, Princeton: Princeton University Press, 2007.

• ROSELLO, Mireille. *Postcolonial Hospitality. The Immigrant as Guest*, Stanford: Stanford University Press, 2001.

ROTHBERG, Michael, SANYAL, Debarati and SILVERMAN, Maxim. *Nœuds de mémoire: Multidirectional Memory in Postwar French and Francophone Culture*, New Haven: Yale UP, 2010.

ROUAUD, Jean. "Mort d'une certaine idée", *Pour une littérature-monde*, Michel Le Bris and Jean Rouaud (eds.), Paris: Gallimard, 2007, 7–22.

ROUSSO, Henry. *The Haunting Past. History, Memory and Justice in Contemporary France*, tr. Ralph Schoolcraft, Philadelphia: University of Pennsylvania Press, 2002.

RUFF, Isabelle. "Le Clézio revient à l'île de ses origines", *Le Temps*, 1 March 2003.

RUSCIO, Alain. *Le Credo de l'homme blanc: regards coloniaux français XIX^e–XX^e siècle*, Paris: Éditions Complexe, 2002.

SAID, Edward. *Beginnings. Intention and Method*, New York: Basic Books, Inc., 1975.

——. *Orientalism*, London: Vintage, 1978.

• ——. *Culture and Imperialism*, London: Vintage, 1994.

SALHI, Kamal. *Francophone Post-Colonial Studies*, Lanham: Lexington Books, 2003.

SALMON, Christian. *Storytelling: la machine à fabriquer des histoires et à formater les esprits*, Paris: La Découverte, 2007.

SAUGERA, Éric. *Bordeaux, port négrier, XVIIe–XIXe siècles*, Paris: Karthala, 2002.

• SCHAMA, Simon. *Landscape and Memory*, New York: A.A. Knopf, 1995.

SCHLANGER, Judith. *La Mémoire des œuvres*, Lagrasse: Verdier 2008.

SCHMITT, Carl. *The Concept of the Political*, tr. George Schwab, Chicago: University of Chicago Press, 1996.

SCHOENTJES, Pierre. *Ce qui a lieu. Essai d'écopoétique*, Paris: Wildproject, 2015.

SCOTT, David. "Antinomies of Slavery, Enlightenment, and Universal History", *Small Axe*, No. 33 (Vol. 14, No. 3), November 2010: 152–162.

SEMUJANGA, Josias. *Dynamique des genres dans le roman africain. Éléments de poétique transculturelle*, Paris: L'Harmattan, 1999.

• SERRANO, Richard. *Against the Postcolonial: "Francophone" Writers at the Ends of the French Empire*, Lanham: Lexington Books, 2005.

SHERINGHAM, Michael. "Ambivalences de l'animalité chez Marie NDiaye", *Une femme puissante. L'œuvre de Marie NDiaye*, Daniel Bengsch and Cornelia Ruhe (eds.), Amsterdam, New York: Rodopi, 2013, 51–70.

SILVERMAN, Maxim (ed.). *Race, Power and Discourse in France*, Aldershot: Avebury, 1991.

SIMON, Claude. *Discours de Stockholm*, Paris: Minuit, 1986.

SOLÉ, Robert. "L'écriture physique de Marie Darrieussecq", *Le Monde des Livres*, le 20 mai 2010, http://www.lemonde.fr/livres/article/2010/05/20/l-ecriture-physique-de-marie-darrieussecq_1360601_3260.html (accessed February 20, 2017).

SPIVAK, Gayatri Chakravorty. *In Other Wor(l)ds*, London and New York: Routledge, 1987.

———. "Echo", *The Spivak Reader*, Donna Landry and Gerald Maclean (eds.), London and New York: Routledge, 1996, 175–202.

———. *Death of a Discipline*, Calcutta and New Delhi: Seagull Books, 2004.

• ———. *Nationalism and the Imagination*, London, New York, Calcutta: Seagull Books, 2010.

◑ STOLER, Ann Laura. *Along the Archival Grain: Epistemic Anxieties and Colonial Common Sense*, Princeton: Princeton University Press, 2009.

STORA, Benjamin. *La Gangrene et l'oubli*, Paris: La Découverte, 1991.

———. *La guerre des mémoires: la France face à son passé colonial*, Paris: Éditions de l'Aube, 2007.

TALBOTT, John. *The War without a Name, France in Algeria, 1954–1962*, New York: Alfred A. Knopf, 1980.

THIBAULT, Bruno. *J.M.G. Le Clézio et la métaphore exotique*, Amsterdam, New York: Rodopi, 2009.

• THOMAS, Dominic. *Black France: Colonialism, Immigration, and Transnationalism*, Bloomington: Indiana University Press, 2007.

———. *Africa and France: Postcolonial Cultures, Migration, and Racism*, Bloomington: Indiana University Press, 2013.

TODOROV, Tzvetan. *Nous et les autres*, Paris: Seuil, 1989.

———. *La Peur des barbares. Au-delà du choc des civilisations*, Paris: Robert Laffont, 2008.

TOURET, Michèle (ed.). *Histoire de la littérature française du XXᵉ siècle*, tome II – après 1940, Rennes: Presses Universitaires de Rennes, 2008.

—— and DUGAST-PORTES, Francine. *Le Temps des Lettres. Quelles périodisations pour l'histoire de la littérature française du 20ᵉ siècle?* Rennes: Presses Universitaires de Rennes, 2001.

TROUILLOT, Lyonel. *Le Doux Parfum des temps à venir*, Arles: Actes Sud, 2013.

VIART, Dominique. *Une mémoire inquiète. "La Route des Flandres" de Claude Simon*, Paris: Presses Universitaires de France, 1997.

—— and VERCIER, Bruno. *La Littérature française au présent. Héritages, modernité, mutations*, Paris: Bordas, 2005.

VIRILIO, Paul. *Speed and Politics: An Essay on Dromology*, New York: Semiotext(e), 1977.

———. *The Aesthetics of Disappearance*, New York: Semiotext(e), 1991.

WABERI, Abdourahman. "Les enfants de la postcolonie. Esquisse d'un nouvelle génération d'écrivains francophones d'Afrique noire", *Notre Librairie*, Vol. 135, 1998: 8–15.

• WALDER, Dennis. *Postcolonial Nostalgias: Writing, Representation and Memory*, London and New York: Routledge, 2011.

WALKER, Keith L. *Countermodernism and Francophone Literary Culture. The Game of Slipknot*, Durham, NC: Duke University Press, 1999.

WATTS, Richard. "Senghor's Prefaces between the Colonial and the Postcolonial", Vol. 33, No. 4, Winter 2002: 76–87.

WEBER, Eugen Joseph. *The Hollow Year: France in the 1930s*, New York: Norton, 1994.

WHITE, Hayden. *Figural Realism. Studies in the Mimesis Effect*, Baltimore: The Johns Hopkins University Press, 1999.

WINSTON, Jane Bradley. *Postcolonial Duras. Culture Memory in Postwar France*, New York: Palgrave, 2001.

YEE, Jennifer. *The Colonial Comedy. Imperialism in the French Realist Novel*, Oxford: Oxford University Press, 2016.

YOUNG, Robert J. C. *Postcolonialism: An Historical Introduction*, Oxford: Blackwell, 2001.

◦ ———. "Postcolonial Remains", *New Literary History*, Vol. 43, 2012: 19–42.

ŽIŽEK, Slavoj. *Violence. Six Sideways Reflections*, London: Profile Books, 2009.

# Index